Breakfast in Bridgetown

Breakfast in Bridgetown

The definitive guide to Portland's favorite meal
2008 edition

Paul Gerald

Bacon and Eggs Press
Portland, Oregon

Bacon and Eggs Press
PO Box 9243
Portland, OR 97207-9243
www.breakfastinbridgetown.com

ISBN: 978-0-9797350-0-4
Library of Congress Control Number: 2008932673

Photo credits:
Plate of food on cover by Mark Nomura
Portland skyline on cover by Jerry Koch Photography
Restaurants by Paul Gerald

DISCLAIMER

This book is meant only as a guide to select restaurants serving breakfast in the city of Portland. It does not guarantee your safety or satisfaction; you dine at your own risk. Bacon and Eggs Press, Second Cup Productions, and Paul Gerald are not liable for property loss or damage, personal injury or illness, or death that may result from accessing or eating in the restaurants described in this book. Please be aware that diners have gotten sick in Portland restaurants. Also, all the detailed information in this books—hours, addresses, website, menu items, and so on—were confirmed to best of the publisher's ability before publishing the book. Because the restaurant business is volatile, it is the reader's responsibility to confirm all relevant information before eating in any restaurant described in these pages.

Dedication

This book is dedicated, with immense admiration and gratitude, to everybody who grows it, delivers it, preps it, cooks it, brings it out, and cleans it up.

Also to Corky Corcoran and Craig Schuhmann, the two finest breakfast companions a guy could have.

But most of all, to Jenny Boyce, whose warmth, sweetness, and love — combined with the occasional kick in the pants — helped me finish this book and have some of the happiest times of my life.

Publisher's Note

All the facts in this book — addresses, phone numbers, prices, and so on — were confirmed with the restaurants, to the best of our ability, in late spring 2008.

We strongly suggest a call to your chosen place before you go to make sure it is still around, that the wait has not gotten out of control, or that it still serves that certain something you read about and must have.

Another way to check the latest information is on the book's Web site, BreakfastInBridgetown.com. In fact, if you find a mistake or have an update — or if you have a suggestion of any kind — please contact the author via the Web site.

And finally, please bear in mind that this is the book's first edition. It will be expanded and (we hope) improved upon as we go.

Happy dining!

Contents

The Restaurants

CONTENTS

Acknowledgements

I wrote and published this book myself, and I can't recommend that process highly enough. In fact, I'm not sure I can recommend it at all.

Write a book for a publisher, which I've done, and you do a big chunk of work and then get a few scraps of money—but almost no headaches or risk, other than poverty. Ah, but commit to publishing it yourself and you get all the risk, all the control, all the work, and (you hope) all the rewards. You are also going to need a *lot* of help.

At least 90 percent of what I have learned about publishing books was taught to me by the fine folks at the Northwest Association of Book Publishers. They meet once a month for the sole purpose of helping people market and publish their own books. Check them out at *NWABP.org*. It was there I found the book's editor, Sue Mann of Working With Words; its designer, Jennifer Omner of ALL Publications; the marketing expert Ken Rowe of Elements Publishing Services; and the indispensable Bob Smith of BookPrinters Network, who knows everything and everybody involved in printing books.

The rest of my publishing knowledge, such as it is, came from Russell Helms of absnth, Inc., a full-service book

ACKNOWLEDGEMENTS

production company (see *absnth.com*). He put up my Web site and helped design the book's cover. The company does everything else involved in publishing, as well.

But before all of that, I needed to know where to eat breakfast. That information came from a constant stream of sources, but special mention must go to Linda Faino, who seemed to send me a clipping or e-mail weekly, to the extent that in the final weeks before publication I had to ask her to stop. I thank her immensely, nonetheless.

Next, of course, were all those meals, the dozens upon dozens of breakfast outings ranging from private to intimate to large-scale wacky. With the possible exception of my expanded understanding of French toast, the finest thing about writing this book has been going out to breakfast with various combinations of these people:

Denise Archer and Nigel Wehling; April Bertelsen; Gary Bishop; Jenny Boyce; Penny Bush-Boyce; Drea Brandom; Elizabeth and Lily Caldwell; Dave Cohen; Kinnari and Soren Cowell-Shah; Jason Cross; Lori Davis; Jan Dance; Kerri Dee; Tom Eggers; Brian and Linda Faino; Jennifer Fields; Derek Fisher; Craig Frerichs; Brooke, Sidney, and Porter Gaab; John Gardner; Christina Gardner; Donovan Gardner; Jane Garbisch; Signe Geneser; Patrick Gihring; Delon Gilbert; Tom Horton; Nancy Howds; Carol Humpage; Steve Istre; Julia Jordan; Cheryl Juetten; Amber and Ruby Kara; Lori King; Amy Kuntz; Allan Lehmann; Manuela Leu; Rob Lloyd; Bob Malone; Beth McNeil; Becky Miller; Sarah Miller; Steve Moellering; Mick Mortlock; Jean Nelson; Tom Nelson; Judy Olivier; Ron Paul; Diana Robinson; Kaitlyn Schaumberg; Toni and Paul Schimming; Jeff Schneider, Craig Schuhmann, Caroline

Smith, Trina Fairbanks, Jason Wehling, Anthony Stevens; Sharon Streeter; Alice Sufka; Jason Thomas; Betsy and Kaia Tucker; Rick Vazquez; Christian Wadlington; Phil Wentz; Amy and Dan Winans Caleb Winter; Leslie Woods; Robb Wynhausen; Elena Yingling; Jeff Young; and Chela Zini Caban.

With all that done, it was, of course, time to write. During that time I had the loving support of many friends, especially the folks around The Big House: Steve Sherlag, Julie Cusumano, and the three cutest girls in town: Anna, Lena, and Sophia. I also thank The Food Dude of *PortlandFoodandDrink.com* for giving me an audience along the way, and Liz Hummer of *LivePDX.com* for letting me share some chapters and blog entries with her readers, as well.

Rick Vazquez did a heck of a job as my No. 1 fact-checker, and Jane Garbisch, Sharon Streeter, and Bernadette Price kicked in for a few chapters, as well.

And finally, I have some love for the various places where I holed up on occasion to write: the Vagabond Lodge in Hood River, Red Wing Coffee Shop, Concordia Coffee Shop, Costello's Travel Cafe, Alberta Street Tea House, my office at ActivSpace, and Summer Lake Hot Springs, where I wrote most of the front-of-book material in between bird watching and warm, soothing soaks.

Why a Breakfast Book?

Where Do You Like to Go for Breakfast? This simple question has launched a multitude of conversations around town and also a singular, oddball quest in my head: to profile our town by describing where and how we eat breakfast.

Breakfast in Bridgetown represents my first attempt. It is not a comprehensive guide to every place in Portland serving breakfast, and no doubt many readers will fail to find in these pages a place of which they are quite fond. This is something I have to live with—for now.

The seeds of this idea lie in my 10-year career as a travel writer for the *Memphis Flyer*. The editors there were nice enough (or maybe desperate enough) to let me write whatever the hell I wanted, as long as I did a couple of 850-word pieces per month. In the process of writing some 300 articles, a theme developed: describe a place by describing a meal eaten there, usually breakfast, which I did for articles about Las Vegas, an Amtrak train, Hong Kong, Santa Barbara, and so on.

And then one day I was sitting with my friend Craig at the Beaterville Cafe when it occurred to me that I had never written a piece about breakfast in Portland. Then I thought about all the places Portland has for breakfast. And then I thought, Hey, I should write a book!

Frankly, I had no idea what I was getting into. I recall a quaint time when I thought maybe I could stretch it to 50 places. Before long, with a steady stream of suggestions coming in from newspapers, the Internet, friends, and strangers, my list went well over 70, then 100. Then 150. Then 200.

I decided that for this first edition I would limit the scope to places in the city of Portland. Then I did what I could, limited though that is. If you know of a place I need in the next edition, please get in touch.

What Is it with This Town and Breakfast?

I have no firm answer, even after consuming about 200 breakfasts over nearly two years while researching the book. But I suspect it consists of three things: we're a social group who like to get out and do stuff, we like to start with some community and nutrition, and our wonderful city has both attracted and nurtured a lot of great chefs who can make money off us. Put it all together and it's good times at the breakfast table.

Breakfast combines so many great things: tastes, smells, the fine balance between savory and sweet, friends, and the start of a new day. And in Portland it combines everything from the neighborhood mom-and-pop outfit to the fancy, New-Age weekend brunch served at some of the finest restaurants in the city—or in America, for that matter.

What This Book Isn't (or, Why No Stars?)

I am neither a restaurant critic nor a foodie, and I don't have a sophisticated palate or any inside scoop on what's happening behind the scenes—mainly because I am lazy, unsophisticated, and don't care about such things. I worked in the restaurant business for just two horrible weeks as a prep cook—neither I nor the industry was unhappy about my career ending—so I am also not an expert in that sense.

Thus, you are not reading the advice of an expert. In fact,

you won't even see ratings because I honestly believe that my opinion of a place, which is based on my preferences, almost certainly has no connection to your opinion of a place. (Though if you really care, I listed my 10 favorites in the back) I do have this going for me, though: I am pretty certain I've eaten breakfast in more Portland restaurants than any other human being. And I have both the receipts and the expanded gut to prove it.

There are restaurants in this town that, now that the book is done, I have no intention of visiting again, just because they aren't my kind of place. But a lot of those places are packed all the time, so what does my opinion mean? There are also places I absolutely adore, and you could easily find people who think they're the worst in town. Again, what would a rating system tell you? Besides, how do you have the same rating system for a mom-and-pop diner and a haute cuisine weekend brunch?

Instead, I refer you to my aforementioned quest: to simply describe how and where Portland eats breakfast. I describe, you dine. Better for everybody.

I should let you know that with only two exceptions (when I was profiling places for *LivePDX.com*) my experiences were not influenced in any way by restaurant staff; none knew I was writing a book when I visited, and none paid for my meals. I am also not putting my photo in the book, which is to keep some level of anonymity and also to obscure the damage done to my physique by 200 breakfasts.

Some places I went to only once, some I went to several times, and there is almost no system to explain it. There's your grain of salt.

Why Isn't (Your Favorite Place) in the Book?

I should make one thing clear: there was no system of any kind applied to this project. I started with a plan that quickly and completely fell apart, and then I just started eating, writing, and finding out about more places to eat in and write about. In the last week before I gave all the final text to my poor editor, I was still going to places I had only recently found out about.

So at the risk of sounding like a simpleton, some places just didn't make it in this time. I never was going to have 200 places in the book, and at some point (with the bank account tanking and the cholesterol soaring) I just needed to finish the damn thing and start hiking on the weekends again lest my new lifestyle (or my doctor) kills me.

So if you're wondering why a particular place isn't in, it's not at all reflective of the place—it's just that for any number of reasons I didn't get around to it before the first edition was done. Or maybe it opened too close to publication date.

Note the emphasis on *first* edition: there will be more editions. Meanwhile, I bet that for every place you like and I didn't visit, there are half a dozen in here that you didn't know about at all.

I also intend to add a donut category and probably a dim sum/pho category. What I will not do is wander into that great, gray area known as the Coffee Shop. I know a lot of places in town with outstanding espresso drinks and fine baked goods, plus even the occasional breakfast sandwich. But if I tried to write *that* book, my doctor wouldn't have to bother killing me.

My Cry for Help

Since this is just the first edition, and since the person who writes a book usually has the least amount of perspective on it (especially at deadline), I am publicly and humbly asking for assistance.

Of course, I want to hear restaurant suggestions; I still find out about new ones every week and I'm usually not happy about it, because I could work on this dang book forever! But I also want to know how I can make the book better and more suited to your needs. What ideas do you have for organization, information, and presentation? Do you have any news tips I should know about? Is something out of date or just plain wrong? Maybe you'd like to do a little writing for a future edition?

Even if you just want to bitch at me, you are strongly encouraged to get in touch. I'm blogging regularly at *BreakfastInBridgetown.com*, and I look forward to hearing from you.

Enjoy!

Paul Gerald
June, 2008, Portland

About the Categories

I've tried to give you a quick take on what kind of place each restaurant is. However, you may get the impression that two dissimilar places are in fact similar, so I put places into more than one category, including the fabulously scatterbrained New/Hip/Old School designation I gave to Milo's City Cafe. (You'll just have to read the review . . .)

Here's what I'm thinking when I assign each category:

New doesn't mean it recently opened. The category is more like "New Portland" and refers to a place that has the hippie/yuppie/foodie feel to it, serves Asiago cheese and whatnot, and generally represents the changes Portland's food scene has undergone in the last, say, 20 years. Examples: Simpatica, Zell's, Tin Shed.

Old School places have generally been around a while, though not necessarily any longer than a New Portland place. A lot of folks would call them diners, but that's too narrow for my purposes. When an Old School place says cheese and coffee, it probably means Tillamook Cheddar and Farmer Brothers. Examples: Pattie's Homeplate, Fat City, Original Pancake House.

Mom and Pop places are often Old School as well. But where the Original Pancake House is clearly Old School, the owner doesn't seat you and you're not eating food Dad cooked, Sissy brought to you, and Mom took your money for. *That's* a Mom and Pop place. Examples: Johnny B's, Beaterville, Hollywood Burger Bar.

Classy doesn't necessarily mean crazily expensive, though these places do run more expensive than average. At the very least, Classy means a place has tablecloths, the staff is in black and white, candles or flowers are on the tables, and an omelet may be about $10 or more. Examples: Cafe du Berry, Roux, Fenouil.

Hip probably sounds like I'm stereotyping. But Hip means it's the kind of place where you can chill for a while and the people generally known as Hipsters often eat there — a Hipster being identified by the trademark thick-rimmed glasses, vintage clothing, sideburns, sneakers, and late rising hour. And if you're offended by that description, you're probably a Hipster. Examples: Juniors, Cricket Cafe, Stepping Stone.

Buffet is another catch-all that throws together some strange combinations. Sometimes it means literally a buffet table filled with food, or a world of options from multiple vendors. Really, Buffet is a state of mind. Examples: Salty's, Farmer's Market.

Weekend means breakfast (many call it brunch) is served only on weekends. Or, in some cases a Weekend designation means breakfast is served all week but staff does something special on weekends — often a buffet or fancy brunch. Examples: Screen Door, Petite Provence, Roux.

Kiddie means the place goes out of its way to accommodate kids. I can't think of a place that doesn't want kids, but these places have a play area, or extensive kids' menus, or just generally a kid-friendly vibe about them. Some even have kids working there. Examples: Daily Market and Cafe, Bumblekiss.

Veggie, as you might imagine, means the place is particularly friendly to nonmeat-eaters. Most places have a vegetarian omelet, but Veggie here means vegetarians and vegans will have more than a couple of choices. A few places really hang their hat on this category. Examples: Vita, Paradox Palace, Blossoming Lotus, Jam.

Restaurants by Location

In addition to category, I sorted Portland's breakfast places by location, with the understanding that all location names are negotiable to some extent. In some cases I didn't use the "real" name of the neighborhood; rather, I used the name of the area's main street because neither I nor anyone else really knows where these neighborhoods begin and end.

With this list, you should be able to figure out locations. As always, please remember that this is a first edition! Your feedback is strongly encouraged at *breakfastinbridgetown.com*.

Each restaurant is also listed with its categories in parentheses.

Downtown: South of W Burnside St. and within I-405.
Bijou Café (New/Classy/Veggie): Page 58
Daily Café (New/Hip/Weekend): Page 103
Farmer's Market (Buffet/Veggie): Page 118
Heathman (Classy): Page 157
Kenny and Zuke's (Hip/Old School): Page 187
Mother's (Classy): Page 208
Porto Terra (Classy): Page 247
Veritable Quandary (New/Classy/Weekend): Page 298

E Burnside: So close to E Burnside St. that it doesn't seem like it's in NE or SE.
Doug Fir Lounge (Hip/Old School): Page 112
Old Wives' Tales (New/Veggie/Kiddie) : Page 220
Screen Door Cafe (New/Weekend/Classy) : Page 265

N/Inner: North Portland south of N Killingsworth St.

FlavourSpot (Weekend): Page 130
Gravy (New/Hip): Page 148
Mississippi Station (New/Classy): Page 205
Moxie (Weekend/Hip/Veggie): Page 211
Overlook Restaurant (Old School): Page 226
Roux (Weekend/Classy): Page 256
Trebol (New/Weekend/Classy): Page 292

N/Outer: North Portland north of N Killingsworth St.

Beaterville (Hip/Mom & Pop/Veggie): Page 49
Cup and Saucer Cafe (Hip/Veggie): Page 100
FlavourSpot (Weekend): Page 130
John St. Café (Mom & Pop/Old School): Page 178
Pattie's Homeplate Café (Mom & Pop/Old School): Page 235

NE/Alberta: On or near NE Alberta St. between MLK and NE 33rd Ave.

Autentica (New/Classy/Weekend): Page 40
Cup and Saucer Cafe (Hip/Veggie): Page 100
Francis (New/Classy): Page 133
Helser's (New/Hip): Page 160
Podnah's Pit (Old School/Weekend): Page 244
Tin Shed (New/Hip/Veggie): Page 280
Vita Café (Hip/Veggie/Kiddie): Page 304

NE/Broadway: On or around NE Broadway and NE Weidler St. between MLK and Hollywood District.

Cadillac (Old School/Classy): Page 85

Milo's (New/Hip/Old School): Page 202
Pambiche (New/Hip/Weekend): Page 229

**NE/Fremont: On or around NE Fremont St.
between MLK and NE 82nd Ave.**
Acadia (New/Classy/Weekend): Page 31
Alameda Café (New/Classy): Page 34
Bumblekiss (New/Kiddie): Page 79
Prescott Café (Mom and Pop/Old School): Page 250

**NE/Hollywood: Around the Hollywood District,
roughly NE Sandy Blvd. from 30th Ave. to 50th Ave.**
Biscuits Café (Old School): Page 61
Daily Market and Café (New/Kiddie): Page 106
Hollywood Burger Bar (M&P/Old School): Page 163
Laurelthirst (New/Old School/Veggie): Page 193
Tosis (Old School): Page 289

**NE/MLK: On or around NE MLK Blvd. south of
NE Killingsworth.**
Bridges (New/Hip/Veggie): Page 73

**NE/Outer: Northeast Portland beyond about
NE 60th Ave.**
Cameo Cafe (Mom and Pop/Old School): Page 91
Gateway Breakfast House (M&P): Page 139
Salty's (Weekend/Buffet/Classy): Page 259

**NW: In Northwest Portland, outside the
Pearl District.**
Basta's (Weekend/Classy): Page 46
Besaw's (New/Old School/Classy): Page 55

Biscuits Café (Old School): Page 61
Joe's Cellar (Old School): Page 175
Kornblatt's (Old School): Page 190
Meriwethers (Weekend/New/Classy): Page 199
Rose's (Old School): Page 253
Skyline Restaurant (Old School): Page 274
Stepping Stone (Hip/Mom and Pop): Page 277
Virgo and Pisces (Weekend/New): Page 301

Pearl District: North of W Burnside St. and within I-405.
Blossoming Lotus (New/Veggie): Page 64
Bluehour (Weekend/New/Classy): Page 67
Byways (Hip/Old School): Page 82
Daily Café (New/Hip/Weekend): Page 103
Everett Street Bistro (New/Classy): Page 115
Farmer's Market (Buffet/Veggie): Page 118
Fenouil (Classy/Weekend/New): Page 127
Fuller's (Mom & Pop/Old School): Page 136

SE/Belmont: On or near SE Belmont St. between SE 12th Ave. and SE 50th Ave.
Cricket Café (Hip/Veggie): Page 97
Paradox Palace (Hip/Veggie): Page 232
Pine State Biscuits (Old School/Mom and Pop): Page 241
Utopia (New/Hip/Veggie): Page 295
Wild Abandon (Hip/Veggie): Page 310

SE/Division: On or near SE Division St. between SE 12th Ave. and SE 82nd Ave.
Broder (New): Page 76
Detour Café (New/Veggie): Page 109

Petite Provence (Weekend/Classy): Page 238
Tom's (Old School): Page 286

SE/Hawthorne: On or near SE Hawthorne St. between SE 12th and SE 50th Ave.

Bread and Ink (New/Classy/Kiddie): Page 70
Cup and Saucer Cafe (Hip/Veggie): Page 100
Hawthorne Café (New/Hip/Veggie): Page 154
Jam on Hawthorne (New/Hip/Veggie): Page 172

SE/Inner: Between the river, SE 12th Ave., and SE Powell Blvd.

Daily Café (New/Hip/Weekend): Page 103
Genies (New/Hip/Veggie): Page 142
Hotcake House (Old School): Page 166
J&M Café (New/Veggie/Classy): Page 169
Johnny B's (Mom & Pop/Old School): Page 181
Juniors (Hip/Veggie): Page 184
My Father's Place (Hip/Old School): Page 214
Niki's (Old School/Mom and Pop): Page 217
Sanborn's (New/Classy): Page 262
Simpatica (Weekend/New/Classy): Page 271
Zell's (New/Classy): Page 313

SE/Outer: Southeast, just a little farther out, but not in Sellwood.

Arleta Library Café (New/Mom & Pop): Page 37
Bar Carlo (New/Hip/Veggie): Page 43
Biscuits Café (Old School): Page 61
Country Cat (Weekend/New): Page 94
Toast (New/Mom and Pop): Page 283

SE/Sellwood: South of SE Powell Blvd. and/or in the Sellwood Neighborhood.

Bertie Lou's Cafe (Mom and Pop/Old School): Page 52

Fat Albert's Cafe (Mom and Pop/Old School): Page 121

SW/Inner: Southwest Portland, outside I-405 but fairly close to downtown.

Café du Berry (Classy): Page 88

Fat City (Mom & Pop/Old School): Page 124

Golden Touch (Old School): Page 145

Marco's (Classy): Page 196

Original Pancake House (Old School): Page 223

SW/Outer: Farther west from downtown than SW/Inner.

Biscuits Café (Old School): Page 61

Hands on Café (New/Classy/Mom and Pop): Page 151

Seasons and Regions (Weekend): Page 268

Weber's Crossing (Mom and Pop/Old School): Page 307

Let's Eat Out(side)!

Feel like dining under the, um, legendary Portland sun? Well, then, turn your books sideways, and here are your options for outdoor seating among the places covered in the book.

Name	Location	Scene
Acadia Cafe	NE/Fremont	Uncovered sidewalk tables
Alameda Cafe	NE/Fremont	Umbrella sidewalk tables
Bertie Lou's	SE/Sellwood	Picnic tables on the street
Besaw's	NW	Covered patio
Biscuits	NE/Hollywood	Covered picnic tables
Blossoming Lotus	Pearl	Uncovered sidewalk tables
Bridges Cafe	NE/MLK	Uncovered tables near MLK
Bumblekiss	NE/Fremont	Umbrellas on a quiet patio
Cameo Cafe	NE/Outer	Deck with some cover
Cricket Cafe	SE/Belmont	Uncovered sidewalk tables
Cup and Saucer	NE/Alberta	Uncovered sidewalk tables
Daily Market & Cafe	NE/Hollywood	Open tables on the street
Detour Cafe	SE/Division	Shady, covered patio
Farmer's Market	Downtown	The whole Park Blocks
Fenouil	Pearl	Uncovered patio next to park
FlavourSpot	N/Inner	Both locations no cover
Francis	NE/Alberta	Quiet patio with some shade
Fuller's Cafe	Pearl	Open tables on the street
Hands on Cafe	SW/Inner	Lovely garden patio
Hawthorne Cafe	SE/Hawthorne	Patio above Hawthorne

Helser's	NE/Alberta	Uncovered sidewalk tables
John Street Cafe	N/Outer	Shady, quiet garden patio
Kenny and Zuke's	Downtown	Uncovered sidewalk tables
Kornblatt's	NW	Uncovered sidewalk tables
Laurelthirst	NE/Hollywood	Uncovered sidewalk tables
Meriweathers	NW	Quiet patio with some cover
Mississippi Station	N/Inner	Quiet patio, no cover
Moxie	N/Inner	Side yard with picnic tables
Pambiche	NE/Broadway	Covered tables, heat lamps
Pattie's Homeplate	N/Outer	Uncovered sidewalk tables
Petite Provence	SE/Division	Uncovered sidewalk tables
Podnah's Pit	NE/Alberta	Uncovered sidewalk tables
Salty's	NE/Outer	Deck overlooking the Columbia
Screen Door	E Burnside	Uncovered Patio near Burnside
Seasons and Regions	SW/Outer	Patio, covered and heated in winter
Tin Shed	NE/Alberta	Shady patio and big fireplace
Trebol	N/Inner	Patio with some cover
Veritable Quandary	Downtown	Garden patio, no cover
Vita Cafe	NE/Alberta	Big patio with some shade
Wild Abandon	SE/Belmont	Big patio with some shade

How to Use this Book

In addition to category and location (see pages 20 and 22), I give you a little more info on each eatery. Here's a quick guide.

Feel (in italics): If I had to quickly summarize its essence, this is what I'd say.

Price range: Average price range for a typical meal consisting of a main dish, beverage, and about a 20 percent tip.

Wait: Not a science, of course, but a good guess based on what I've seen and heard from customers and staff.

Seating: How many and what kinds of seats; outdoor options available.

Large groups? How staff will handle a group of six or more.

Portion size: Again, not a science, more of a quick impression.

Changes: How open to making changes, like "hold the cheese" or "pancakes instead of toast." Also any charges that might apply.

Other drinks: Espresso? Fresh juices? Cocktails? Smoothies? Anything special?

Feel-goods: Free range, grain fed, shade grown, local, organic, etc.

Health options: Vegan/vegetarian options, egg substitutes, allergy-sensitive options.

WiFi? Not that *anyone* would want to bring a computer to breakfast, of course . . .

Acadia

New/Classy

Perfectly New Orleans: loud, classy and over the top
1303 NE Fremont St. (NE/Fremont)
503-249-5001
Brunch served Sundays only, 10:30 a.m. to 2:30 p.m.
creolapdx.com
$15–20 (All major cards)

━━━━━━━━━◆━━━━━━━━━

As Jenny and I walked to Acadia one fine Sunday morning, I was a little worried about how the meal might go. I had just told the folks at Acadia there would be nine—my dentist and his wife, a Buddhist friend, a fellow writer, two of Jenny's friends, and my old boss from FedEx—and most had never met.

A table was already set for us, a fleur-de-lys on each glass—a subtle French touch that was the last subtle thing we'd see all day. The staff was friendly and seated the five who were already there. About that time the jazz trio started playing; a bit loud, perhaps, but we just raised our voices to match it. We had three former Missourians, a Louisiana native, and a Tennessean, so all Arkansas jokes were deemed acceptable. Then it turned out two of us spoke French, we had several kinds of artists, and we were all politically way left. We even had a wacky element: among our names we had Sharon, Shari, Jerry, and Jenny, which is really fun to say.

Pour some strong coffee on the group and throw in a wildly entertaining waiter, and soon the Breakfast Magic started to flow. I have eaten more than a hundred breakfasts to research this book, and the meal we had at Acadia was one of the tastiest and, without doubt, the longest, loudest, most over-

the-top one of the bunch—which is exactly what one would expect from brunch at a New Orleans bistro. In fact, coming in a close second was the Breakfast Crew's mad journey to another New Orleans place, Roux.

While we were waiting for the rest of the Crew (who never showed), the waiter said "How about some beignets?" As I would do several times, I spoke for everyone and blurted out a "Hell yes!" Soon three big, warm, puffy pastries covered in powdered sugar appeared on the table. Briefly. Anybody ever had turtle soup? Let's get some out here! Steve, our Louisianan, was impressed Acadia had actual snapping turtle; in fact, Acadia's chef picks up a package of Louisiana seafood once or more a week at PDX.

The soup was dark, rich, and meaty, the consistency of legitimate Mexican chili. Yummy. I wondered how the seafood gumbo was. Bring it out! Not the best offering: a little thinner and blacker than we expected but nice and spicy; still, the rice was on top contrary to tradition, and Steve and I exchanged raised eyebrows. But by this time our musician was telling stories about playing with Jerry Lee Lewis in the '50s, and Steve told us the painting on the wall of an outdoor feast was by George Rodrigue, whose kids Steve used to play with back in Lafayette. So we were lettin' the good times roll, though for the record folks at other tables were being considerably more sedate.

When it came time to order, 40 festive minutes after we were seated, we attacked like a team. Jenny went for the special omelet, with crawfish, asparagus, Parmesan, and a touch of the Creole Mustard Hollandaise. I got the smoked pork special, with a hash of sweet potatoes and caramelized onions and a side of grits that were appropriately slathered in butter but still the low point of the meal. Jerry went for an omelet with fried green tomatoes, and we all tried to out-French one another pronouncing "Marigny." Steve took a shot at the Crawfish Etouffe: a risky endeavor so far from the bayou, but he was fairly impressed, especially by the crawfish. Sharon got the special quiche of bacon, broccoli, and goat cheese with a side salad. We tossed around small share plates and loved all of it.

And Shari got the Pain Perdu. Technically, this is what we Yanks call French toast, but this stuff wasn't French or toast. It was a celebration of American indulgence: a softball-size slab of moist brioche over which the kitchen had poured a serving of Bananas Foster and a "dollop" of whipped cream that could be measured in cups. It was ridiculous: pecans and banana liqueur and cream and cane syrup all over the place. The waiter said no one had ever finished it alone. We admired it. We were afraid of it. We loved it.

And we decided it was Acadia's signature.

Wait: None that I've seen; reservations are taken, though.
Seating: 20 tables inside and a few tables on the street.
Large groups? Yes.
Portion size: Nuts.
Changes: Within reason.
Coffee: Kobos, but if you ask you'll get New Orleans-style stuff with chicory.
Other drinks: Espresso and a wide range of cocktails.
Feel-goods: Fresh seafood straight from Louisiana.
Health options: Please. This is New Orleans food!
WiFi? No.

Alameda Cafe

New/Classy

The French invade New Mexico

4641 NE Fremont Ave. (NE/Fremont)

503-284-5314

Daily 8 a.m. to 9 p.m.; breakfast until 11 a.m. on weekdays, 2 p.m. on weekends.

$12-14 (all major cards, no checks)

———————◆•◆———————

My first impression of the Alameda Cafe, before I even sat down, was that it was full of itself. That's pure stereotyping, I admit it. When I see white tablecloths, paintings of flowers on the walls, actual flowers on the tables, the staff wearing black, and bottles of wine in a display on the counter, I think "Great, welcome to Pompous Valley." Had I looked at the menu and seen an omelet with blue cheese, eggs Benedict with chili-infused hollandaise, and French toast named for Santa Fe, I might have left.

Then I sat down and noticed that on top of the white table-cloth was paper for kids to draw on; they were even given crayons. Then I saw a hefty special (available before 10 on weekdays) of eggs, toast, and potatoes for $4.95. Then I saw that all the omelets, scrambles, and even the eggs Benedict, were less than $9. Then I thought, "Hey, being kid friendly and serving big portions for reasonable prices isn't pompous!" It helps when the wait is almost nonexistent, the bacon crisp and peppery, the potatoes big and chunky and oven roasted, and the prices only about one to two dollars above Portland's average.

The Alameda suits its neighborhood perfectly. Is the neighborhood defined by grand homes along Alameda

Ridge? Is it the streets north of Fremont without sidewalks? Yes and yes. Is it Stanich's old-school burgers? Is it Starbucks and the Alameda Brew Pub? Yes and yes, again.

Such is this cafe's food, which is part stylish (the Southwestern Benedict also comes with sweet and spicy corn bread) and part, well, kind of down-home. You can, for example, build your own omelet with any three ingredients for $8.95 with potatoes and toast. More places should make this perfectly reasonable concession to common sense.

The Alameda has goofy stuff like the Klickitat Omelet with blue cheese, apples, and bacon. And there's a braised mushroom omelet with spinach, sweet onions and Swiss cheese, which you should stay away from unless you really love mushrooms. And the hollandaise is prepared with par-cooked eggs (I don't even know what that means).

But then there is the basic scramble with cheese, mushrooms, and onion; a Belgian waffle that's only $4.95; oatmeal with bananas, raisins, and brown sugar for $4.95; and granola or yogurt with fruit for $5 or $6.

And the French toast. Giving in to their elegant, stylish side, they couldn't just do French toast; they had to fancy it up. And yet they didn't do anything *too* fancy. They make it with thick baguette bread, dipped just enough to hold a crust of cinnamon and sugar-crushed corn flakes, then fried. As my friend Beth said, it looks like pieces of cod. It's called Santa Fe Railroad French Toast because, apparently, the recipe originated on the old Santa Fe Railroad.

The first time I had it, I wasn't sure what to make of it. I like my French toast soaked, and this was dry in the middle. The second time? Well, now I'm thinking that the cinnamon is a nice touch, the crunch of the crust plays well with the soft bread, the syrup takes care of the moisture, and it reminds me simultaneously of Navajo fry bread and breakfast cereal with Saturday morning cartoons. Clearly, more research is required.

Wait: Small on weekends, mostly outside with some cover
Seating: 49, all tables.
Large groups: With notice.
Portion Size: Hefty.
Changes: Within reason.
Coffee: Stumptown.
Other drinks: Mimosas, homemade Bloody Mary mix, tea, fresh-squeezed juice.
Feel-goods: Some veggie options, tofu.
Health options: 2% milk.
WiFi? No.

Arleta Library Bakery Cafe

New/Mom & Pop

Almost hate to pass it on . . .

5513 SE 72nd (SE/Outer)

503-774-4470

Tuesday through Friday, 8 a.m. to 2:30 p.m.; breakfast served all day. Weekend brunch from 9 a.m. to 3 p.m.

arletalibrary.com

$11–15 (Visa, MasterCard)

———————◆●◆———————

Early in 2007 my friend Rick, a former restaurant and catering guy, started telling me I needed to check out a place in his neighborhood called the something library cafe. At first, all I heard was Rick's neighborhood (outer Woodstock) and "library." What food, I wondered, could there possibly be at SE 72nd and Harold? And who eats at a library? I had visions of stale croissants over by the periodicals.

But Rick knows his food, so out I went, all the way from my home near Alberta Street, and I took a friend. How was it? The short answer is that my friend, who also lives in Northeast, now takes her boyfriend there all the time. I've been back a few times as well. When I was looking for a place to live, I seriously looked in that neighborhood so I could walk to Arleta every day.

It could just be that it's new or that it's in a part of town novel to the breakfast crowd. But I think the reason is that it's cozy and quiet, friendly, usually staffed by the owners, uses local ingredients, and serves fantastic food. And it's the least pretentious place you'll ever walk into; in fact, much of the décor is recycled doors, and the walls remain unadorned.

Inside, you're immediately greeted with what may appear to be the usual assortment of pastries; but this is, remember, the Arleta Library *Bakery* Cafe. The delights are all made in-house: when I was there they had a moist date scone, morning glory muffins, almond anise biscotti, triple ginger snaps, coconut macaroons with bittersweet chocolate, sour cream coffee cake, and always something new. My favorite is the coffee cake, which uses various fruits, mostly those in season. One day it was pineapple, another time blueberries, and without exception the crust was perfectly crunchy and the inside moist but light. Just what you want, along with the French-press Stumptown, while waiting for your order.

If the cake doesn't make you feel good, then you can bask in the mission of the place, which, according to the Web site, includes the ambitious hope that the restaurant "will continue the trend toward revitalization in the area." Arleta is also committed to "sustaining its neighborhood and food-shed by purchasing as much organic food from local farmers and producers as possible and by paying its employees an equitable, living wage." In 2007 Arleta also partnered with Your Backyard Farmer *(yourbackyardfarmer.com)*, which helps people start organic gardens in their yards.

Such innovation would be admirable even if the chefs weren't fantastic. In fact, everything we've eaten has been not only delicious but also cooked just right, whether it's the roasted red peppers in the Tuscan Scramble (with spicy sausage and Romano cheese) or the Library Fries, which are like big Jo-Jos done right: soft inside but just crunchy outside, with a light dose of salt and rosemary. A special scramble with Swiss chard, mustard greens, collard greens, red and white Russian kale, and spinach was a spicy trip through the shades of green, like walking through an old-growth forest. (The Florentine, a version with ricotta and Parmesan, is on the weekend brunch menu.) The sweet potato biscuits and rosemary sausage gravy come with a thin slice of slow-roasted pork loin that our waiter said had been in a brine "for a few days."

Topping off everything is a shot glass-size of wonderful jam of the day; once it was apricot-pineapple-ginger, another time roasted nectarine with rosemary.

Like any new love, I am already jealous about the Arleta. I hardly want to tell people about it. Word is it has applied for a liquor license and is planning an expansion, at least a patio. I already feel sentimental about its small, charming Old Days, when only a devoted few of us knew.

Wait: Up to 30 minutes on weekends.
Seating: About 30, all at tables, with garden seating expected in 2008.
Large groups? No, but try the catering.
Portion size: Solid.
Changes: Sure.
Coffee: French-press Stumptown.
Other drinks: Fresh juices, homemade lemonade.
Feel-goods: Most ingredients are local and organic.
Health options: Good options for veggies.
WiFi? Possibly from a coffee shop next door.

Autentica

New/Classy/Weekend

Mexican sophistication, Portland relaxation
5507 NE 30th (NE/Alberta)
503-287-7555
Brunch served weekends 10:00 a.m. to 3:00 p.m.
autenticaportland.com
$15–20 (all major cards, maximum of two per table)

———◆—•—◆———

Among the many signs that a neighborhood is changing, one that will really catch your eye is a man doing Tai Chi in the middle of the street. That's what we found when we arrived at the corner of NE 30th and Killingsworth in search of Autentica and found a wellness fair going on, with booths from local yoga classes and meditation programs. Yep, I thought, this end of Killingsworth ain't what it used to be!

A Mexican brunch ain't what I thought it was, either. I can be an idiot at times, and this was one of them. Somebody said "Mexican brunch" to me and I thought huevos rancheros and maybe a breakfast burrito. Autentica, it seems, is just what its name means in Spanish: "authentic." And it's a serious restaurant that happens to serve dishes from the owner's hometown of Guerrero, Mexico.

The owner, Oswaldo Bibiano, cooked at Basilico, South Park, and Pazzo, and he uses local meats and produce, has vegetarian and vegan options as well as freshly made tortillas — a treat, if you haven't had them. The result is one of the more widely liked places among the online critics, whose opinions can be summed up best as "The food is so good that the slow service hardly matters."

Never daunted by slow service, because we ourselves are

slow, the Breakfast Crew headed out for the Upscale Killingsworth Strip. (Yes, that's the real estate world's name for the part of Killingsworth with all the thirtysomething white moms pushing strollers.) At 10:30 on a lovely Saturday morning, we

perused the fair, shot a curious glance at the line outside Cup and Saucer, and walked into the mostly empty Autentica.

Long before Alice uttered the day's first astonished "Damn!" upon biting into her *sope*, we knew we had found something pleasantly out of the ordinary. For one thing our waitress was better at speaking Spanish than English, but fortunately Rick, who grew up in Puerto Rico, was with us. Confused by the menu, which was filled with words and dishes we didn't know, we simply told Rick to ask her to get us something we couldn't get anywhere else. (I had spotted huevos rancheros on the menu but wanted something new). Her response, translated, was, "Everything here is something you can't get anywhere else."

Indeed. About that menu: there's *menudo,* or spicy tripe soup, as well as a quesadilla of the day and enchiladas. I had no idea there are enchiladas for breakfast, but after trying these (chicken stuffed, with a red mole sauce, iceberg lettuce, avocado, radishes, and Oaxacan cream), I would have eaten them at any time of day. As for the *sope,* which elicited Alice's "Damn," it was a little like an open-faced soft taco with refried beans, cheese, onions, salsa, and your choice of meat. We were amazed at the number of flavors in that little thing!

It all sounds like the Mexican food you know, right? Well, how about this: a cactus salad with crispy pork skin, onions, tomatoes, avocado, and fresh cheese. Or a crispy tortilla shell filled with octopus and prawns, topped with spicy cabbage salad. Or a *torta* that features pickled jalapeños. Or huevos *ahogados,* which is eggs poached in a traditional chicken broth with cilantro, lime, onions, and serrano peppers.

Alice, Rick, and I ordered four dishes among us, shared them all, and then kicked back and had a long, rambling discussion without ever feeling pressured to go. (This is the positive side of slow service and a relaxed atmosphere: you get to hang out!) We admired the down-to-earth nature of the menu and the place, with its earth-tone walls and ceramic dishes and photos of family on the walls.

The small bar and open kitchen give Autentica a mildly sophisticated feeling, but it still has a very relaxed vibe about it. You pay a few more dollars than, say, Cup and Saucer, but the food is so much better and the scene so much more chilled out that you'll be glad that you, too, found out about Autentica.

Wait: None that I've seen.
Seating: About 38, all at tables, plus a few tables outside and a patio out back with room for 16.
Large groups? Yes, but some notice would help.
Portion size: Big.
Changes: Didn't ask.
Coffee: Cafe Umbria.
Other drinks: Cocktails, juices, homemade Sangria.
Feel-goods: Only free-range organic eggs and local ingredients are used.
Health options: Many vegetarian options, and some dishes can be made vegan.
WiFi? No.

Bar Carlo

New/Hip/Veggie

Decent breakfast, or frontier outpost?
6433 SE Foster Blvd. (SE/Outer)
503-771-1664
Weekdays 7:30 a.m. to 3:00 p.m.; weekends 8:00 a.m. to
3:00 p.m.
barcarlo.com
$12–15 (all major cards, no checks)

———————◆·◆———————

Sometimes people treat a restaurant as something other than
a restaurant. In the case of Bar Carlo, which opened in 2007,
it seemed like everybody treated it as an opportunity to make
socioeconomic statements about the neighborhood it's in.
Local media ran articles that read like reports from Lewis
and Clark just in from the land of savages, telling us there
are actual reasons to go "out there."

Think I'm exaggerating?

The Mercury's blog: "Foster: not just for felons. . . . SE
Foster is starting to get some attention (and this time it's the
good kind). . . . you'll finally get a chance to check out that
cool Russian restaurant building that's always piqued your
interest when you drove by." (Note the assumption: it was
unthinkable to *stop in* at the Russian restaurant.)

The Mercury's (mostly positive) review: "If Bar Carlo was
in my neighborhood, I'd go there all the time. I probably
wouldn't make the trip out to SE 64th and Foster for lunch
alone — though on a weekend, faced with the brunching
hordes at Zell's or the Tin Shed, I just might be persuaded
to make the trip." (For the record, the drive from Zell's "all
the way" to Bar Carlo takes all of 11 minutes.)

A *Willamette Week* review of new restaurants in the area referred to it as a "fast-food vortex" and a "dusty, urban frontier."

That *Willamette Week* story set off quite a discussion in its online comments area, with readers lobbing grenades like "gentrification" and "meth houses" and "white trash." Others ridiculed the area's new name, FoPo (for Foster-Powell). Purely entertaining—and none of it has anything to do with the food at Bar Carlo.

The initial positive buzz about Bar Carlo came when any restaurant serving fresh, local, organic ingredients didn't need to do much else to get praise. By 2008 such actions were nearly a requirement for a new place. Other than its (irrelevant) location, what set Carlo apart was a wide variety of egg-based dishes—four sandwiches, six scrambles, and three omelets, plus daily specials and two Benedicts every weekend—in addition to French toast, and waffles. Prices are generally around $8 per dish, which is reasonable, but portions are not exactly gut-busters, either.

When I visited in late 2007 and early 2008, Carlo still had an unfinished feel. Work was still being done on the room next to the dining area, which will eventually offer nighttime with kind of a pub feel. And the main room itself was still a bit raw—or maybe it was finished and we had just expected more decoration. (Of course, it's an outpost on a "dusty frontier.")

Two people's opinions: My girlfriend and I went there twice and found no lines, friendly staff, strong tasty coffee, and food that made us shrug. Like I said, in any other neighborhood this would be a fairly run-of-the-mill place, with loyal followers and others who find it disappointing. And Bar Carlo does have both.

A smoked salmon scramble was long on salmon and had a nice combination of grilled red onions and fresh dill, but the eggs were a smidge overdone so they kind of fell apart. The King Melt sandwich (eggs, bacon, mild peppers, mascarpone, tomato, and basil on a butter bun) lacked zing and was on a rapidly wilting roll. On the weekends crepes are added, and although I had one with champagne-orange soaked pears and mascarpone that was not good at all, other diners have said good things.

That's what Bar Carlo is to these eyes: a pretty standard Portland breakfast place that a lot of folks like. It just happens to also be in the crosshairs of some weird sociological energy.

Wait: Mostly on Sundays, with the side room to be available for waiting soon
Seating: About 50, all at tables.
Large groups? Yes.
Portion size: Underwhelming.
Changes: Minimum fee of $0.50.
Coffee: Self-serve Stumptown.
Other drinks: Tea, espresso, Dragonfly Chai, juices, and sodas, cocktails
Feel-goods: Ingredients are local and organic whenever possible.
Health options: More for vegans on the weekends, but plenty for vegetarians.
WiFi? Soon, they say.

Basta's

Weekend/Classy

Classy, Italian, and not crowded!
410 NW 21st Avenue (NW)
503-274-1572
Brunch served weekends from 10:00 a.m. to 2:00 p.m.
(Lunch also available from noon to 2:00 p.m.)
bastastrattoria.ypguides.net
$12–16 (all major cards, no checks)

It was a typical, energetic Saturday morning on Northwest 21st Avenue: young couples strolling hand in hand, folks walking their dogs, a line at Ken's Artisan Bakery, and joggers weaving through it all. I was looking for a place called Basta's, which I had heard served a nice brunch.

When I passed its address, I saw a strange-looking place that may have once been a fast-food joint. Could *that* be it? Well, I thought, it does have off-street parking. I walked in to find a few things I rarely see at a weekend brunch in Portland: classy decor, a real bar-evening vibe, and a wealth of empty tables. I was there about six months after Basta's started serving brunch, but the waitress told me the place is rarely crowded. "Go tell everybody," she said.

When she brought the menu, I saw more rarities: a small menu, mostly Italian dishes, and all the main courses priced at just $9. The day was getting less ordinary all the time: A classy Italian brunch in the middle of Northwest, with easy parking and no lines? What's going on?

I got an excellent cappuccino made with Illy espresso (the regular coffee is Stumptown) and ordered the Uova alla

Fiorentina, which, according to the menu, was "true eggs Florentine served overeasy with lemon poached asparagus, brown butter sauce, parmigiano reggiano  and black truffle salt." Other options included Uova in Tegamino (organic eggs drizzled in olive oil and baked in clay with San Marzano tomatoes, fresh mozzarella, garlic, and fresh basil) and Mozzarella in Carozza (fresh bread-battered eggs stuffed with fresh mozzarella with tomato sauce.

Also on the menu: Frittata of the Day and Scramble of the Day (both served with a side of polenta, house-made sausage, rosemary potatoes, pepper bacon, or toast), True Belgian Waffle (with leavened dough, not batter) with huckleberries and cream that people rave about, and Polenta Dumplings with sausage, gravy, and two eggs. And each was just $8! Basta's roasts their own pigs and makes their own sausages, pepperoni, Pancetta and breads.

I relaxed and enjoyed the Mediterranean frescoes, wrought iron touches, retro couches and chairs in the waiting area, and the huge wine selection over the bar. Jazz was playing and the staff was in black, so it really had a kind of evening feel to it, especially since it was so quiet. And yet right outside was all the hustle and bustle of Northwest 21st Avenue.

I remembered where I had heard about Basta's: from online foodies. A poster at *PortlandFoodAndDrink.com* called it "a delicious Italian slant on breakfast" and raved about the Bloody Mary "made with habanero vodka garnished with all kinds of pickled vegetables." The blogger at Alt.Portland said it was his favorite Italian place in town. The folks at *PortlandFood.org* generally agreed that it was good (though perhaps a little salty) and reasonably priced. And everybody agreed it's a wacky thing to find in a former Tasty-Freez.

When my food arrived, I could immediately see why everybody liked the place—and again how different it is. This is not your typical American breakfast fare. I had two perfectly cooked over-easy eggs with a light, brown butter sauce spiked with salt, asparagus that was done just as perfectly (crisp outside, soft inside, and a touch of lemon), and a piece of toast that was thick but light, brushed with butter with just the right amount of crunch. Dang!

Sitting with my perfect little meal amidst the pleasant surroundings, enjoying the brisk show outside, I just had to lean back and feel grateful that Portland breakfast could still surprise me.

Wait: None that I've seen.
Seating: About 60 in tables and booths.
Large groups? Yes, but call ahead
Portion size: Reasonable for the price.
Changes: Not so much.
Coffee: Stumptown.
Other drinks: Illy espresso, wine, cocktails, fresh juice, including seasonal fruit juices like pomegranate.
Feel-goods: Many local and organic ingredients, free-range chicken.
Health options: Vegetarians would do well here.
WiFi? Yes.

Beaterville Cafe

Hip/Mom and Pop/Veggie

They put the fun *in funky.*
2201 N Killingsworth St. (N/Outer)
503-735-4652
Hours: Daily 7 a.m. to 2 p.m.
$9-12 (Visa, MasterCard, no checks)

Folks often ask how I got the idea for a book about breakfast in Portland. Well, for more than 10 years I have been the travel writer for the *Memphis Flyer* back in Tennessee. I have written about 300 articles, and along the way a theme developed: I often described a place by describing a meal I had, because a place's essence shines through its restaurants. Generally, that meal was breakfast: breakfast on Amtrak's Empire Builder; breakfast at the Excelsior Hotel in Hong Kong; breakfast in Baker, California, a run-down stopover between L.A. and Vegas.

And one day I was sitting at the Beaterville Cafe with my friend Craig. Already that morning, the front room of the cafe had come to a standstill because a regular had come in with photos from a vacation in France. I also noticed a stream of UPS drivers heading for the back room. The waitress told me the drivers were a regular Bible-study group, and I told Craig, "See, friends coming in from a trip and people meeting every week to get religion: *that's* the kind of thing you write about when you write about breakfast." Then it occurred to me that I had yet to write a "Breakfast in Portland" travel column, and in the next moment this book was born.

So the short answer to the birth of this book is, "I got the idea sitting in Beaterville," and I couldn't think of a more appropriate place for that to happen. And it's not a coincidence; it's hard for me to think of the Beaterville and not have the phrase "perfect Portland breakfast place" come to mind. Maybe not the best or most innovative, but the most Portland, like a drizzly day is perfect Portland weather or like Bud Clark was our perfect mayor. Beaterville is a little strange, really friendly, colorful in both the paint way and the people way, and in a part of town that is seeing both grass-roots changes and intensive urban planning.

It has a good story, as well. A *beater,* you may know, is an old beat-up car that is street-legal but barely runs. And, of course, our fair city has a club—people who are into this kind of thing—and, of course, they occasionally parade their beaters, which is a perfect Portland thing to do. Beaterville's owner is one of these folks, and he still keeps some of his beaters out back, as well as who knows what assortment of automotive parts on the walls. And an odd collection of art. And a backwards clock.

Oh, and the food is excellent. The car theme is carried into the menu, which includes nine yummy, filling "scramblers" (get it, like Ramblers?) such as the Valiant (salmon, black olives, tomatoes, and Cheddar) and the Onassis (tomatoes, spinach, red onions, garlic, Greek olives and feta cheese).

There are also eight omelets, hashes, several combos, and plenty of vegetarian options. (Tofu and egg substitutes are available in all the scrambles and omelets at no extra charge). The French toast has a little crispiness to it and comes slathered with blueberries.

None of this stuff is likely to knock your socks off, but it's all solid and consistent, and there's no more relaxed, fun place to hang out than Beaterville. As you've probably figured by now, I ain't no foodie, much less a food critic. But I have spent years visiting places and eating there, looking for something interesting to write about. And when I think about Portland breakfast, I usually think about Beaterville.

Wait: Long-ish on weekends, with space inside and some cover outside.

Seating: About 60, mostly tables but some comfy two-person booths.

Large groups? Should be better after a scheduled 2008 expansion.

Portion size: Solid.

Changes: Egg dishes can come without toast or potatoes for $1.50 less.

Coffee: Portland Roasting.

Other drinks: Numi Tea, espresso, fruit smoothies.

Feel-goods: None in particular.

Health options: Egg substitutes and tofu available for $1.

WiFi? Yes.

Bertie Lou's

Mom and Pop/Old School

1940s diner with a dash of goofiness
8051 SE 17th Ave., Portland (SE/Sellwood)
503-239-1177
Monday through Friday 7 a.m. to 2 p.m.; Saturday and
Sunday 7:30 a.m. to 2 p.m.
$7–11 (Visa, MasterCard, checks)

————————◆•◆————————

There's a sign on the wall in Bertie Lou's that captures the
essence of the place: "Unattended children will be given a
shot of espresso and a free puppy." It conveys both the reasonable (control your kids) and the whimsical. Think about
it: is there anything cuter than a wound-up kid with a puppy?
That would be *fun*, right?

It's like that through the place and throughout the menu.
Another item on the wall is a picture of Bertie and Lou
standing at the same counter in the 1940s; though they are
long gone, their presence brings in a second level: If there's a
neighborhood breakfast place anywhere in Portland in nearly
original condition and still in its original neighborhood, it's
Bertie Lou's. The only major change is that the second room,
which was a barber shop also owned by Bertie and Lou, now
has eighteen seats at tables to go along with the six at the
counter.

Well, that and the 1940s version probably didn't say,
"Parties of 24 or more require a reservation and 80% gratu-
ity." Probably also didn't say you could get a half-order of
biscuits and gravy that's "no biscuits . . . or no gravy." Or that
the fruit cup is "good for you—not for me." Or that you can

52

get a signed copy of the menu for $10 . . . plus $50 for framing, $25 for packaging, and $50 for delivery.

Get the picture? There's definitely a sense of humor about Bertie Lou's as well as a very friendly vibe, at least during the week when it isn't swamped. Sit at the counter and join in the conversation with the regulars and the staff because Bertie Lou's isn't the place for a private conversation. At Bertie Lou's, about 25 percent of the diners at any given time can reach out and touch the cook.

There's nothing fancy about the food—seven omelets and scrambles, four Benedicts, a couple of breakfast sandwiches, waffles, a burrito—but it's all solid. Egg Beaters and soy bacon are available for non-meat eaters, as is a veggie scramble "made with one, some, or all of the following, depending on what we have at the time you order: mushrooms, eggplant, zucchini, spinach, tomatoes, peppers, onions, and provolone."

Two items do stand out, if only for their difference: the

potatoes are deep-fried reds, golden brown on the outside and soft on the inside, just about perfect to this Southern palate. In one dish, they're grilled with onions and peppers and laid over a bed of sautéed spinach. The other standout is the French toast, which they make with two croissants sliced lengthwise and served with fruit and thick maple syrup. If that isn't enough sugar for you (and if it isn't, I think I'd like to meet you), usually there are cinnamon rolls and bear claws.

So sit back, chat with the folks at the counter, have some sugar and locally roasted coffee, then look at that old picture on the wall and ask yourself how much has really changed. Oh, and control your kids or else you might take home more than a full belly.

Wait: Long on weekends, entirely outside.
Seating: 6 at the counter, 18 at tables in the other room; four tables outside in summer.
Large groups? Would be a hassle.
Portion Size: Reasonable.
Changes: Reasonable.
Coffee: Blue Joe.
Other drinks: Tazo tea.
Feel-goods: Bear claws feel good, right?
Health Options: Egg Beaters, soy bacon, some veggie options.
WiFi? No.

Besaw's Cafe

New/Old School/Classy

Where new cuisine meets Old Portland
2301 NW Savier St. (NW)
503-228-2619
Monday 7:00 a.m. to 3:00 p.m. Tuesday through Friday 7:00
a.m. to 10:00 p.m.; Saturday 8:00 a.m. to 10:00 p.m.; Sunday
8:00 a.m. to 3:88 p.m. Breakfast available daily until 3 p.m.
besaws.com
$10–15 (all major cards)

———————◆•◆———————

My personal history of breakfast in Portland began with
Besaw's. I came to town during the flood of 1996, when an
end-of-the-world rain had been coming down for days and
I was adjusting to a new place to live. I was staying with a
friend who lived on the edge of Forest Park, and each morning we'd stumble down to Besaw's to warm up. I'd get the
Farmer's Hash, apple-cranberry juice, and coffee, and Chip
and I would sit for hours, read about the flood, and marvel at
my new home. Any place where a guy could get good food,
friendly service, chill out with the paper, then go walking in
a 4,000-acre forest was a place to call home.

And why should you care? Well, it's impossible to dis-
cuss breakfast and Portland history without getting Besaw's
into the mix. It's been there since 1903, when two French-
Canadian loggers got seed money from Henry Weinhard to
start a tavern. In fact, back in the corner on the right there's
a photo that shows Besaw's with a steeple on top, before
a 1922 fire took out the second floor. (I met the energetic
young owner, who was working with the Besaw family to get

more of these old photos on the wall.) And, as with every historical building in town, there allegedly was a brothel upstairs. When Prohibition came the guys switched to food, and they've never looked back.

So when you sit down at the 18th-century oak bar to enjoy your classic Portland breakfast—Wild Smoked Salmon Scramble, Farmer's Hash, Forest Mushroom Omelette—you're literally surrounded by Portland history. You'll even see Cousin Maurice's Eggs on the menu, a brie-scallion-tomato dish that's also a staple at Zell's because the two restaurants have swapped ownership and staff over the years.

The weekend wait can be historic as well, but the staff serves coffee outside, and it's quite a social scene out there. Inside you'll find the perfectly Portland combination of class and chill. The staff is in black and makes a fine Bloody Mary, but the clientele is as likely to be mountain bikers in from Forest Park as high-end shoppers ready to cruise Northwest 23rd Avenue. You can sit inside under the ceiling fans or out back on the covered patio, and you'll find the menu extensive and the dishes full of fresh, local ingredients.

The salmon scramble is spiced with dill and smoothed by cream cheese. The potatoes are big chunks of reds tossed with garlic and rosemary. The mushroom omelet has shitake, portobello, and button mushrooms. The Farmer's Hash, a longtime favorite, is three eggs scrambled with potatoes, roasted garlic cloves, bacon, onions, peppers, and Cheddar cheese. It's fine thing to eat on a rainy day.

The priciest entrée (two eggs, potatoes, and either grilled wild salmon or a six-ounce Strawberry Mountain Organic Steak) is only $12.50, so it's not a budget-busting place. And for $6.50 or less you can get organic oatmeal, organic home-made granola, banana-pecan buttermilk pancakes, three big pieces of French toast made with apple fritter bread from local Sunrise Bagels, or a big, tasty Belgian waffle.

And, sitting under the twirling fans listening to the creaking wood floor, you can try to decide (as my friends Linda and Rich and I did) if Northwest Portland reminds you more of a relaxed San Francisco or a hilly Back Bay in Boston. Then you can hop the streetcar to go downtown, stroll the scene on Northwest 23rd, or head up to Forest Park for a woodsy walk. In other words, you can relax, eat well, and feel right at home.

Wait: Way long on weekends after about 9 a.m.

Seating: 60 inside and 20 on the patio, all at tables. A few seats at the bar. Plus there are 6 sidewalk tables.

Large groups? A mild hassle on weekends.

Portion size: Large.

Changes: Easy.

Coffee: Stumptown.

Other drinks: Espresso, Tao of Tea, fresh juices, Italian soda, Dragonfly Chai, Mimosas, and Bloody Marys.

Feel-goods: The menu says "Fresh, local and organic ingredients whenever possible."

Health options: Egg substitute for $1.50, some gluten free options

WiFi? No.

Bijou, Cafe

New/Classy/Veggie

You can be healthy/progressive and *be a "real" restaurant!*
132 SW 3rd Ave., Portland (Downtown)
503-222-3187
Monday through Friday, 7:00 a.m. to 2:00 p.m.; Saturday and Sunday, 8:00 a.m. to 2:00 p.m. Breakfast until 2:00 p.m. daily.
$14–17 (Visa, MasterCard, local checks).

———————◄●►———————

The best way to sum up the Bijou Café's standing in Portland's breakfast scene is this: Out of 36 restaurants listed in *Frommer's* Portland guide, only three serve breakfast: the Heathman, Peanut Butter & Ellies (which made it as a kiddie/novelty place), and the Bijou.

And the best way to explain how that happened is to have a bite of the Willapa Bay Fresh Oyster Hash. Four or five cornmeal-dredged grilled oysters sit on thin strips of onion and potatoes, with parsley and a dash of lemon. Sorting through all this for variations on the perfect bite might be the highlight of your day. It's serious food. It's also $12.50, with no toast or other sides.

The Bijou might not have been the first place in town to stress locally raised and organic ingredients. But has been around since St. Patrick's Day, 1978), and it sure does look, feel, and act like the granddaddy of the New Portland restaurants. Both the crowds and the prices seem to back up that assertion.

The old brick walls and exposed wood beams say history; the modern art on the walls say style; the coat racks on each booth actually host coats and say utility; the blue-and-white checkered tablecloths, old-timey sugar pourers, and muffins in a basket say down-home. You'll see businesspeople going over charts, friends planning a wedding, tourists poring over maps, conventioneers reuniting, and regulars chatting with the staff.

The Bijou is darn near the prototypical Portland breakfast place. It's not necessarily the best, and it's certainly not the cheapest, but it's perhaps the one place you'd take your parents or other visitors who want a nice, safe dose of Portland's organic, progressive, friendly, homey culture without the tattoos, hairy armpits, and all-out vegan fare. Your waitress might be wearing rainbow stockings, though.

Another telling tidbit: They serve Heritage Farms bacon, Grafton Village sharp Cheddar cheese, Nancy's yogurt, Tracy's Small Batch granola, Kookoolan Farms chicken, and Dagoba hot chocolate, and they don't offer a word of explanation regarding what these ingredients are. It's like what was once a radical idea — using artisan and (presumably) local ingredients raised in a healthy way — now doesn't even need an explanation.

It's also true that a lot of folks in town think this is all very uppity and just an excuse to charge $8.75 for bacon and eggs or $10.25 for a cheese-and-mushroom omelet (ah, but they're *crimini* mushrooms!). And grilled orange-anise bread "baked for us by Pearl Bakery" and called *gibassier*? Please.

It's not a slacker, stumble-in hung over and surf the Web for two hours kind of place. It's like, I don't know, a grown-up restaurant—but a relaxed, Portland breakfast restaurant. The Roast Beaf Hash is made with vegetarian-fed beef ($11.95). Daily-special muffins (I had Banana-hazelnut) are made fresh. Brioche, French, or whole wheat toast; cornmeal, buckwheat, or buttermilk pancakes, all with real maple syrup.

Maybe the place just grew up. And maybe the "New Portland" is doing the same. The whole *Frommer's* thing feels like a stamp of approval from a parent. *Frommer's* calls the Bijou "comfortably old-fashioned, yet thoroughly modern." Tough to add to that.

Wait: Long on weekends; sometimes a wait during the week. Small indoor waiting area.

Seating: About 80, mostly tables, and there are 12 counter spaces.

Large groups? Could be a seriously long wait. No reservations.

Portion Size: Big (and they'd better be!).

Changes/Substitutions: Within reason.

Coffee: Cafe Femenino (organic).

Other drinks: Illy espresso, Dagoba hot chocolate, Tao of Tea, fresh organic OJ and Grapefruit, Nudsen's Organic Vegetable Juice.

Feel-goods: Heavy emphasis on organic and local ingredients.

Health options: Tofu, granola.

WiFi? No, but you can pick it up from next door.

Biscuits Cafe

Old School

Just a big ol' all-American place
Four locations in Portland:
    5137 NE Sandy Blvd. (NE/Hollywood), 503-288-8271
    103 NW 21st Ave. (NW), 503-295-3729
    460 SW Miller Road (SW/Outer), 503-297-3880
    9201 SE 91st Ave. (SE/Outer), 503-777-2800
Also in Oregon City, Beaverton; Canby; Vancouver, Washington; and Grapevine, Texas.
Monday through Saturday, 6:30 a.m. to 2:30 p.m.; Sunday 7:00 a.m. to 2:30 p.m. (Hours are for all locations; breakfast served all day.)
biscuitscafe.com
$10–15 (Visa, MasterCard, no checks)

———◆•◆———

Whenever I tell people that Biscuits Cafe has a location in Texas, they always say, "Yeah, I can see that." When I add that it's in a town called Grapevine (a suburb of Dallas), they kind of chuckle. I mean, how much bigger can you get than Texas, and how much more American than a suburb called Grapevine?

And that may be all you need to know about Biscuits Cafe: it's big, it's American, and it's mostly in the suburbs. So to a lot of folks that means it's a comfortable, charming place with gigantic portions, friendly staff, and a consistent theme. To others it is at best boring, at worst generic food that barely rises above fast food with servers who often don't know what they're doing.

Biscuits has spread from its first location in Oregon City,

which opened in 1998, to now include nine locations. The owners met while working at Sambo's in 1968, and after a stint in management at Kings Table Buffet, they moved to Oregon and hired their son, who had just graduated from Western Culinary Institute. And in case we haven't hit on enough Americana themes yet—family, marriage, upward mobility, chasing your dreams, moving West—wait until you see the menu at Biscuits.

Consider the Joe's Scramble, with spinach, onions, tomato, bacon, potatoes, and Parmesan with a choice of biscuit, pancakes, or toast. You can get up to three biscuits with gravy and add meat, hashbrowns, or red potatoes. The Breakfast Specialties, served with red potatoes or hashbrowns and a choice of biscuits, pancakes, or toast, consist of eggs with New York Strip, Polish sausage, pork loin, chicken fried steak, ham, bacon, sausage patty, or hamburger patty.

Folks, we're not even halfway through page one of the two-page breakfast menu! As I'm sure they like to say in Grapevine, *yeeee-ha!* We got yer corned beef hash, yer sweet potato pancakes, yer blueberry pancakes, *and* yer buttermilk pancakes. We got yer almond-crusted French toast on sourdough bread or with berries and whipped cream. And waffles, too, o'course—got them three ways too! We got us a seniors' and kids' menu too. And folks, we have twelve omelets and four Benedicts, including a corned beef hash Benedict (dang!) and the Country Benedict with buttermilk biscuit, sausage patties, and poached eggs all smothered in gravy. Jes' try gettin' up on yer mount with all'a *that* in yer belly!

Okay, I'm being silly, but you get the idea on the food,

right? And the portions! You should have seen my friend Jane when her French toast showed up. It was six big slices of, yes, Texas toast, with a side of four slices of bacon. I had thought that $7.99 was a bit high for ham and eggs, until I saw it and realized I'd be having the leftovers for dinner.

The decor of the place is no more challenging or ambitious than the menu is. The theme is old-timey, and the effect is a little goofy and made up. I thought it was sentimental and fine for what it is. At the NE Sandy Boulevard location, we saw folks dressed up for church and three generations of families eating together, and I'm pretty sure Jane and I were the only people headed for a hike in the Gorge after breakfast.

I've seen complaints about the staff, mainly running along the lines of "nice but not too professional." I haven't seen the latter, but in a rapidly growing chain I imagine that sometimes you'll run into some new staff.

What is a stretch is imagining a place that doles out more Americana and food per buck.

Wait: A little on weekends after about 10:00.
Seating: Varies per location.
Large groups? Absolutely.
Portion size: Texas size.
Changes: Yes.
Coffee: Farmer Brothers.
Other drinks: Stash tea, iced tea, hot chocolate, sodas, cappuccinos and mochas from a machine.
Feel-goods: None.
Health options: Egg whites and substitutes available for a small fee.
WiFi? No.

Blossoming Lotus

New/Veggie

"Bringing Peace to Life"
925 NW Davis St. (Pearl)
503-228-0048
Breakfast served 8:30 a.m. to noon daily.
blpdx.com
$7–11 (Visa, MasterCard, no checks)

———————◆—•—◆———————

To list the Blossoming Lotus as a breakfast place seems to demean it. Even calling it a place that serves breakfast doesn't remotely do it justice. How about this? On its Web site, the Lotus calls itself "a vortex of positive and loving vibrations for all to experience." Seriously.

Portland's Blossoming Lotus (there's one on Kauai, also) is in the lobby of Yoga in the Pearl, and from the fountains, the healthy-happy staff, the bamboo, and the sunshine to the stylish hard-body Pearlites, it's just about the healthiest damn place in town. And there's not one ounce of snootiness about it.

And, yes, the Lotus does serve breakfast—only five breakfast-specific options—but the larger lunch menu is also available starting at 11:00 a.m. Of the food, the Web site says, "Our cuisine is prepared and served with mindfulness, gratitude and the intention to heal and nurture. . . . Respect for the earth and the principles of nonviolence guide us to utilize the abundance of the plant kingdom in all of our recipes."

If you'll allow me to cut through the New-Agey stuff, everything served is organic and vegan—even the beer. Ditto the "soft serve," which is made with soy milk. And then there's the word *live*. It kind of jumps out at you from the menu, like when my dessert-oriented eye wandered to an offering called "Live Pecan Pie."

Although it's fun to think of a pecan pie hopping around, refusing to be eaten like the lobster on the old "Muppet Show," at the

Lotus *live* means "raw," and many of the selections, including two on the breakfast menu, are raw. And lest you think *vegan* means "veggie burgers" and *raw* means "salad," how does this sound for breakfast? Breakfast Parfait with live granola, fresh fruit, and cashew nut creme. Buckwheat and Walnut Granola with fresh and dried fruit and nut milk. A breakfast burrito (tofu, black beans, and veggies), and good ol' hot oatmeal with maple syrup, fresh fruit, raisins, and Brazil nut milk.

Since the lunch menu is available all day, you should wander off into the world of wraps and bowls and sandwiches; there's only one non-dinner entree above $8, and everything will leave you glowing with health — even if you feel like only a visitor in the world of health, yoga, and raw food. I think of trips to the Lotus not just as a cheap, healthy meal with some great people-watching, but rather as time spent among folks who usually keep guys like me at bay. Facing the young, smile-adorned staff, I feel guilty asking for coffee — as if I should promise not to scratch myself or talk about football while I'm there.

I exaggerate to make a point: The Blossoming Lotus isn't just about nutrition; the cafe refers to itself as a "model" and the official slogan is "Bringing peace to life." Sitting in the sunny, relaxing cafe, you can see it's meant both ways: bringing a little peace to your life and trying to give life to a larger peace.

Wait: You order at a counter, but it can be tough to get a seat at times.

Seating: About 20 at tables, a few outside.

Large groups? Wouldn't work.

Portion size: Smaller than most.

Changes: Fine.

Coffee: None, but there's a coffee shop across the street.

Other drinks: Teas, chai, home-made milks (rice, soy, Brazil nut and Hemp nut), smoothies, fresh juices, beer, wine, sake.

Feel-goods: Everything is organic and vegan; most of it is local.

Health options: Bountiful; many dishes are raw.

WiFi? Yes.

Bluehour

Weekend/New/Classy

Approachable sophistication

250 NW 13th Ave. (Pearl)

503-226-3394

Brunch served Sundays from 10:00 a.m. to 3:00 p.m.

bluehouronline.com

$15–23 (all major cards, no checks)

———————◆•◆———————

I can offer but one man's—well, one table's—opinion on brunch at Bluehour, and it is this: Eating brunch at Bluehour felt like listening to a famous recording by Miles Davis. I became immensely comfortable, felt sophisticated, concentrated hard, and believed that something good and impressive was happening. In both jazz and fine cuisine, however, I must depend on the opinions of experts. To my ears Miles Davis sounds nice and is obviously talented, but the experts tell me he's also important, influential, monumental, and historic. Bluehour is a beautiful restaurant with very good food and excellent service, but the experts tell me it's a lot more than that.

They tell me that its owners, Bruce Carey and Kenny Giambalvo, changed the Portland dining scene forever with his previous place, Zefiro. After Zefiro closed, Carey opened Bluehour, with its million-dollar interior featuring Italian space-defining curtains, supremely tall windows, and leather Bellini chairs. (Note: I don't know what a Bellini chair is.)

So we all agreed that Bluehour is important, as (I am told) was Davis's album, *Kind of Blue*. Relative to the Portland breakfast scene, however, Bluehour operates in a sphere all its own. In October 2007 Bluehour did something right out of

 a Hollywood movie by hosting a $125-per-person benefit for wild cheetahs, with two actual cheetahs in the restaurant. And during the economic slowdown of 2008, Carey told the *Willamette Week* he had instructed his staff to find a Pinot noir for less than $50.

I figured the lowly Breakfast Crew would need reservations to eat at this place, and maybe a loan from the World Bank. Neither was true; half the restaurant is saved for walk-ins, and, as an example, the Eggs Benedict (with house-smoked pork loin) is $12.

But first you have to *see* the place! The ceilings soar, the curtains ripple, and various nooks are adorned with large sprigs from flowering trees. A lily awaited us at our table. It attracts a crowd unlike any other place in Portland. I saw a woman in pearls! And visiting movie stars eat at Bluehour, probably because it's the only place that reminds them of L.A. or New York. I don't know that we saw anybody famous, but one good candidate was a guy in jeans, black boots, wrinkled white shirt, sport coat, and perfect three-day beard.

The staff is everywhere and nice looking, in sleek white aprons held together in back by metal clips. We found the service to be phenomenal. When Jerry dropped a knife, in the time it took me to crack a joke about his lack of sophistication, somebody was standing next to him with a new, clean knife . . . on a platter. Shari had a pancake that was a little overdone, and it took about two minutes to bring out another, perfectly done and with a new complement of huckleberry sauce. Or maybe it was compote. Or coulis. I can never tell.

Ah, yes, the food. Forgive my getting carried away

with the setting. It seems to happen to others, as well. The *Oregonian*, for example, said Bluehour had a "solid, sometimes inspired kitchen." But they might have also said Davis was a little flat on a solo, and how would I know?

We all thought the food was good, and Jerry loved his French omelet with its smoky truffle flavor. Our waitstaff brought us yummy almond tea cakes as an *amuse bouche*, certainly the only one I've seen at breakfast. The rest of the items, at least the titles, are quite common; it's a true brunch, with sandwiches and salads in addition to breakfast stuff like omelets and Benedicts and hashes and pancakes and a waffle. None of us were as blown away by what was on the plate as we were by what was going on around us. But we sure had fun eating whatever was there, if that makes sense.

Although the prices aren't obscene, look out for the drinks: we paid $3.25 each for coffee and $3.50 for a glass of orange juice. But you have to expect prices like that at a place like Bluehour. I mean, this isn't a "breakfast place," right? It's an institution, a landmark, a breakthrough, a *scene!* It's nice of them to let us common folks in too.

Wait: Little to none, but they do take reservations.
Seating: Vast.
Large groups? Absolutely, but call for reservations.
Portion size: Stylish.
Changes: Within reason.
Coffee: Stumptown; French Press available.
Other drinks: Espresso, cocktails, juices.
Feel-goods: Local ingredients, including organic eggs.
Health options: Not a whole lot for vegetarians.
WiFi? How crude!

Bread and Ink Cafe

New/Classy/Kid-Friendly

A classy old lady down on Hawthorne

3610 SE Hawthorne Blvd. (SE/Hawthorne)

503-239-4756

Breakfast served Monday through Friday 8 a.m. to 11:30 a.m.;
Saturday 8 a.m. to 12:30 p.m.; Sunday 8 a.m. to 2 p.m.

$12–16 (all major cards, checks)

———————◆•◆———————

Down in New Orleans there are restaurants called Old Line. They aren't cutting edge and a lot of folks consider them stuffy, but they are immensely popular and traditional. The Grand Dame is 100-year-old Galatoire's, with its tuxedoed staff twirling under massive chandeliers, jackets required for male patrons, and families who've had the same waiter for two generations. But here's the kicker: it's on Bourbon Street! So when you walk out of your 19th-century luxury dining experience, you have a decent chance of hearing Jimmy Buffet karaoke or seeing somebody puke.

On a lesser scale, the Bread and Ink Cafe may be the Galatoire's of the Portland breakfast scene. It opened "way back" in 1983, and was sort of a pioneer on then-run-down Hawthorne. Today, it's definitely aiming for the area between classy and casual. It has fresh flowers to greet you and high-backed green chairs with armrests. Its white-tablecloth reputation has labeled it as a high-end, expensive place—but the drawing paper on the tables mark it as kid-friendly. And when you walk out of the Bread and Ink, you have a decent chance of hearing drums or seeing somebody in a Guatemalan skirt.

I took my girlfriend, Jenny, there for a leisurely weekday breakfast at a time when I had a night job and she was out of school. When she arrived, I got kind of swept up in the fancy atmosphere—rising to give her a kiss and pulling out her chair for her. We were served quickly and efficiently, and our server put up with a lot of my goofy questions: Why is the Kentucky Pork Sausage called that? (It's just a name.) What about the Santa Fe Chicken Sausage? (it's got a Southwestern flavor to it.)

I should tell you that in my research no other place got quite the negative online reviews for service like the Bread and Ink. The reviews spanned several years and may or may not have been the result of Southeast Portland slackerness running into high expectations. Among the more serious food-oriented sites and blogs, it's often damned with the "ain't what it used to be" designation. On the other hand, it's packed every weekend.

As of late 2007, you can even get a little something on the street. They opened the Waffle Window (8 a.m. to 5 p.m. on weekends) with a wide range of sweet waffle flavors like chocolate dipped, apple pie, and banana Nutella waffle. All of these run from $2 to $3.50.

Inside, the options range from the basic Skillet Scramble (red onions, herbed potatoes, Italian sausage, spinach, and Cheddar cheese with a side of fresh fruit) to the more sophisticated Smoked Trout Scramble with onions, pepper bacon, spinach, and Jack cheese topped with horseradish sour cream. There's also an omelet unique to Portland, as far as I know: the Apple Omelet of Granny Smiths with caramelized onions, pepper bacon, and Gruyère cheese. Alas, the kitchen was out of it when I visited—another complaint that popped up on the Internet, by the way.

I had to "settle" for the Brioche French Toast, which was a whopping four slices of super-moist raisin bread soaked in a cinnamon-vanilla custard. In my experience only the over-the-top offering at Café du Berry is less in need of syrup. The Tomato, Avocado, and Pepper Bacon Scramble that Jenny ordered was longer on other ingredients than on eggs, which we didn't mind since the ingredients, especially the bacon, seemed to pack more flavor than in the average scramble.

When I looked around, I realized (this was at 11 a.m. on a Friday) that I was the only male! Seven tables were occupied, two of them with kids, and they were girls, too! That's when I realized I had gone through the looking glass, transcended the pseudo-hippie Hawthorne, and arrived in the land of the leisurely. Me and the ladies, having a late breakfast!

Still caught up in the moment and feeling a bit Old Line, I took Jenny's hand and said, "I wonder what all the employed folk are doing today?"

Wait: Long on weekends.
Seating: 75, all at tables. **Large groups?** Sure.
Portion size: Medium. **Changes:** Within reason.
Coffee: Kobos. **Other drinks:** Espresso, tea, fresh juices.
Feel-goods: Local ingredients.
Health options: Nothing stands out.
WiFi? Yes.

Bridges Cafe

New/Hip/Veggie

It was cool before MLK was cool
2716 NE MLK Jr. Blvd. (NE/MLK)
503-288-4169
Weekdays 7:00 a.m. to 2:00 p.m. Weekends 8:00 a.m. to
3:00 p.m.
bridgescafeandcatering.net
$9–13 (all major cards)

———————————◆•◆———————————

What is happening these days on Martin Luther King, Jr.
Boulevard—all the new construction, redevelopment, and
old homes getting fixed up—was only a twinkle in some city
planner's eye when Bridges Cafe first opened in 1994. Back
then, the owner wanted to start a food-import business. But
the bank wanted to finance something like a restaurant to
get the neighborhood going. In fact, when Bridges opened
it was one of only two restaurants in almost two miles along
MLK. The building had, according to an article in the
Portland Business Journal, "no plumbing and no electricity;
big chunks of plaster fell off the walls. To save money, (the
owner) bartered with local plumbing and electrician compa-
nies—lunches in exchange for their services."

A crowd of regulars formed, and the new owner teamed
up with the owner of another business to start events called
Saturday Stroll and the Dog Days of Summer to get people walking around and noticing the neighborhood's
businesses.

Word spread around the city: there's this cool place to
eat breakfast up on MLK! From the beginning Bridges was
known for a laid-back atmosphere, good Benedicts, local

organic ingredients, and the best mimosas around. And believe me, in the mid- to late-1990s this was exciting news in pretty much any Portland neighborhood, let alone MLK.

Bridges hasn't changed that much. It still has the same tile tables, the same big windows, the same type of staff that can seem alternately goofy or surly, and the same down-to-earth menu: three Benedicts (Carlton Farms Canadian bacon, smoked wild salmon, and florentine); four omelet or scramble options; a range of basics like oatmeal, granola, and biscuits and gravy; and seven specialties that range from waffles and challah French toast to catfish hash, a breakfast burrito, and Eggs Fiesta, a Mexi-mix served on cornbread.

It's funny to think that this kind of menu was once worth driving across town for, but it was. Of course, a lot has changed since 1994, and as a result, Bridges's star has faded somewhat while the rest of the neighborhood has blossomed. A typical modern take on the place was a review on the Web site *altportland.com,* which called it a "sunny little breakfast joint" and started out, "I hate to damn Bridges with faint praise, but it's a neighborhood joint . . . reasonably friendly, generous with the food . . . consistently not bad."

Since I have fond memories of Bridges (I'm fairly sure I saw my first hipster there), I went back to check it out. I walked in at about 10:30 a.m. on a weekday, just like the old days, and saw a guy hunched over his computer, two contractors talking shop, an older couple looking around as if they'd never been there, and four young women talking about their favorite teacher. The waiter came over and asked if I wanted coffee, then pirouetted off with a flourish. He returned to do a high-altitude pour into my mug and I thought, well, they've still got style.

The specials that day, each about $8 or $9, were old standards: a bacon-onion-mushroom-Cheddar scramble and a garlic-spinach-roasted red pepper-Jack cheese scramble. I ordered my old favorite, the Catfish Hash, and the rest was a trip down memory lane. It's still a big pile of potatoes with grilled onions and peppers and chunks of fried catfish in a stiff batter spotted with sesame seeds, topped with two perfectly poached eggs and Creole Hollandaise, which is a spicy version of the sauce, still one of the best sauces in town. It's still served with big slices of yummy toast that somehow play perfectly with the savory festival on the plate and the house-made marionberry jam. And all this for $9.75!

Neighborhood joint, indeed. An old friend in a rapidly changing neighborhood, I say.

Wait: Pretty long on weekends after about 10:00 a.m., with limited space inside and cover outside.
Seating: 40 seats, two booths. Some outdoor seating in summer, but street noise can be loud.
Large groups? Yes, but not the best place for it.
Portion size: Big.
Changes: Within reason.
Coffee: K&F. **Other drinks:** Soda, apple juice, espresso, Dragonfly Chai, cocktails, mimosas, bottled beer.
Feel-goods: Many ingredients are local and organic.
Health options: Good options for vegetarians.
WiFi? Yes.

Broder

New

Absolutely the best Swedish breakfast in town
2508 S.E. Clinton St. (SE/Division)
503-736-3333
Breakfast served daily 9:00 a.m. to 2:00 p.m.
$12–15 (Visa, MasterCard, cash)

When Broder opened in 2007, so many people wrote about it that it was a little overwhelming, especially since so many dishes were completely new to the Portland breakfast scene and some were completely unknown. When was the last time you saw a breakfast menu with pickled herring, meatballs in sherry cream, Duroc ham, Pytti Panna, or Aebleskivers?

Allow me, then, to summarize what every review had in common: Broder is a cute, popular place that serves authentic Swedish cuisine — the reviewer knows because of various Swedish connections or experiences — that, when you eat it, will make you feel like you've tapped into Scandinavian culture and want to ride a reindeer or something. And it's a million times better than IKEA.

Some folks think it's great food at a good price, but others think it's a novelty restaurant with bland food. The *Oregonian*, in a generally positive review, wondered why the food couldn't be more interesting, even if a little less authentic. The *Mercury* said, "Breakfast at Broder is a dainty affair, with modest portions and an emphasis on adorability. But the preciousness wears off if you realize you've ordered the most expensive breakfast item on the menu and you're still hungry."

So Broder is different; it's not a gut-bomb place, and it's not greasy, and breakfast is served on boards. The latter, I must admit, is what Elena and I were excited about when we went to check it out. We just wanted something on a board. And I wanted to eat there with Elena because she's a tall blonde, which I thought would accentuate my Scandinavian experience.

Broder is definitely a tiny, cute place, aiming for a cross between old-timey (dark wood and light fixtures that everyone compares to antlers) and the sleek-modern-Euro feel, with white tiles, stainless steel, and lots of powder blue that reminded me of flying on KLM. The square shelf units will remind you of IKEA, the napkins are tied with twisty ties, and the bathroom is labeled "WC." Handwritten specials on a mirror offer AM Booze called Damenel Dansk (whatever that is) and desserts like Swedish Cream, Danish Butter Cream, Applesauce Cake, and Bread Pudding.

The menu, at least at breakfast, is surprisingly close to what you're used to seeing, just with little twists and different names. Turns out Aebleskivers are Danish pancakes, and they are little fried balls of dough served with lingonberry jam, lemon curd, and syrup on the side. We thought they were great. Options for baked scrambles (served with walnut toast and a choice of roasted tomatoes, green salad, or potato pancake) include smoked trout and red onion, wild mushroom and caramelized onion, or Duroc ham and homemade ricotta. (I looked it up online, and it turns out Duroc is a type of pig, prized for its marbled meat.) And yes, everything is served on a board. Cute, huh?

The signature dish is the Swedish Breakfast Bord, a

sampler plate of rye crisp, walnut toast, salami, smoked trout, grapefruit, yogurt and honey, lingonberry jam, and hard cheese, for $10. The rest of the menu, like I said, is close to standard American fare, just not quite the same. There's Pytti Panna (it's Swedish hash) with potatoes, peppers, green onions, ham, and roast beef topped with baked eggs and served with walnut toast ($9). Swedish Waffles come with butter, syrup, and seasonal fruit. The Breakfast Sandwich has Duroc ham, Gruyère, marjoram cream, and roasted tomatoes topped with baked eggs ($8).

Elena and I were not blown away by the food, which means we didn't know and appreciate the subtleties of Scandinavian cuisine or they were really more novelty than taste. But it's a fun, cute place to eat in a cool little neighborhood. And if you can avoid the lines, and maybe bring a cute, tall blonde with you, it's a charming little place to eat breakfast.

Wait: Up to 30 minutes on weekends. Most waiting is outside.
Seating: 30, all at half-booths.
Large groups? No.
Portion size: Smallish.
Changes: Within reason.
Coffee: Stumptown.
Other drinks: Fresh Lemonade, Orange Juice and Grapefruit Juice, Wine and Beer, Cocktails.
Feel-goods: Menu says, "We always use cage-free eggs and organic produce and meats whenever possible."
Health options: Not much here for vegetarians.
WiFi? No.

Bumblekiss

New/Kiddie

Sweet, happy, sunny day!

3517 NE 46th Ave. (NE/Fremont)

503-282-6313

Weekdays 8:00 a.m. to 2:30 p.m. Weekends 8:00 a.m. to
3:30 p.m. Breakfast all day.

$10-14 (Visa, MasterCard, no checks)

When you hear a name like Bumblekiss, you know you're not
talking about a place that takes itself seriously. If anything,
the name practically screams "bring your kids!" And when
you want to evaluate how a place does with kids, there's no
better way than to call in the Play Group.

The Play Group is a group of moms who meet on
Wednesdays to get out of the house, get the kids together,
share the work and play, and have some adult time. So the
group's a lot of fun and really cute, if not always manageable.
When you see the group doing its thing at Bumblekiss, you
realize the two were made for each other.

Bumblekiss is in an old orange-painted house just up
from NE Fremont Avenue; it sports a Ping-Pong table in
the garage and a driveway filled with tables under umbrellas. In the single room inside, you're greeted with orange
plastic chairs (cheerful and unbreakable), yellow walls with
a constellation of mirrors, and an orange ceiling from which
hangs a collection of coloring-book pages. So we're off to a
happy start.

When our group announced itself as 11 — that's out of 20
seats inside — the waitress didn't even flinch and just started

moving tables around. Done this before, I reckoned. Out of more than 200 breakfasts I ate for this book, no waitress did more with less help and in a more cheerful manner than the Play Group's heroine at Bumblekiss. We ordered in three waves, asked for changes, and paid with about four cards; she was happy and efficient the whole time.

The food fit in with the mix of adult and kiddie that Play Group is all about. A little basket of yummy mini-muffins (blueberry-banana and lavender-coconut plus a third flavor that changes daily) included oat-based options for protein and health and an apple-pecan special that was sweet enough to send a kid bouncing around the room. The kids' menu (with room for scribbling) featured four items at $4.25 each: pancakes with chocolate sauce and maple syrup for dipping, an egg-French toast combo, Chicken-Apple (sausage) in a Blanket, and Green Eggs and Ham, the color courtesy of some blueberry extract. Although the adults agreed that the kid portions were too big, the youngsters offered up such feedback as Porter's "Mmmmm." Lily, who was by now wearing some of the Little Dipper's chocolate sauce, added, "This is good!"

The moms talked of hair and shopping and trips to the zoo; I sampled the oatmeal (a slight berry flavor), one of five benedicts (this was a veggie version with a nice light sauce and a big slice of tomato), the French toast (cinnamon-swirl with berries all over it) the fantastic pancakes (moist and rich), and the pepper bacon, which I'm happy to say was both tasty and a little too spicy for the kids. Hence, more for me.

The *Willamette Week,* soon after Bumblekiss opened, wrote

a review that called it "an adorable neighborhood place" but suggested that maybe the chefs were trying to do too much, especially with the number of ingredients in some of their dishes. The Sweet Stuff Scramble, for example, has chicken apple sausage, yellow onions, diced green apple, mozzarella, and blue cheese. The Farmer's Benedict has a tomato slice, basil pesto, feta cheese and hollandaise sauce. Some of these tastes might kind of run together; then again, they're all well cooked and tasty.

My theory, as the Play Group's trip to Bumblekiss suggested, is that a little managed chaos can be fun, especially when it's playful and colorful and cute.

Wait: Short on weekends.
Seating: 20 at tables inside, 5 with umbrellas outside
Large groups? Yes.
Portion size: Reasonable.
Changes: Easy, and all the scrambles come with potatoes or fruit and Grand Central Baking toast or a side order of French toast or pancakes.
Coffee: Organic, shade-grown, farmer direct, Tanager Song Coffee from Portland Roasting Company (also for sale at $12.50 a pound).
Other drinks: Mighty Leaf tea, weekly mimosa specials (no other liquor), and beer.
Feel-goods: They use "organic and local ingredients whenever possible," as well as free range meats and cage-free eggs.
Health options: Egg beaters and tofu available for scrambles. They use no hydrogenated oils and say they have neither a fryer nor a microwave.
WiFi? No.

Byways Cafe

Hip/Old School

Can you resist the kitsch? What about the French toast?

1212 NW Glisan St. (Pearl)

503-221-0011

Monday through Friday 7:00 a.m. to 3:00 p.m. (breakfast
until 11:00); Weekends 7:30 a.m. to 2:00 p.m. (breakfast only,
no lunches).

$8–11 (Visa, MasterCard, no checks)

———————◆•◆———————

Dan and Amy are self-proclaimed "foodies." They actually
met at the Culinary Institute of America, ran a restaurant,
and spent most of a year at a restaurant school in Bologna,
Italy. So I took them to Byways Cafe to get their impression.
In retrospect, I think it might have been like taking a classical musician to a Grateful Dead concert.

The Byways isn't as wacky as a Dead show, and Dan and
Amy are not snooty by any means. But they are all about the
food: how it's prepared, the state of the ingredients, the presentation, etc. And the Byways has more of a "what's up?"
vibe, if that makes sense. So seeing these two fairly serious
people sit in a springy booth that makes the table a little too
high, under a collection of national park pennants, and with
their coffee in a House of Mystery-Oregon Vortex mug . . .
well, it was worth a chuckle.

When Amy said the amaretto-infused French toast with
honey-pecan butter probably wasn't on real brioche and it
might have had some freezer burn, and Dan sort of grudg-
ingly admitted that his omelet was well cooked, it was a little
like a non-Deadhead pointing out that Bob Weir forgot the

words to "Truckin'." I wanted to say, Yeah, but it was still fun, right?

Maybe I'm just a sucker for kitsch, particularly of the travel variety. When I see a place decorated with souvenirs from the 1910's to the 70's like plates from various tourist sites, luggage, a globe, postcards, View-Masters on the tables, the cases along the walls filled with trinkets, and Roger Miller on the stereo, it could smother previously frozen semi-brioche with butter and syrup and still make me happy. (For the record, I have no idea if the brioche was frozen. Also for the record, I thought the French toast was great. And finally, I don't smoke pot anymore.)

The place even has a history of kitsch. It used to be Shakers, a similar breakfast place with, instead of all the travel knickknacks, the biggest, freakiest collection of salt and pepper shakers you'll ever see.

It's funny: My notes from three research trips to Byways include phrases like "chic greasy-spoon: just a marketing theme?" and "down-home feel, food not exceptional." And yet I *like* the place; hell, I kept going back to "research" it! It's like listening to a tape of a Dead show I had a good time at and finding out they repeated verses and missed solos and all the other stoner stuff they did. Does that stuff even matter? Maybe I'm just a rube.

So now I think back on the meals I've had at Byways. One time I had eggs, sausage, and mushy-yummy blue corn pancakes, topped with the honey pecan butter and organic maple syrup. But were those 'cakes supposed to be mushy? Another time, while waiting for a friend who was late I had a blueberry crumble muffin my notes say was "more crumble than blueberry, but good. Dry and sweet." Of course I ate the whole thing.

Now I'm confused. The rest of the menu is just classic stuff—hashes, scrambles, taters, and so on—and I have always enjoyed chatting up the staff. I guess I'm just a little more slacker than foodie, just like I'm a lot more Deadhead than symphony. And Byways seems to fit all that: it's kind of a "whatever" place in the middle of the foodie-infused Pearl, and I'm glad it's there, even if I don't know if it's any good.

Wait: Can get long on weekends, almost entirely outside and uncovered.

Seating: About 50, in tables and booths.

Large groups? Would be a hassle on weekends.

Portion Size: Big, not huge.

Changes: Within reason.

Coffee: Stumptown.

Other drinks: Various brands of teas, including Tazo, Stash, and some British teas, hand-packed milkshakes.

Feel-goods: House-made baked goods.

Health Options: Egg whites and tofu available for $1.

WiFi? No.

Cadillac Cafe

Old School/Classy

The one place everybody knows about
1801 NE Broadway (NE/Broadway)
503-287-4750
Weekdays 6:00 a.m. to 2:30 p.m.; weekends 7:00 a.m. to
3:00 p.m.
$14–18 (all major cards except Discover, no checks)

———————◆•◆———————

Whenever I visit my hometown of Memphis, certain tradi-
tions must be observed. Along with the heat, the humid-
ity, the sentimental moments, and the family-related stress,
I regularly stuff myself on barbecued pork.

Although folks in North Carolina, Kansas City, and
Texas will argue, folks in Memphis think they have the best
barbecue in the world. And when Memphians think of *tradition* and *barbecue* together, one place always springs to mind:
Charlie Vergos's Rendezvous. When visiting the Bluff City,
you pretty much *have* to eat there, after which you have a
drink at the Peabody Hotel and then go boogie to the blues
and R&B on Beale Street.

But here's the thing: the lines at the Rendezvous are
insane, sometimes up to two hours. Old-timers rue the massive expansion that happened in the 1990s, and not many
locals actually think it's the best barbecue in town. It's just
The Place to Go. In fact, part of the reason everybody goes
there is that, well, everybody goes there.

What does all this have to do with Portland? Simple: The
Cadillac Cafe is the Rendezvous of our breakfast scene. The
lines are insane, the vibe feels pretty corporate, some folks

say it used to be cooler in the old location . . . but seemingly everybody has been there.

Simply put, the Cadillac is widely adored. It gets more reviews — and more positively glowing reviews — than almost any other place in town on Web sites like Citysearch and Yelp. Folks flip over the size of the portions and the variety of choices: eight specialties like Filet Mignon Steak and Eggs, Cajun Catfish, and a breakfast burrito in addition to seven omelets and eight items listed as "Simple Fare," including basic egg plates, granola, porridge, pancakes, and French toast.

About that French toast: it's the Cadillac's calling card, and I add my voice to its chorus of praise. It's done two ways: three pieces soaked in custard egg batter for $7.50 (or $9 with seasonal fruit and roasted hazelnuts) or Hazelnut French Custard Toast, which is covered in hazelnuts and powdered sugar and served with one egg and either bacon or chicken apple sausage for $9. You can also get a slice of either kind as part of the Bunkhouse Vittles, a combo plate with sausage, potatoes, and two eggs ($9.25). I was told by a waiter that the French toast bread was developed in the mid-1990s specifically for the Cadillac.

The main gripes against the Cadillac boil down to either "Why would I wait 90 minutes for breakfast?" or "It's more of a suburban chain feel than a 'real' Portland breakfast place." To the former I say, I have to agree. If you're standing in line for an hour and a half on a weekend, it's because you've already decided you love it, you're determined to check it out, or you're entertaining some out-of-town guest who just *has* to experience the tradition.

To the "real Portland" argument, well, that just depends on your style. The Cadillac definitely has an upscale, cosmopolitan, kind of gay flowers-on-the-tables vibe, made a little theme-y by the presence of a pink Cadillac. It is not, in other words, a hippied-out place like the Utopia or the Cricket or a serious foodie palace like Simpatica.

And yet the Cadillac is pure Portland, in an older, richer, Irvington kind of way. But why should I bother to describe it, anyway? There's a 90 percent chance you've already been there and made up your own mind. And if you haven't, well, I suppose you should. If you want a big dose of Portland culture, a Cadillac run would be a pretty solid start.

Wait: Legendary on weekends: up to 90 minutes in good weather.

Seating: About 100 at a counter and tables, plus an enclosed patio.

Large groups? With notice.

Portion size: Massive.

Changes: Options abound.

Coffee: Kobos.

Other drinks: Espresso, breakfast martinis, hot liquor drinks, Oregon Chai, freshly squeezed juices and lemonade, Tazo Tea, sparkling cider.

Feel-goods: None that's touted.

Health options: Substitute fresh fruit or tomatoes for potatoes or toast ($1); staff will make two-egg or white-only omelets.

WiFi? No.

Café du Berry

Classy

French café, with French prices and French people working there
6439 SW Macadam Ave. (SW/Inner)
503-244-5551
cafeduberry.citysearch.com
Breakfast hours are Monday through Friday 7 a.m. to 3 p.m.,
Saturday and Sunday 8 a.m. to 3 p.m.
$12-15 (Checks, all cards)

———————————◆●◆———————————

Café du Berry is a challenge. I went there once and had an outstanding scallop-and-shitake-mushroom omelet, with a light cream sauce, potatoes, and fruit. Rick, Jean and I shared an order of French toast, for which I would have viciously fought anyone.

But the omelet, which wasn't on the menu, was $14, which the server didn't mention. Sure, I could have asked, but a $14 omelet? The server didn't mention the sauce, either, which was tasty but doesn't generally appear on omelets. In fact, whenever he came to the table, we were left somewhat dazed by his rapid-fire, straight-to-the-point, not-even-looking-at-us delivery. He greeted us, described three specials, poured water, and was gone in about 5.2 seconds. So, is that efficient or rude?

But the food was outstanding. Well, mine was. Rick's salmon was overdone, and he needed a knife to get through the English muffin, which was both a little stale and a little overdone. Jean didn't happen to like the potatoes, though I did: they were the mashed potato-type hashbrowns, grilled in a patty with a slightly peppered taste. But Jean rightly pointed out that for $7.95, the French Toast with Potatoes and Fruit was one piece of the (amazing) toast, one smallish helping of potatoes, one strawberry, and half of a banana. That ain't much for $7.95.

The table was cramped. But the hollandaise sauce was good. The padded chairs were comfy, but I had to lean forward every time somebody walked by. The service was quick and efficient, even if it never smiled. The white table-cloths and shirred eggs and frittata and New York café watercolors on loan from a foundation of some sort all said "attitude," but most customers seemed like neighborhood regulars and random visitors, not the snooty art crowd. (We had to ask about shirred eggs, by the way: they are baked to over easy, then served with a light tomato sauce underneath.)

The three of us had a plate each, two had coffee, I had an excellent apple-raspberry juice, we had the extra side order of French toast, and *without the tip* the bill was $50!

So, what to do about this place? Was it good? Yes. Great? No. Overpriced? I'd say so. Were we seated quickly and served efficiently? Yes — and this was a Saturday at 9:30 a.m. Would I go back? Yes, but only for the French toast. In fact, I briefly considered moving to the neighborhood for the French toast.

So I decided to do this: Let you, gentle reader, make up your own, now slightly more informed, mind as to whether you'd like to try Café du Berry . . . and then insist that you eat their French toast.

It's a French custard dessert recipe, made with Hawaiian egg bread thoroughly soaked, then grilled to just crisp on the outside, with a touch of lemon in the finish, dusted with powdered sugar, and served warm, syrup be damned. I could add details like the firmness of the bread and how it played perfectly with the bouncy delight of the custard, but I'm on my way to have some right now.

Wait: Not bad, mostly outside.
Seating: 20 downstairs, 40ish upstairs with booths.
Large groups? Upstairs with some notice.
Portion size: Seemed small for the price.
Changes: We were too scared to try.
Coffee: Kobos.
Other drinks: Espresso, tea, cocktails.
Feel-goods: None that I noticed; it's French food!
Health options: I think if you eat the custard-based French toast, or the béarnaise sauce, or the hollandaise sauce 10 times you get a punch card for a free angioplasty.
WiFi? No.

Cameo Cafe

Mom and Pop/Old School

It's a, um, kitschy Korean Roadhouse!
8111 NE Sandy Blvd. (NE/Outer)
503-284-0401
Daily from 6:30 a.m. to 3:00 p.m. Breakfast served all hours.
cameocafe.com
$14–18 (all major cards)

———◆———

Folks can argue long and hard about the best or worst breakfast places in Portland, and some would put the Cameo Cafe on either of those lists. But I don't think anybody can deny that the Cameo is one of the strangest places in town to eat breakfast. I used to drive by it and figured it was a roadhouse or greasy-spoon joint; there's a cheap-looking motel behind it, and its location at the hub of highways around NE 82nd and Sandy Boulevard gives it a feel of being "out there" someplace.

But inside, the décor practically screams Grandma, with flowered wallpaper, tea sets on shelves, and clay figurines of chefs over the stove. The *Mercury* said it "looks a little like an insurance office," and my friend Jane said it looked like an ice cream parlor. Keep looking and you'll spot a bulletin board covered with signed photos of Miss America contestants who apparently ate there. There's also an accordion, a flashing carousel, a parasol, and more clay figurines of hillbillies, Cupid, and a naked lady.

When you sit down and check for the specials, there's another shock. Nothing can prepare you for the words *Kimchee Omelet.* Jane asked me what kimchee was, and I told

her it's a very spicy fermented cabbage dish popular in Korea. She asked, "And they make an omelet with it?" I can't tell you what it's like because I've never convinced anyone to order it. But when I first saw it, I wondered, What kind of place is this?

Well, it's a, um, kitschy Korean roadhouse. I guess.

Our waitress, Darlene, who to single-handedly serve everybody in the place while dispensing stories, information, and smiles. For example, other than the owner, the only person who knows the recipes for the secret family sauces is the dishwasher, who apparently has worked seven days a week for 16 years. And the hot sauce is called Oh Baby Hot Sauce.

After you peel through the layers of oddness, you'll see that the Cameo is in most ways a pretty straightforward breakfast joint, with big portions and high prices. It shares the famous "acres" of pancakes from the old Cameo West, but Cameo East's Full Acre is listed at Market Price (I forgot to ask why, but it's $10.95). The 'cakes come with apples, bananas, strawberries, raspberries, or peaches.

But there is a Korean thread running through the menu. There are tofu pancakes (made with mung beans and rice), for example, with vegetables and cheese. And there is Sue Gee's FUSION Pancake (that's how it's written on the menu) with rice and vegetables in a "special prepared batter" with cheese. And then there's what I had, the Pindaettok, which is pronounced pin-day-tuck and is, according to the menu, "a Korean word meaning pancake."

I was on my way out of town for a hike, which might be the only time that a soy-based pancake with vegetables, beans, spices, and ground rice in a "flavored batter," cooked thin and crispy and with something called Duck Sauce on the side, sounded about right. It also comes with two eggs, bacon, and two pieces of their yummy, multigrain, house-made STRONG BREAD. (Again, that's how it appears on the menu).

The Cameo also has the usual assortment of waffles (plus a coconut option), French toast, and about a dozen combinations of egg, meat, and carb. But the Pindaettok defined the place for me. I had never heard of it, wasn't quite sure what it was, and was not at all used to spicy vegetables at breakfast.

But I also liked it, and there was more of it than I could eat. And walking out of a breakfast place, all filled up and ready to hike, was the first nonstrange thing that happened to me that day.

Wait: None.

Seating: About 40 inside at tables and a counter, a few covered tables outside.

Large groups? Not so much.

Portion size: Big.

Changes: Within reason; there's also a $1 charge to split plates.

Coffee: Farmer Brother's.

Other drinks: Tea, juices, hot chocolate, old fashioned RC off the tap.

Feel-goods: The house bread is preservative free.

Health options: Pretty good range for vegetarians.

WiFi? No.

Country Cat Dinnerhouse

Weekend/New

A new happening in a newly happening area

7937 SE Stark (SE/Outer)

503-408-1414

Brunch served weekends from 9:00 a.m. to 2:00 p.m.

thecountrycat.net

$13–17 (all major cards)

You could just about drive right past the Country Cat and never notice it. In fact, chances are you've driven right past the whole Montavilla neighborhood and not noticed it. But Montavilla is becoming a "happening" place, and the Country Cat is part of it.

But more on that later. What you need to know about the Country Cat is this: the generic exterior hides an exquisite interior made of wood, with shades of blue and brown, spacious booths, hanging lights, and an open kitchen. It's modern, yet comfy.

Likewise, the menu at first seems rather down-home: pancakes, a Benedict, a basic breakfast, a scramble, biscuits and gravy, and lunch items like chicken wings, a ham sandwich, and fried chicken (more on that later too). Again, though, the details tell you that you're dealing with something different: the pancakes come with things like syrup-glazed bananas or roasted apple maple syrup. The scramble might be of wild mushrooms and goat cheese; the ham sandwich is the Blackstrap Molasses Ham Sandwich with pickled red onion, herbed cream cheese, and whole grain mustard. The Cast Iron Skillet Fried Chicken comes with mixed greens and toasted pecan spoonbread (much more on that later).

The hash might be of duck confit with leeks and collard greens.

See where I'm going here? The Country Cat aspires to be two things, really: a cozy neighborhood place *and* a new-Portland-style cutting-edge restaurant. The chef/owner, who cooked for years at Wildwood, told the *Mercury*, "There's somewhat of a void here, and we wanted to be able to fill it, to raise the bar a little bit."

At the Country Cat, a pig is butchered once a week; bacon, ham, and other meats are made on site. Almost all other ingredients are local. The whole vibe says traditional dishes with top-quality ingredients. After it opened in 2007, most early reviews had a theme: Gosh, an actual good restaurant in *this* neighborhood!

The picky folks over at *PortlandFood.org* went nuts over the place. Some were from the neighborhood and were excited about the Cat in conjunction with the Academy Theater, a wine bar, and a new farmers' market on Sundays. Others were just fired up about such serious cooking with fresh, local produce and an ever-revolving menu based on the season.

And then there is the fried chicken. Just about everybody mentions the fried chicken, for two reasons. One is the decent chance that it will be some of the finest fried chicken you've ever eaten, unless you're a purist and believe that fried chicken should still have the bones and skin. The Cat's is a brined, skinless piece of thigh meat with seasoned breading; at brunch (for $10) one piece comes with a mixed green salad and a slab of toasted pecan spoonbread, which is at the same time moist and cakey and firm and soft and sweet and crispy. It, and the chicken, are drizzled with real maple syrup, and the result led one online poster to gush, "OMG this was about seven kinds of yum, like a delicious marriage between my favorite parts of both soufflé and cornbread."

At dinner, apparently, the chicken is $18, and this is where some folks get a little sideways about the Country Cat. The theme here is, "What's a place, much less in this neighborhood, doing charging $18 for fried chicken?" Some folks even lobbed the nuclear bomb of such conversations: *gentrification.*

I don't wade into such conversations. If a guy can get $18 for fried chicken, I say more power to him. All I can tell you is that the chicken is darn good, as was everything else we had at the Cat, and who cares what neighborhood it's in? My friend Alice spent the whole meal saying, "Wow, this is good," and "I need to come back here for dinner."

Wait: Not bad.

Seating: 67 in tables and booths.

Large groups? Yes.

Portion size: Not overwhelming (some would even say small).

Changes: Yes.

Coffee: Stumptown.

Other drinks: Espresso, Tao of Tea, Bloody Mary, Mimosa, fresh juice.

Feel-goods: Plenty of local ingredients, and much of the meat is prepared on site.

Health options: Brunch menu is open to suggestion for veggie options.

WiFi? Yes.

Cricket Café

Hip/Veggie

Dude, dig the size of this menu!

3159 SE Belmont Ave. (SE/Belmont)

503-235-9348

Breakfast served daily from 7:30 a.m. to 3:30 p.m.

$10-13 (Visa, MasterCard)

The Cricket Café has long been known for a few things: long waits, decent food, big menu and portions, and slow service. I have seen all these in action at various times. Try it sometime: Ask your friends if they've been to the Cricket, and they'll probably say, "Yeah, the food is alright, but I waited forever and the service was comical."

The Cricket is nearly the perfect Southeast breakfast place: good ideas, good food, slow pace (for better or worse), good folks, a little rough around the edges. For example, the first time I walked in, I was greeted by a lovely person who seated me immediately (it was a weekday), and then a fly landed on me. Welcome to the crunchy side of Southeast. Colorful artwork of baked goods and outdoor scenes adorn the simple white walls. Bamboo blinds block the summer sun and Belmont Street traffic noise. But the ceiling and concrete floor are crisscrossed with cracks.

Workers and creative types come in for the free WiFi, and you'll also see the big sideburns, flannel shirts, and horn-rimmed glasses of the so-called hipster set. One day the cook in the open kitchen had a classic Elvis swale of hair. The place bills itself as pet friendly, too.

The Cricket roasts its own coffee and buys from local

growers and farmers, which suggests a commitment to health and community. It also serves a large list of "liquid breakfast" cocktails, and it's Happy Hour all day Wednesday. The baked goods are made from scratch, and they're known for absurdly good cinnamon rolls, which are only available some weekends. The apple bread is served warm, soft in the middle, and crunchy outside—rather like the whole place, now that I think about it.

I went there once on a weekday around 10 a.m. and the place was nearly full, suggesting fine slackerness. But on that occasion, five young, energetic people worked the place and did a great job. Another time we got there at 9 a.m. on a weekend to beat the crowds, and thanks to seemingly overwhelmed service, didn't make it out until 10:30, by which time about two dozen people were waiting for tables.

And the menu! It's a Denny's level of variety: 22 omelets, scrambles, hashes, skillets, plates, and specialties, *plus* you can build your own omelet, scramble, or potato dish. And there are two other wonderful touches: $3.99 specials before 9 a.m. and $3.55 to-go orders. And you won't leave hungry. You can get the Big Farm Breakfast with potatoes, pancakes, *and* toast, if you want. The bacon is thick and crispy. The pancakes are thin but very flavorful and crisp around the edges, served with pure maple syrup. They have home fries (simple, lightly peppered, with the smaller pieces crunchy) as well as crispy shoestring hashbrowns. The granola is excellent—of course. The fruit bowl is large and the fruit fresh, but none is peeled; again, that just seems to fit the theme.

Still, what I am going to remember about the place are two things. One is the relaxed vibe that exists, whether it's crowded or calm. The other is an interaction we had with the punk, I mean, the young man pouring water for us. There was some music playing, and we were discussing whether it would be called rap or hip-hop. (We're very white.) Pitcher Boy mumbled loud enough for us to hear, in a voice dripping with disdain, "Just call it *music*." Then he walked off, and we all looked at each other for a moment, caught between shock and humor. Then we remembered where we were, shrugged it off, and dove back into our food.

Wait: Long on weekends after about 9:30 a.m.; some chairs and cover outside, very little room inside.
Seating: 47 inside at tables, plus 3 picnic tables outside.
Large groups? Easy for medium sized groups.
Portion size: Honkin'.
Changes: Fruit or pancake for potatoes and toast; otherwise, the menu says "We have plenty of choices for you, so please, no other substitutions!"
Coffee: Roast their own.
Other drinks: Numi tea, Tao of Tea, Dragonfly Chai, cocktails.
Feel-goods: Local fruits, veggies, cheeses, butter, and meats.
Health options: Egg Beaters or tofu in any dish for $1; vegetarian gravy, vegan and vegetarian options.
WiFi? Yes.

Cup and Saucer Cafe

Hip/Veggie

Like an old friend: dependable and nonthreatening
3566 SE Hawthorne Blvd. (SE/Hawthorne), 503-236-6001,
7:00 a.m. to 9 p.m. daily.
3000 NE Killingsworth (NE/Alberta), 503-287-4427,
8:00 a.m. to 9:00 p.m. daily.
8237 N Denver (N), 503-247-6011, 8:00 a.m. to 3:00 p.m.
Breakfast served all day in all stores.
$10–13 (Visa, MasterCard, checks)

———————◆———

Here's a typical Portland breakfast scenario: You wake up medium-late, like 10 in the morning. You want some breakfast, but you don't want to spend 15 bucks. You want something more than a coffee shop, something less than a fancy brunch. You live in Southeast or Northeast, and you don't want to go too far. You figure the lines are already huge at the local giants. You talk it over with your friends, you waver for a minute, and then somebody says, "Screw it, let's just go to the Cup and Saucer."

Now, you might think I just demeaned the Cup and Saucer. Not so. In fact, here's another way of saying the same thing: The Cup and Saucer is *The Princess Bride* of Portland breakfast places. Get some friends together to pick a movie sometime, let them hash it out for a while, and then say, "What about *The Princess Bride*?" I guarantee that, even if you don't rent it, more than one person will smile and say, "Oh, I love that movie!" It's got something for everyone.

That seems to be how Portland feels about the Cup and Saucer. It's friendly and casual, and it's in three very happening neighborhoods. It's hippie, hipster, kid-friendly, and dependable. It serves breakfast at all hours, and the menu is bursting with options. Chances are, nothing you eat there will be the best you ever had, but chances are even better that whatever you walk in wanting, they'll have it.

The 18 egg or tofu plates include just about every ingredient you can think of, and you can add The Works (Cheddar, salsa, and sour cream) to your side potatoes for $3. Split plates for the 18 come with a scone and a side of potatoes for $2.75, and you can substitute fruit for your potatoes for $2. Oh, and there are five house specialties (smoked salmon and Florentine Benedicts, biscuits and vegetarian gravy, *huevos rancheros* and the Super Saucer, which is two eggs, a meat choice, and a pancake), challah French toast, granola, oatmeal, and four pancakes: buttermilk, blueberry, vegan cornmeal, and a daily special. More than a dozen side orders include brown rice, sautéed veggies, muffins, toast, and tortillas.

See what I mean? Just try to go into the Cup and Saucer and find nothing you want. I am a pig and generally get the Lucky Scramble #13: mushrooms, green onions, bacon, Cheddar, and potatoes scrambled with three eggs. My girlfriend can't eat sugar or wheat, so she digs on the Basil Pesto Scramble with spinach and sun-dried tomatoes. And, for the record, before I even read this review to her, she said, "That place is like a generic breakfast place, but it's pretty good!"

Other than the variety and dependability, the Cup and

Saucer is known for scones and the spin on breakfast potatoes. The scones . . . well, they're called the Cup and Saucer Classic Buttery Vanilla Delight. Need to know more? A basket of three is $2, so don't skip them. The potatoes are a combination of russets and sweet potatoes, with cloves of roasted garlic thrown in. They come with most dishes and are $3.50 as a stand-alone.

And, of course, since this is the Cup and Saucer, there are eight items (both meat and vegan) you can add to your potatoes, all for $2 or less. With The Works they're $7.50. And there are three styles of french fries.

And now I'm hungry and need a break, so I think I'll just walk over to the Cup and Saucer.

Wait: Medium on weekends, with some space inside and cover outside.
Seating: About 50 in each location.
Large groups? A better bet at the NE location.
Portion size: Reasonable.
Changes: Easy.
Coffee: Portland Roasting Company.
Other drinks: Espresso, Dragonfly Chai, Italian sodas, cocktails.
Feel-goods: Plenty of organic options.
Health options: Egg substitute; tofu; vegan and vegetarian options abound.
WiFi? No.

Daily Cafe

New/Hip/Weekend

Possibly the perfect Pearl place

902 NW 13th Ave. (Pearl)

503-242-1916

Locations also at:

1100 SE Grand Ave. (SE/Inner) 503-234-8189

3355 SW Bond Ave. (Downtown) 503-224-9691

Breakfast served at all locations weekdays 7:00 a.m. to 11:00 a.m.; Saturday 9:00 a.m. to 2:00 p.m. Sunday brunch at Pearl location only, 9:00 a.m. to 2:00 p.m.

dailycafeinthepearl.com

$7–12 Monday through Saturday, $17-20 on Sundays (all major cards)

———————————◆———————————

Whatever your feelings about the Pearl district, I bet they hit fever pitch when you eat at the Daily Cafe. Is it a modern, efficient, Euro-style cafe, or is it bland and sterile? Is it chock full of computer-slinging hipsters or home to a new generation of young families? Is it a pass-through cafe with no food of great interest or a destination restaurant with reasonable prices?

To my eyes it's all of those things, which is why it may be the most perfectly Pearl place to eat breakfast. The Pearl has cafes where workers gather for quick meetings and stroller-pushing moms take breaks from shopping, and it also has fancy restaurants that attract diners from all over the city. And in a way, the Daily Cafe is both.

During the week breakfast at the Daily Cafe is a very casual, quick affair; you order at the counter from a menu

on a chalkboard, grab a seat, and the ultra-friendly staff will bring it out. The choices are similar to the weekend brunch, only fewer. One day there were griddle-cakes with granola and cranberries; two eggs with home fries, eight-grain toast, and marionberry jam; a breakfast panini with bacon and pepperjack cheese; granola; a daily-special quiche; and oatmeal.

Nothing much to that, right? One time I had a frittata with roasted red peppers, caramelized onions, spinach, Cheddar, fries, and eight-grain toast, all for only $7.95. I was in and out in less than an hour and on my way to my nearby office. I've had better frittatas (like at the Detour Cafe); this one was a little too squishy, and having Cheddar on it seemed beneath a Pearl place. But then I remembered: especially during the week this is a Pearl *cafe*, a place where you can eat in a flash for less than $10 or linger for two hours with your computer and free coffee refills.

On weekends, though, the Daily Cafe is a different animal entirely. The lines form early and stay long, and although the options and prices go up, it's still a value. The $13.95 fixed-price menu includes one appetizer, one entrée, and a basket of house-made pastries. There's even more staff and full table service, and I don't know if it's the enhanced experience, but it sure seems like the food gets better. One time, for example, I had a whipped mascarpone and dried black fruit compote with cherries, currants, and plums. I also had some laughs with the waitress about how to pronounce *mascarpone*.

I wondered if the folks at Fenouil in the Pearl could have had that kind of fun.

Other appetizers that day were fresh papaya with a wedge of lime and some mint; granola with fruit and nuts; a fruit salad; Irish oatmeal; and the "best ever mug of hot chocolate," with "62% bittersweet chocolate bar, Madagascar vanilla and Natalie's house made marshmallows." Okay, so there *is* a little Pearl snootiness going on.

The options for the next course were a broccoli scramble, huevos rancheros, a basic omelet, a two-egg classic breakfast, and a smoked salmon plate with a grilled bagel, capers, cucumbers, red onions, tomatoes, and cream cheese. I had a stack of three buttermilk griddlecakes with orange marmalade and ricotta, and I was astonished how filling they were. My waitress told me that the only types of people who finish that stack are skinny women who run marathons and teenage boys.

I would have added stoned college students, but I'm not sure they go to the Pearl. Maybe they will after they grow up and get a little more sophisticated.

Wait: Long on weekends after about 9:00 a.m.
Seating: More than 100, all at tables. **Large groups?** Yes.
Portion size: Reasonable for what you pay.
Changes: Not a lot of options. **Coffee:** Cafe Umbria.
Other drinks: Soda, mineral water, juices, tea, milk.
Feel-goods: Some organic, locally raised ingredients.
Health options: Not much here for vegetarians and less for vegans.
WiFi? Yes.

Daily Market and Café

This restaurant changed its name to **New Deal Cafe** in 2009 and eliminated the market, but otherwise is the same place.

New/Kid-Friendly

The paper, the kids, the dog, some shopping, not much going on.

5250 NE Halsey Blvd. (NE/Hollywood)

503-546-1833

Monday through Friday, 7 a.m. to 4 p.m., weekends 8 a.m. to 4 p.m. Breakfast served all day.

$7–10 (Visa, MasterCard)

———————◆●◆———————

Close your eyes and try to locate NE 52nd and Halsey. What's around there? What's that neighborhood even called?

When the Daily Market and Café opened in the spring of 2006, the *Portland Tribune* said it "will be a fine addition to this rather barren (except for houses) stretch of Halsey." Barren, they said—except for houses. As if houses don't count. I mean, nothing there but . . . people . . . just . . . living there.

I asked the staff what the neighborhood was called, and several of us had a little conference. We knew we were east of Lloyd District, south of Hollywood, south of Alameda, north of . . . whatever is south of here.

"It's Rose City," somebody said.

"But all of Portland is Rose City, right?"

And that's when it hit me. The Daily Market Café sits in the middle of a perfectly generic, maybe a generically perfect, Portland neighborhood. And now there's a little neighborhood market and café they can hang out in.

As my friend Jane and I worked through our meal, chatting with table neighbors and watching kids in the play area, this "perfect Portland" thing became a theme. The décor is light and airy, a combination of wood tables (cozy!) and plastic chairs (modern!) splashed in happy, cheerful oranges and yellows and greens that make the place feel like a chip off the New Seasons block.

The place is welcoming and cheerful, with high ceilings, plenty of light, fresh pastries under the glass, folks sipping self-serve coffee and surfing the WiFi, and a high percentage of customers who seem to know the staff.

The menu is written on a chalkboard above the counter. Keeping things grounded are a few classic scrambles — $7.25 with potatoes and toast or biscuit — and this being Portland, they use Naturally Nested eggs (egg whites and tofu are also available). The Basic has mushrooms, peppers, onions, Cheddar cheese, and meat/veggie sausage or tofu. The Vegetable Garden comes with broccoli, corn salsa, garlic, mushrooms, and roasted pepper sauce; the Mediterranean has basil, feta, tomatoes, garlic and Kalamata olives. French toast. Pancakes. Biscuits and Veggie Gravy. A Breakfast Sammich Burrito.

Nothing earth-shattering, in other words, but classic. Dependable. Tasty. Then there's the progressive-good idea side dishes, all about $1.50: a single pancake, some sausage, coconut oatmeal, a biscuit, some potatoes, a piece of French toast . . . a peanut butter and jelly sandwich! You have to love a place where folks of all ages can get a PB&J for a buck and a half. We liked the food a lot, and it showed up quickly. The French toast was made with rustic white bread (wholesome!) and done old-school: crisp on the outside and eggy throughout (Mom!).

The café was opened by the owners of the Laurelhurst Theater, one of the best examples of another fine Portland idea: theaters showing second-run movies with cheap ticket prices, where you can buy pizza and beer and eat *while watching the movie.* The Laurelhurst is the perfect combination of old-timey theater and New-Agey good ideas. And the Daily Market is a local market with the usual conveniences, New-Age Portland style: Kettle chips, locally made floating beeswax candles, Clif Bars, Luna Bars, Seventh Generation toilet paper (exclusively), Tom's *and* Jason's toothpastes, and Tofurkey.

And if you're eating with Poochie, you're close to Normandale Park, which has the ever-popular leash-free zone. So of course Daily Market has a daily dog treat special.

What would you expect from a local market and café, especially when it's in a neighborhood that's named for a city known for good ideas and is a great place to live?

Wait: Little to none.
Seating: About 50, inside and out.
Large groups? If you can get several tables at once.
Portion Size: Medium-big.
Changes/Substitutions: Sure!
Coffee: Stumptown.
Other drinks: Espresso, juices, tea
Feel-goods: Organic ingredients.
Health Options: Tofu, egg whites available
WiFi? Yes

Detour Cafe

New/Veggie

A literally hidden gem

3035 SE Division St. (SE/Division)

503-234-7499

8:00 a.m. to 4:00 p.m. daily

detourcafe.com

$9–13 (Visa, MasterCard, checks)

———————◆•◆———————

I was sitting with a couple of long-time Portlanders at the Detour Cafe, reminiscing about what the city used to be like: more working-class, more small-towny, perhaps more old-fashioned. Tom, for example, said it was tough to find a good bacon-and-egg sandwich anymore.

And then it occurred to me that one of these days I'll be sitting around in who-knows-what kind of breakfast place, telling folks I was there when the organic/local-grown/sustainable revolution happened—a time when so many good places opened all over town that a yummy, cool place like the Detour Cafe could exist right under my nose and I wouldn't even know about it. And I mean that literally: starting in 2001, this little place hid behind all the vegetation on its porch for six years before I knew of its existence, and the only reason I have for its relative anonymity is that the folks in the neighborhood didn't want the rest of us to know about it.

The Detour represents everything the "new" Portland is all about. Its Web site says, "We use free range eggs, organic flour, and when possible, organic and/or locally farmed produce and meats. We also feature freshly baked pastries of all kinds, housemade vegan soups, and Stumptown coffee." It then goes on to offer links to such things as Gathering

Together Farm, the Oregon Humane Society, Planned Parenthood, art studios, bands, you name it. How "new Portland" can you get?

The Detour is cute and friendly, with yellow and green dominating the décor and plastic chairs and tables giving it a semi-goofy feel, and on the shady porch the overhanging plants cut down on the noise from Division Street. Detour has good baked goods, including one of the finest Cheddar biscuits in town ($2 to take one with you), spiced with scallions and sweetened with corn.

What really sets the Detour apart, though, can be stated in four words: build your own frittata. As soon as I saw my smoked-salmon-and-goat-cheese three-egg frittata sitting on my plate with roasted potatoes and whole wheat toast (all for just $7.75), I thought, "Why doesn't everybody do this?" My frittata was the perfect combination of egg, cheese, and meat with just a little crust from the baking and plenty of fresh, cream cheese goodness.

The basic option is any two of 24 frittata ingredients, so a vegetarian can do well. Extra ingredients are only 50 cents, and you get roasted onions for free. You can get any three of the same ingredients from the same list with potatoes for only $6, so even the vegans can get their groove on (there's a daily vegan soup, as well). And for only $3.25 you can get toasted focaccia with cream cheese, tomatoes, and fresh basil.

The portions aren't overwhelming, but everything looks nice and colorful. Chela's French toast was made with cardamom bread, which sort of grounded the sweetness from the custard dip; the topping of cherry compote, toasted almonds, and organic maple syrup brought it home wonderfully. A half-order for $4.25 was just what she wanted.

Tom even found his bacon-and-egg sandwich. But it was a BELT, with two eggs sunny side up, bacon, tomato, mixed greens, with house-made mayo and focaccia ($6.25). Other sandwich options included the Original, with baked eggs, cream cheese, roma tomatoes, fresh basil, and pepper bacon; the All Fired Up, with spiced cream cheese and red peppers; and the Don ($8.25), with portabella mushrooms, onions, and feta mixed into the eggs and topped with Italian sausage, avocado, tomato, and basil.

Everything was fresh and tasty and down-home in that "new Portland" way. Somehow, that seemed to wrap up the Detour perfectly: a new place that satisfied old longings.

Wait: Long on weekends, with some cover outside and self-serve coffee.

Seating: Six tables, three semi-booths, a few counter seats, and the porch.

Large groups? Not your best option.

Portion size: Reasonable, especially for the price.

Changes: Three different creamed cheeses; the spicy and the herbed are $.50 extra. Veggie sausage and wild smoked salmon available on The Don for $.50.

Coffee: Self-serve Stumptown.

Other drinks: Espresso, Lisa's Chai, Tao of Tea, Kombucha, sodas, and juice.

Feel-goods: Organic, local ingredients and cage-free eggs.

Health options: Plenty here for vegetarians and vegans.

WiFi? No.

Doug Fir Lounge

Hip/Old School

Live music and good food, at the same place

830 E. Burnside (E. Burnside)

503-231-9663

7 a.m. to 2:30 a.m. daily. Breakfast served 7 a.m. to 3 p.m.

dougfirlounge.com

$10–14 (all major cards)

———————◆———————

Perhaps you've heard that the Doug Fir Lounge, that "music place" on East Burnside, serves breakfast. And perhaps when you heard it, you thought, "Bar, club, breakfast . . . no thanks." Well, the Doug Fir is trying to be more than a music place, and its food is definitely beyond bar chow.

So what is the Doug Fir? First and foremost, it is a music place featuring bands that this 40-something has absolutely never heard of. Maximo Park's bus was parked outside when I ate at the Doug, and had the entire band been sitting at a table next to me singing its number 1 song, I wouldn't have known them.

Like any music place, the Doug is trying to be young and hip — trying too hard, if you ask its detractors, who also bemoan its stylishly casual approach to service. Supporters generally chime back with, "Chill out, it's a rock and roll place." Even among rock and roll places, though, it's going for a particular niche. The shows start on time downstairs in the smoke-free room and are finished around midnight, attempts to draw a wider range of audiences. Its owners told *Willamette Week* that their goal was to make the club itself a destination "like Disneyland."

You might think you've walked into LoggerLand when you come into the ground-floor restaurant. Or maybe RetroLoungeLand. The walls and ceiling are a fancy-looking version of a log cabin, bulbous chrome fixtures drop amber light on Formica tables and round booths, and the colors are various shades of brown, from the two-tone padded chairs to the etchings on the ubiquitous mirrors. In the lounge area you'll find couches, padded ottomans, and a fireplace. It's Retro Maximo.

The menu is as classics-oriented as the décor. There's a Logger Breakfast of eggs, roasted rosemary potatoes, and various options for meats and breads. There are classic waffles and pancakes as well as French toast made with croissants and a touch of orange zest; all three come with a choice of maple syrup, blackberry compote, or cherry compote. Three Benedicts (ham, spinach, or smoked salmon) are served with a lime-chili hollandaise that has a nice little bite to it. Four scrambles are named for defunct local clubs. I had the smoked salmon hash and found it a little long on the new potatoes but still flavorful, with the salmon mashed up and creamy, mildly spiced with capers and red onions.

If you want some real entertainment, go over to Citysearch. com and read what folks have said about the service. On my quiet weekday trip I had no problems, but it's clear some folks have — or maybe they were expecting something else.

There's also a great exchange about a bartender who by all accounts has a foul mouth and a "screw-you attitude." She even said so herself in a response to the post.

As for the feel of the place, I found the defining moment to be when the heavily tattooed (and entirely pleasant) bartender shut off the start of Lynyrd Skynyrd's "Freebird," put on some '70s funk instead, started flirting with a two-year-old boy to try to get him to eat, and served a (reputedly strong and expensive) Bloody Mary to a scruffy-looking, twitching dude in a flannel shirt sitting at the bar with a very attractive young woman. Somehow, everything about the Doug Fir was right there: the family eating a hearty breakfast, the pre-9 a.m. booze, the guy who may well have been with the band, the staff dancing on the line between rockin' and professional, and the whole place moving to a funky '70s groove.

Wait: Maybe a little on weekends.
Seating: About 60 at tables and booths, plus a bar.
Large groups? More than six might be tough, but they do host events.
Portion size: Decent.
Changes: Easy.
Coffee: Stumptown.
Other drinks: Cocktails, Stash Tea, Red Bull.
Feel-goods: Many of the ingredients are local.
Health options: Not much here for vegetarians.
WiFi? Yes.

Everett Street Bistro

New/Classy

A casual hangout, Pearl style
1140 NW Everett Street (Pearl)
503-467-4990
Breakfast served daily, 8:00 a.m. to 3:00 p.m.
everettstreetbistro.com
$12–16 (Visa, MasterCard, no checks)

The four ladies were having quiche and enjoying the toddler who kept trying to get into the kitchen. The woman in the corner, in her matching workout suit, was groovin' to the Motown. A gray-haired gent was working on a crossword. The waiter was telling another woman about his pet rabbit and how much they both (he and the rabbit) like spinach.

I felt a little out of place in my flannel shirt, baseball cap, and jeans, but it sure was nice to be stylin' it up in the heart of the Pearl. And if the Pearl, that "upscale" development with the semiprecious name, has its own casual hangout, it's the Everett Street Bistro. It also fits that such a place would call itself, as the Bistro does, a "European style charcuterie." (I had to look that word up, and it means, very roughly, "a place that serves a lot of meat.")

I had always taken the place for a glorified coffee shop. When I got a menu with two dozen cocktails on it, I felt I had been corrected—until I saw that it was a dinner menu. I asked for the breakfast menu, and by golly, the cocktails were on there too! So it's all about leisure at the Bistro.

The menu is full of options hovering around $9. There's Grand Marnier French Toast and a Dutch Baby, and you can

also choose from two quiches (you *knew* this place would serve quiche, right?) with bacon-mascarpone or a daily special. Ten egg-based dishes assure your protein needs will be met, whether you're feeling light (a seasonal Caprese Scramble with tomatoes, mozzarella, and basil) or heavy (Corned Beef Hash or Eggs Benedict Sardou).

Reviews of the Bistro usually start like this: There's an amazing dessert case when you walk in, the place is lovely, and the crowd runs upward in both age and apparent income. From there, opinions vary on the food, but none are very strong one way or another, though a lot of folks think the lunch and dinner menus are a little too pricy for what is served. I think the Bistro tries to be everything to everybody, within the context of the Pearl district, so maybe it isn't really good at any one thing in particular. As for the prices, they're cheaper at breakfast, and besides, I can only imagine what the rent must be at the corner of NW 11th Avenue and Everett.

I chose the Crabcake Benedict with Spinach and Creole Hollandaise (a special), and took some satisfaction from it being served on *pain au levain*—even though I had no idea what *pain au levain* is. I was just happy to relax in my wicker chair in the bright, airy room, surrounded by the sophisticated black-and-white decor with chandelier-style lanterns on the walls, enjoying the company of my fellow Pearlites. Well, we were all eating in the same place, anyway. I felt like I should go shopping afterward, or hit a gallery or something.

I've had better Benedicts and paid less for them too. And I wouldn't always want to be the youngest and worst-dressed person in a place. But the food was just fine, and I did get to see the gray-haired gent flirt with the four ladies on his way out, and I laughed with the ladies at one of the waiter's jokes, and for a few moments I got to feel like a stylish Pearl District Denizen, just passing a drizzly Wednesday morning with my Crabcake Benedict, wondering what the working folk are up to.

Sometimes breakfast really is about the scene, after all.

Wait: Maybe a little on weekends.
Seating: About 40 in booths and tables inside, some sidewalk seating when the weather is nice.
Large groups? Yes; notice would help.
Portion size: Reasonable.
Changes: Within reason.
Coffee: Sleepy Monk.
Other drinks: Espresso, juices, and a huge variety of cocktails.
Feel-goods: None that they brag about.
Health options: Vegetarians could do okay here.
WiFi? No.

Farmers Market

Buffet/Veggie

Yuppies, farmers, and old hippies—and sometimes you can't tell 'em apart.

Address: Saturdays at Portland State University (April to December), Wednesdays on the south Park Blocks at Salmon Street (May to October), Thursdays in the Pearl District at 10th and Johnson (June to September)

Phone: None

Hours: 8:30 a.m. to 2 p.m.

portlandfarmersmarket.org

$5 up to whatever you want to spend (Cash at the booths or use a debit card to buy tokens to use throughout the market).

My friend Julia told me somebody at the farmer's market at Portland State made good breakfast burritos. So I thought, Hey, that'd be cool: get something to eat and shop for produce. I mean, that's a farmers market, right?

Wrong, by a bunch! I was there an hour before I even found the burritos, and by then I wasn't hungry anymore. That's because I had been wandering around noshing on smoked salmon, strawberries, fresh bread, jam, peas, sausage and bacon right off the grill, carrots, cherries, apples, dried apple chips, and countless kinds of cheese. And that's just what they're giving away! You could absolutely graze your way through breakfast; this is *not* the farmers market my Mississippi grandparents took me to.

The market is enchanting: the baby Thai broccoli, Yukon gold potatoes, radishes, honey, dozens of berries made

into jam, spelt bread, super-
scrumptious Hood strawberries, various kinds of cherries.
And that's not to mention
all the smiling, attractive,
healthy-looking people selling
the stuff. I could see myself
turning into one of the people I saw pulling wagons with
the tops of garlic and sweet
onions and five kinds of lettuce sticking out.

For $20 (I showed restraint) I bought a 16-ounce organic
coffee; an orange croissant that was pure heaven (sold by
people who also had an Oregon croissant with almond paste,
sugar coating, and marionberries); a French toast bread pudding with praline topping, maple syrup, and fresh strawberry
slices; two pints of Hoods; two pints of sugar snap peas; and
three sweet onions. The Hoods didn't last the day, and the
peas and onions will soon be appearing in a wok near me.

Along the way several defining moments came to me.
One was walking past a divine spread of organic greens and
herbs and roots with sprawling bouquets of flowers across
the way, and suddenly smelling bacon being grilled — and
then hearing somebody say, "Ah tell ya, once ya taste this
h'yer bacon, it is *ovah,* ahmon tellya. You gawn *buy* some-a
that there bacon." I was smelling pig and hearing Texas, and
it was hell gettin' away from that booth.

Another such moment came while admiring different
types of honey and a honeycomb-shaped candle carved out
of beeswax, then noticing a jar filled with little crystals of

bee pollen. After I made the requisite "not as good as A pollen" joke, I asked the bespectacled fellow behind the counter what's up with the pollen. He said people just eat it, then pointed to a little card that listed the nutritional qualities of bee pollen: it's 40 percent protein and rich in free amino acids, vitamins including B-complex and folic acid, and many other wonders. And how did he get it? He puts a filter on the door of a hive that's big enough for a bee with one piece of pollen but not two. When the bee arrives, it dumps one piece so it can enter the hive. How cool is that?

Finally, there was the moment sitting near the old-timey country fiddle band, watching all the people, when my friend Jean pointed out, correctly, that about one-third of the population we could see was between the ages of 1 and 2. With all those young couples getting those toddlers out of the house, and all the locally grown food, our overall impression of the place was fertility and bounty.

Wait: Every stinkin' year until spring!
Seating: Eternal, including benches and tables.
Large groups? Made for 'em.
Portion Size: Whatever you like.
Changes: Way too many options already.
Coffee: All over the place.
Other drinks: Espresso, juice, tea, you name it
Feel-goods: The whole thing.
Health Options: Ditto
WiFi? Who cares?

Fat Albert's Cafe

Mom and Pop/Old School

No nonsense, from them or you
6668 SE Milwaukie (SE/Sellwood)
503-872-9822
Monday through Friday, 5:30 a.m. to 2 p.m.; Saturday and
Sunday 8 a.m. to 3 p.m. Breakfast served all day.
$8–12 (Cash and checks only)

———————◆•◆———————

Let's get one thing straight about Fat Albert's: Nobody is
going to kiss your ass there. The staff will seat you, feed you,
and move you out, all the while doing it professionally and
efficiently. And you'll get only a single page of options to
choose from; that's one way to keep both the kitchen and you
moving right along. So sit down, eat, and then go do whatever it is you're supposed to be doing.

Another thing, as a sign will inform you as soon as you
walk in: Cash and checks only, and incomplete parties will
not be seated.

So at this point, perhaps some of you are thinking,
"Gee, sounds a little rough." Well, there can be an edge to
the place. Some of my meeker friends avoid it, and sometimes there seems to be an "in" crowd that's treated better.
Marginally. In this "edgy" sense, the signature dish is the
egg-and-ham breakfast sandwich, which my friend Jeff likes
to get. He once told me, while wiping off the excess moisture with a napkin, that it "went over the butter line," and
even from my side of the table I could see its certain buttery
glow. I loved it, but I'll probably die of a heart attack when
I'm 50. Everything in it was cooked well, and I don't mind
a little edge.

You could also be thinking, "Finally, a breakfast place that doesn't try to be what it isn't, doesn't encourage people to surf on their laptops all day, doesn't try to break new ground in cuisine. A place that just serves good breakfast and gets you going." Well, that's Fat Albert's, too.

Eggs, meat, potatoes, bread, and something sweet. That's the menu. Six omelets, pancakes, the sandwich, bottomless oatmeal, and biscuits and gravy. The omelets are straight to the point: one has good ol' ham and cheese; the Yuppie has sun-dried tomatoes, artichoke hearts, and feta; Kim's Fave has avocado, Cheddar, and bacon; the Salad Eater, with its spinach, tomatoes, onions, and mushrooms, is a nod to the veggie crowd.

I'm not much of a biscuits and gravy guy, but I can tell you that most reviews I've read don't consider them the café's strong point. The pancakes, however, are quite popular: big, fluffy, and a little crisp around the edges (of course). The maple syrup is nice and light; that's because, as the menu says, Fat Albert's uses "<u>real</u> maple syrup" and "<u>real</u> butter." Even the menu has an edge!

In fact, the menu also explains that it's policy to ask you to leave after you're done eating. You'll appreciate this when you're waiting in line for a table, but one online review recounted having fresh silverware placed in front of the reviewer along with the check!

Fat Albert's is built for efficiency. It's small enough that the staff is always right there, and every time I've been there, the food has arrived so quickly I'm always astonished.

No espresso, just a house coffee blend, so the cafe is really just a throw-back, no-nonsense kind of place. Even naming an omelet The Yuppie suggest an odd combination of sentiment and name-calling, which fits the place perfectly.

I had a work lunch there—it's truly a place where someone with a one-hour lunch break could eat—and as we were leaving, I wasn't sure who was paying. We stood at the register, each with a $20 bill at the ready, and after we hesitated for about one breath, the waitress dinged open the register and said, "I know! Why don't you pay separately!" Then she rolled her eyes, took our money without another word, and went back to serving food and coffee.

We were briefly stunned, then remembered where we were, admitted she had a point, and hauled our full bellies back to our day.

Wait: Fairly long on weekends.
Seating: Around 30, including a community table and a counter.
Large groups? No.
Portion size: Decent.
Changes: Within reason.
Coffee: House blend.
Other drinks: Tea and juices.
Feel-goods: None in particular.
Health options: None in particular.
WiFi? No.

Fat City Cafe

Mom and Pop/Old School

In a small town, a long, long time ago . . .
7820 Southwest Capitol Highway, Portland (SW/Inner)
503-245-5457
6:30 a.m. to 3 p.m. every day; breakfast served all day
$8-11 (all major cards)

———————————◆●◆———————————

Here's how you do a Breakfast with the Fellas. You meet too damn early on a weekday, 'cause fellas have to work. You can't meet on a weekend, because fellas have to sleep. You show up on time so you can give a load of crap to the guy who shows up late (generally the single/unemployed one) with lines like "Oh, you decided to join us" or "Good gosh, they'll let anybody in here." You say something about not being awake until you've had your coffee. You order something with eggs and meat, or explain why, and for the most part you get the same thing you always get, or explain why. Any mention of an attempt at weight loss is completely understood and thoroughly ridiculed.

Most important, you don't go to some place that has candles on the tables, or *bistro* in the name, or Asiago cheese. You go to a place like the Fat City Cafe.

Ponder the name for a moment: Fat City. Every time I've been there, the special on the chalkboard was some kind of sausage: Italian, Cajun, Spicy, Smoked. The spicy sausage is precisely that, and a guy can earn points for eating it without complaint. In the fall the place goes nuts and has pumpkin pancakes. I think there's only about a dozen ingredients in the kitchen, and the whole menu is variations on them.

For example, the menu includes omelets, scrambles, and sizzles, and the only difference is consistency and egg-to-potato ratio. The bacon is crisp, the coffee never stops coming, and the waitresses work hard, do a great job, and take no slack.

I eat there with Bob, Phil, Al, and Mick, and one time I told the waitress that we don't hang out with guys who have two syllables in their names. Phil and Mick always get the hash, Bob gets the two eggs with links, and I get the Fat City Sizzle, which sounds like it's from a *Simpsons* episode but is actually a pile of hashbrowns, ham, green peppers, onions, and cheddar with two eggs on top. It's so big it looks like it may have been served with a shovel, and it comes with either a pancake or toast on the side. Carbs schmarbs.

The décor of the place is kind of a road theme, with old signs and license plates stuck up on the wall, plus seasonal decorations and Fat City T-shirts. The bathroom is Pure American Goofy: a super-narrow door between the counter (which is always filled with fellas) and the kitchen, and once you're in you can't even take a step forward before you have to turn right for the barely-bigger-than-the-toilet room. Fellas gotta stand next to the sink to pee, and ladies probably have to put their legs under it to sit down.

If the place looks like it's old and in a small town, it is. Multnomah Village dates to the 1910s, when a community sprang up around an Oregon Electric Railroad station. Today, the Village itself is much more Lady Habitat, with shops and bookstores and whatnot; it's often called quaint.

On your way back to your table, you might notice an *Oregonian* article on the wall: the account of the 1987 Fat City Firing, perhaps the ultimate Breakfast with the Fellas Gone Wrong. In this very booth, the mayor of Portland, Bud Clark, fired his police chief, Jim Davis.

I mean, where *else* would two fellas who needed to talk some stuff out go for breakfast? It wasn't the Alameda Ass-Kicking, was it? Or the Bread and Ink Bashing? Tin Shed Tanking?

Nope. It was the . . . read my lips: Fat. City. Firing. Mmmmmm.

Wait: Medium on weekends, mostly outside.

Seating: Half a dozen booths, a couple of tables, and a counter.

Large groups? Not at the same table.

Portion Size: Heapin'.

Changes: Yes, and splits available with an extra plate of hashbrowns for $1.95.

Coffee: Gourmet Coffee.

Other drinks: Tea, milkshakes, hot chocolate.

Feel-goods: You don't have to eat the whole thing.

Health Options: Ditto.

WiFi? Check back in 30 years.

Fenouil in the Pearl

Classy/Weekend/New
Gosh, look *at this place!*
900 NW 11th Ave.
503-525-2225
Brunch served Sunday from 9 a.m. to 2 p.m.
fenouilinthepearl.com
$15–20 (all major cards)

First of all, if you're wondering, it's "fen-yu-wee." So it's French. And it's in the Pearl.

If you forget either of those critical elements, you will be reminded, often and not subtly. The space — that's what everyone calls it, a "space" — is massive, glamorous, and completely over the top, in keeping with its Pearl location. The impressiveness stretches from the overhead dining area and view of Jamison Square all the way to the saucer with Fenouil logo on which your coffee cup rests, and the little silver dish with small serving spoon in which the salt and pepper reside.

There's a fluer-de-lis on the glasses and *oeufs* (eggs), *les autres* (others), and a Hamburger Parisien on the brunch menu. And we were told how the special is "finished." That's not a word you hear at many breakfast places.

Four of the Breakfast Crew showed up and felt like we needed to sit up straight and not say anything stupid. Jenny wondered if we can keep the little jars of preserves, and when we wondered if staff gives the leftovers to the Pearl District homeless, somebody made the "Let 'em eat preserves" joke.

After we ordered (I did it in poor French), our drinks came

and we were all impressed again. The tea bags were in little paper pyramids with a leaf sticking out the top of each! Jenny called them "little pieces of art," and we all marveled that they cost more than the coffee. We also didn't realize at first that the dish of "little rock things," as David put it, was the sugar. Seemed about right for a French place in the Pearl. (Did I mention Fenouil is French and in the Pearl?)

The food was outstanding, and we all agreed that it had better be. Even if you call it *Oeuf Benedictine au Jambon*, you need to make a solid Eggs Benedict with Ham if you're charging $13 for it. Each *oeuf* dish comes with *un croissant (avec* or *sin chocolat)* or weekly-special pastry (I had a marionberry-lemon-cream-cheese roll). All were tasty and fit perfectly on our little saucers, next to the logo. We also had fun watching David pick out just the right-size rock thing to sweeten his coffee.

The menu was moderately grounded and not as terrifyingly expensive as we had feared. For $12.50 you can get a wild mushroom omelet with Pierre Robert cheese, a smoked salmon hash, a black truffle egg scramble with sage, a duck comfit hash with caramelized shallots and Talegio cheese, seafood quiche, steak and eggs, and more than half a dozen lunch items. At $14 only the steak was more.

We particularly enjoyed a $5 fruit plate with pineapple and melon pieces, even though we had to ask what "the stuff on it" was (turned out to be crème fraîche). We felt all grown up, sampling the confit and the compote and Pierre Robert and not really knowing what any of it was. Duck and jam and cheese, we figured. I couldn't contain my sarcastic side, though, and busted out my best Jethro Bodine accent to announce that "this here *jambon grille* is good; tastes jes' lak grilled ham!"

The conversation inevitably led to the subject of gross displays of wealth, unnecessary fanciness, and what we'd do if we won the lottery (eat lots of *jambon grille*, I said). Anthony said he'd get a Toto toilet. When I realized he didn't mean a figurine of Dorothy's dog, he told me all about the Japanese wonder toilet that washes you with a stream of water, and how it costs $1,000 or more.

Then he went to the restroom and came back laughing. "Guess what kind of toilets they have," said with a grin. We all got up together to go check out the bathroom. They don't have the spray-and-wash model, but Fenouil in the Pearl does, indeed, have Toto toilets. Didn't surprise us a bit.

Wait: None.
Seating: 220 or more, all at tables. (65 upstairs, 55 downstairs, plus there's patio area, another 100)
Large groups? With a reservation.
Portion size: Decent. **Changes:** Not much.
Coffee: Cafe Umbria.
Other drinks: Tea Forte, cocktails.
Feel-goods: Cascade Natural beef, Carlton Farms bacon.
Health options: None in particular.
WiFi? *Oui!*

FlavourSpot

Weekend

Little carts exploding with waffles
2310 N Lombard Ave. in the VideoRama parking lot
(N/Outer) and the corner of N Mississippi and N Fremont
(N/Inner)
No phone
Weekdays 6:30 a.m. to 3:00 p.m.; weekends 8:00 a.m. to
3:00 p.m. Mississippi Street cart closed weekdays.
flavourspot.com
$4–6 (cash only)

———————◆•◆———————

Sometime around 2007 two momentous things happened in
Portland: One was that Mississippi Street turned some kind
of psychological corner and started arguing about high-density
housing coming in. The other was that, all of a sudden,
waffles became The Thing.

I was contemplating these trends one sunny morning at
the corner of Mississippi and Fremont, sitting in a plastic
lawn chair on a gravel lot in front of the newest FlavourSpot
cart. Across one street was the Son of Haiti Hall; across
another, an empty lot with a tire swinging from a tree and
what looked like a little homeless camp. I was eating the
sweetest, yummiest thing I'd enjoyed in some time: a Sweet
Cream and Jam Waffle with whipped cream cheese, vanilla,
and organic raspberry jam folded over like a sandwich.

The owner was telling me that somebody had just bought
the lot across the way, and we agreed it would probably be
condos or townhouses within a year. I wondered how long
the Sons of Haiti could hang on.

Here in Portland, we have a lot of good ideas, and often it's a new twist on something very old-fashioned.  Fixing up old neighborhoods instead of sprawling all over creation is one; so is opening a cart that does nothing but crank out a wide variety of incredible waffles—and serves stuff like Postum, Ovaltine (even an Ovaltine Mocha), and "gelatin-free mallow" instead of creepy old marshmallows. FlavourSpot, which opened on North Lombard in late 2006, was so busy by the end of 2007 that its owner opened the bigger cart on Mississippi. Iit's a simple premise: there's some seating, but for about $5 you get a waffle to go and a cup of coffee.

And what waffles! There's a basic one with butter and powdered sugar, another with ham and Cheddar or smoked Gouda. The Sausage and Maple has patties and 100 percent pure maple spread, and it inspires legions of followers. There's also the PB&J, the Lemon Pie with lemon curd and whipped cream, the Fifth Avenue (peanut butter and Nutella), the Black Forest with Nutella and raspberry jam, the S'More with Nutella and gelatin-free mallow fluff, and, incredibly, one called the Ice Cream Sandwich: a waffle wrapped around a chocolate-coated slab of vanilla ice cream.

The whole waffle thing really is interesting. In January 2008 the *Oregonian* ran a big article headlined "Going beyond breakfast with waffles." It revealed that restaurants around town were serving waffles with stuff like curried cream sauce, chile-spiked salsa, smoked salmon and cucumber. A place called Jace Gace apparently drapes spears of steamed asparagus over a cornmeal waffle and covers it with a curry-cream sauce studded with dried cranberries.

David Stokamer, the owner of FlavourSpot, told the *O,* "I look at savory waffles like any sandwich that I would eat on challah bread." He said that on his savory waffles he goes for a touch of sweetness balanced by smoked ingredients, like turkey and bacon paired with Havarti cheese. He said that some stuff, like a roast beef-Cheddar-horseradish waffle he tried, was terrible. One of the occasional specials he came up with: smoked salmon, cream cheese, cucumber, tomatoes, chopped green onions, and capers. And he's still coming up with ideas; he told the *O* that the bigger kitchen on Mississippi will let him "experiment with some of the four pages of combinations he's dreamed up but hasn't tried yet."

I go into all this background because, really, all you need to know is this: There are these two waffle carts in North Portland with food that is cheap and wonderful. What are you waiting for? Don't you want to know what else the man has up his dough-smeared sleeves?

Wait: Can get a little long on weekends.
Seating: A few chairs here and there.
Large groups? Sure, but you order one at a time.
Portion size: Think big sandwich.
Changes: Not so much.
Coffee: Stumptown.
Other drinks: Espresso, Ovaltine, Postum, Lemon- and Limeaid, Italian sodas.
Feel-goods: Lots of organic ingredients.
Health options: Come on, they're waffles!
WiFi? No.

Francis Cafe

New/Classy

Another watershed place on Alberta Street

2338 NE Alberta St. (NE/Alberta)

503-288-8299

Tuesday through Friday, 7 a.m. to 3 p.m.; weekends 7 a.m. to 4 p.m. Breakfast served all day.

francisrestaurant.com

$10–14, with $6.95 specials during the week (all major cards)

━━━━━━━━━◆●◆━━━━━━━━━

Everybody who lives around Alberta Street has, in the last 10 years or so, experienced some kind of "wow" moment. It happens when you realize how much the neighborhood is changing. Maybe it was the advent of the Last Thursday art walk-street fair, or the departure of the Clown House, or Alberta being named Street of the Year in the *Willamette Week* restaurant guide.

For me it was the opening of Francis Restaurant in November 2006. Right across the street from the old Rexall-drugstore-turned-coffee-shop there suddenly appeared a restaurant with white tablecloths, high-backed chairs, wait staff in black and white, and oyster hash with ancho peppers finished with cream and horseradish for $11. Wow.

Not everyone was thrilled, apparently. In a fit of twisted white guilt and antibusiness pique, some nitwit painted "gentrification this way" on the door and busted the lock, which ironically handed Francis some excellent advance publicity as well as large, supportive crowds for its opening. But the word through the neighborhood, whether positive or negative, was that Helser's had clearly been replaced at the high end of the local breakfast scene. We have the chill Cup and

Saucer, the veggie palace Vita, the iconic Tin Shed, the classy but relaxed Helser's, and now Francis, with its designer wood patio and $12.50 house-smoked maple salmon Benedict with pear, sherry, and sage hollandaise sauce. Wow.

I'm not into the white-guilt thing, and I'm completely in favor of nice restaurants. Serving all the PC stuff like hormone-, cage-, and cruelty-free eggs and organically fed beef doesn't hurt, either, and fits the new Alberta vibe perfectly. The question to me was, Is this a place I'll think of when I want just a casual breakfast?

It's definitely classy, and in my shallow quest for stereotypes I noticed there were tables with well-dressed elderly folk, three businesspeople chatting on cell phones, people talking about wine, and a family with two teenagers. Not the typical Alberta crowd — or is it? Is the neighborhood changing that much, or are people driving in to eat at Francis?

When a shirtless dude rode down the street on a seven-foot-tall bike with a jam box blasting classical music, I felt a little more centered.

As for the food, I had to get that salmon Benedict, and I actually found myself writing the following: "The sage gave the hollandaise an earthy ground for the sweetness of the bountiful salmon to stand out." Understand, I wrote this on *Alberta Street*, within blocks of the (a moment of silence, please) Clown House.

Many dishes are fancy twists on traditional treats: an omelet with ham, aged Gouda cheese, and crimini mushrooms topped with crème fraîche and fried onions. Maple brûlé oatmeal with currants and fruit. Vegan biscuits with tempeh gravy. Pan-fried oysters served with horseradish marmalade sauce.

Other dishes are more grounded. Don's Benedict, for example, includes a crunchy biscuit, house-cured ham, and peppery, chunky sausage gravy. Everything is a la carte, so these egg dishes come with a garnish of toast or biscuit (there are gluten-free options on breads), or cantaloupe and honeydew drizzled with mint sauce. The hashbrowns (or skillet-fried grits) are $2 with several add-on options: onions ($2.50), onions and Cheddar ($3.00), or those two plus chili or sausage gravy ($4.00).

I was sitting on the sunny patio, going back and forth between sweet salmon with rich hollandaise and fresh melons with mint sauce while looking at the crowd. And I thought, Wow, this is serious food stuff right here on Alberta. So the answer to my original question was, yeah, this *is* a place I can hang out in!

Wait: A little long on weekends, all outside without cover.
Seating: About 48 inside at tables and 46 on a (usually) sunny patio. **Large groups?** Maybe on the patio. Reservations suggested.
Portion size: Decent, but it is mostly a la carte.
Changes: Sure. **Coffee:** Stumptown.
Other drinks: Italian sodas, cocktails, Bloody Marys.
Feel-goods: All the ingredients are organic, hormone-free, and local.
Health options: Some gluten-free breads and pastries, home-made vegan sausage, and a vegetable hash.
WiFi? No.

Fuller's Coffee Shop

Old School/Mom and Pop

Some call it old-fashioned
136 NW 9th Ave. (Pearl)
503-222-5608
Weekdays 6:00 a.m. to 3:00 p.m.; Saturday 7:00 a.m. to 2:00
p.m. Sunday 8:00 a.m. to 2:00 p.m. Breakfast served all day.
$6–9 (cash and checks only, but there's an ATM on site)

———————◆•◆———————

A common misconception about Fuller's Coffee Shop is that
it's in a place called the Pearl District. The folks at pearl-
district.com say Fuller's is "a reminder of when the Pearl
District was into lifting heavy loads off the docks." But the
Pearl District never did an ounce of heavy lifting; the name
was created as a marketing tool in the 1990s when a ware-
house-brewery district was being turned into a land of condos, art galleries, and boutique shopping.

Although Fuller's is geographically in "the Pearl," it's
really in the 1940s. And although there's nothing wrong with
yoga and doggie day care, it sure is nice to have an old-style
coffee shop around.

Most Fuller's reviews are a variation of "Oh my gosh, all
they have is homemade white and whole wheat bread, and it's
good, and they make real hashbrowns instead of fancy potatoes, and they have pig-in-a-blanket, and you sit at counters
on stools!"

Perhaps I sound snide, and perhaps I am being just that.
I will miss the old warehouse district when it's totally gone,
and I don't think of Fuller's as a reminder of times gone
by. I think of it as a place where people eat breakfast, read
the paper, sit close to one another, and have conversations.

Somehow that has become quaint, which seems a shame. I'm just glad I can still do it.

Fuller's has all your old favorites: pigs-in-a-blanket, strawberry waffles (in season), great hashbrowns, crispy bacon, chicken-fried steak smothered in gravy, huevos rancheros, and that "homemade" bread sliced by a machine you can spot from the counter. Actually, you can spot the whole kitchen from the counter.

The prices, many of them written by hand on the menu, top out around $9. Newspapers are generally strewn on the counter, and on the walls are photos of the same place in 1955, back when it was at Union (now MLK) and Pine. It moved to 9th and Davis in the 1960. The water heater is in the bathroom, an old neon clock/sign hangs above the register, and you can even get a Fuller's T-shirt.

Here's a story I love about Fuller's: Michael Stern, of roadfood.com and *Eat Your Way Across the USA*, had Fuller's in his first book but left it out of a later edition because it had been so long since he had been there and wasn't sure it was still worthy. Then he came back 10 years later and found that it hadn't changed at all! He even found a man at the counter who ate there 30 years ago and said it hasn't changed since then, either—other than the prices.

It's funny that people expect a place like Fuller's to change.

Why should it? Fame and glory? Shoot. It's pretty simple, really: cook basic, good food; charge reasonable prices; treat people nicely; otherwise, stay out of the way and let folks be folks. Labels like "businessman" and "tourist" and "Pearlite" and "guy off the street"—even "waitress" and "cook" and "owner"—tend to disappear at Fuller's counter.

My friend Craig used to work with the homeless population downtown, and he loves Fuller's. I think it's because he sees the Pearl as a land of posers and Fuller's as a place where nobody's full of it and a guy living on the street can be welcomed. I don't see the Pearl so harshly, but to see Fuller's getting some notoriety for being old-timey is somewhat humorous.

After shaking hands with Craig on the sidewalk at 9th and Davis, with another condo tower rising behind the car repair place across the street and a stream of thirtysomethings walking their dogs by us, I rub my bacon-filled belly and hope the old way lives long into the future.

Wait: Medium-long on weekends.
Seating: Two horse-shoe counters with 28 stools, plus a few tables outside in nice weather.
Large groups? If there's room at the counter.
Portion size: Solid.
Changes: Sure, hon.
Coffee: Boyds.
Other drinks: Stash tea, espresso.
Feel-goods: Getting to know folks at the counter.
Health options: Egg substitute is available.
WiFi? Hardly.

Gateway Breakfast House

Mom and Pop

Family, regulars, piles of food and a touch of goofy
11411 NE Halsey St., Portland (NE/Outer)
503-256-6280
Monday through Saturday 6:30 a.m. to 3 p.m.; Sunday
7:00 a.m. to 3 p.m.; breakfast served all the time
$7-10 (Visa, MasterCard, and Discover)

The defining moment of our trip to the Gateway Breakfast House was when Tom's order—pancakes—arrived. I've never seen a table of friends let out a collective "Wow" like the one generated by those pancakes. It was part awe, part humor, and part fear. Tom looked like he had walked into a pickup basketball game and found out he was guarding Shaquille O'Neal.

Diana said they were "pancakes you could sleep on," and when Tom cut somebody a portion, he said, "White meat or dark?" The waitress said that two or three times a year one person eats the whole pancake order.

So, you get the idea. Very. Large. Portions. Seven of us each ordered something, we could have easily fed a dozen people, and the pretip bill was only $53. The Gateway does breakfast the way James Michener writes books.

The Gateway is cozy, crowded on weekends, and has a vibe that's part homey-family and part, well, mildly odd. For example, the nice young women hustling food, the large wreath, and the painted skillets and washboards hanging on the wall all say "down-home." Despite the long lines, the Gateway doesn't keep a seating list; it just sort of . . . works out.

You sit down to a cup of coffee in those truck-stop brown mugs and water in plastic cups. You read the menu and notice both hamburger steaks *and* hamburger patties (at which point you know you're not in for an exotic meal). The ribeye-and-three-egg platter is described as "seasoned."

All of this makes you think the waitress is probably the daughter or niece of the hostess, who's married to the cook, who's minding the place for his old man. I don't know if any of it is true; it just feels that way.

But while I was waiting (30 minutes to seat seven on a Sunday morning at 9:30), I had a chance to read some of the stuff on the bulletin board. Two selections: "If you want customers to remember you, hit them with a 2x4" and "Beatings will continue until morale improves." Hmm.

The building used to be a Chinese place and a donut shop (presumably not at the same time), so the architecture isn't much of a turn-on. The first description I heard, from my dedicated breakfast spotter, Linda, was "strange-looking place with a huge line." Hanging from the ceiling are about two dozen large, white orbs of different sizes, some of them lights, in a pattern that suggests a bizarro solar system, or, as Leslie put it, "The molecular structure of fat." Her thought seemed reasonable when my pork-chop-and-eggs special arrived: two large pork chops, three eggs, a half-plate of hashbrowns, and four pieces of toast.

The size of these portions, I mean . . . Consider the country breakfast. You get a pancake or French toast or a waffle or toast or biscuits and gravy. *And* you get two eggs, hashbrowns, and bacon or links. *And* you get a choice of one pork chop or ham or sausage or pastrami or chicken-fried steak. For, like, seven bucks.

Though we could hardly walk out, we had a good time; good friends, big portions, and cheap prices will do that. The world o' pancakes (my term), for example, was only $3.25 (single big pancake) and the two big pancakes are $4.25. The staff was friendly and attentive, and they volunteered to let us pay separately at the register. (Even our check was about four pages.) We saw kids and old folks and families and loners and regulars and everything, and now I know why they always have a line outside this place: they feed the hell out of you!

Wait: Up to 30 minutes on weekends
Seating: About 60 in tables and booths.
Large groups? Sure, but send somebody early on weekends.
Portion Size: Shock and awe.
Changes: Just tell 'em what you want!
Coffee: Farmer Brother's.
Other drinks: The usual
Feel-goods: Do the by-the-pound price comparison!
Health options: Can't imagine
WiFi? No

Genies Café

New/Hip/Veggie

Look at what these kids are up to!

1101 SE Division (SE/Inner)

503-445-9777

8 a.m. to 3 p.m. daily. Breakfast served all day.

geniescafepdx.com

$9–14 (all major cards)

———————◆—•—◆———————

Whenever I go to Genie's, I am impressed all over again. Now, I must admit there is a tinge of condescension to that. I'm not proud of it, but the truth is I have long thought of the young folk of Southeast Portland more along the down-home, slacker lines of the Cricket Cafe or Junior's Cafe.

When Genies opened, I read a clip in The *Oregonian* about how Genies uses all local ingredients, serves fancy cocktails, and has a chef (a chef!) and a menu with smoked tomatoes, crimini and oyster mushrooms, artichoke hearts, and an Italian sausage frittata with nettles and fiddleheads. Genies also got a lot of press for the cocktails, including an Emergen-C Elixir (orange vodka, EmergenC, muddled lemon, and a splash of cranberry juice) and a Bloody Mary made with jalapeno-infused vodka.

And I thought, Really? At 11th and Division? What's going on in Southeast? So I went to check it out—and was immediately turned away by a Tin Shed-level weekend line. Fortunately, Genies expanded soon after opening; the folks added a small espresso bar and an indoor waiting area, an idea I always thought somebody should act upon. As it turns out, Genies is full of good ideas.

For one thing, look at where the folks get their ingredients: The menu says, "We pride ourselves in using only local cage-free eggs, local farm-raised meats, and local produce wherever possible." Considering the farm bounty and foodie innovation we live in, that's a fine idea.

Then there's the space itself: large, open, and airy, but divided to somehow still feel private, and the choice of sitting in the sun or in a shady corner. The décor is at once clean — almost industrial — yet open and colorful with slight art nouveau touches. The staff and the vast majority of patrons are quite young; I was there once for a crowded Monday lunch and, at 40, was among the four oldest people in the building.

So you've got the energy and the PC ingredients, and then you've got a massive menu: five omelets, seven scrambles, five Benedicts, five "specialty egg dishes," three kinds of pancakes (buttermilk, huckleberry, white chocolate chip hazelnut), French toast made with ciabatta bread, more than a dozen sides, and rotating seasonal specials like a morel scramble with asparagus tips, or huckleberry pancakes. Goodness!

Here's a typical weekday visit (I can't stand the weekend wait): I take a table in the corner and immediately have a cup of strong coffee. I admire both the number and youthful energy of the other customers. After fighting through the menu, I force myself to rule out things like an omelet with locally grown button, crimini, and oyster mushrooms topped with shallots and chives. I settle on the Tasso Benedict featuring Cajun-style ham. For a $2 sweet treat, I toss in a single white-chocolate-chip-and-hazelnut pancake.

I see that on the table we are both old school (Heinz ketchup), local quirky (Secret Aardvark Sauce), and artisan (house-made raspberry jam and orange marmalade). My big plate comes with two large portions of the Benedict and a heaping side of tender, flaky red potatoes seasoned with rosemary, thyme, and parsley. The ham had fat and just a little toughness and spice to it, the closest thing to Southern-style country ham I've found in Portland. Playing that against the thick, creamy hollandaise, clearing the palette with the occasional potato, I lose track of the massive pancake sitting nearby. It's just a little crunchy on the under side, giving it a nice snap to go with the chewy hazelnuts, fluffy cake, and fine sweetness of white chocolate.

By the end I realize, again, that I need to do two things immediately: get over my silly notions about Southeast Portland and get back to Genies more often.

Wait: Long on weekends, with uncovered benches outside but an espresso bar inside.
Seating: About 75 at tables and booths.
Large groups? Absolutely.
Portion size: Whoppin'. **Changes:** Easy.
Coffee: Stumptown. **Other drinks:** Tao of Tea, espresso, beer, and a world of cocktails.
Feel-goods: Everything is local, and much of it is organic.
Health options: Plenty of vegetarian options, and both tofu (free) and egg whites.
WiFi? Yes.

Golden Touch Family Restaurant

Old School

"It's just a family restaurant."

8124 SW Barbur Blvd. (SW/Inner)

503-245-2007

Monday 6 a.m. to 4 p.m.; Tuesday through Sunday 6 a.m. to 9 p.m. Breakfast served all day.

$7–12 (Visa, MasterCard, no checks)

━━━━━◆━●━◆━━━━━

Let's say you have a favorite hike. You do it all the time, even though it doesn't change a whole lot from trip to trip, doesn't have great views, doesn't visit a big waterfall, doesn't even give you a great workout. Maybe you don't even recommend it to a visitor looking for a great hike. You just . . . like it. So you keep doing it.

My good friend Corky and his friend Sam have a favorite hike. It's in the Columbia River Gorge, the loop from Wahkeena Falls to Multnomah Falls. There are longer, steeper, more spectacular hikes, but almost every Sunday for about 30 years Corky and Sam hike that loop—after they eat at the Golden Touch.

I have the pleasure of eating breakfast with Corky often, and 90 percent of the time it's at what we affectionately call the Touch. This is largely because Corky lives nearby and is stubborn, but I don't mind telling you, the Touch is one of my favorite places to eat. It's not about the food, though it is good. In fact, when I told the waitress that I was writing a book about breakfast places and was putting in the Golden Touch, she actually looked at me funny and said, "Really? *This* place?"

Yes, the Touch. And here's why: It's about the least pretentious place in the world, most of the staff has worked there forever and call it a "family restaurant," it has a million options on the menu, and you can get in and out in half an hour. Or you can sit there and shoot the breeze for hours, at which Corky happens to be a master.

Put it this way. A negative review on citysearch.com, while noting the quick and friendly service, said, "The decor suggests a scene from the mid 70s and the bacon flavor is cooked right into the paint and fixtures." To which I say, "Exactly!"

It's the kind of place where you can peruse the extensive menu or just tell the waitress what you want, and she'll probably say, "Sure, that's the [fill in the blank] with a couple changes, no problem." I like the honey wheat cakes special, which comes with a couple of eggs and four pieces of thick bacon (buttermilk, blueberry, and Swedish cakes are also available). Corky always gets a veggie omelet and fruit, and he likes to put Heinz 57 sauce on the omelet. After all these years he hardly needs to order; one time he was still cracking jokes and didn't even realize the waitress had written down his whole order and was looking at me, the two of us sharing an "Isn't Corky funny?" glance.

Sometimes we sit in one of the fancy round booths in the

back room, which is straight out of a 1970s cafeteria. Nora, another fan of the Touch I worked with at FedEx, said she always wanted to sit back there but thought you had to be "special." I told her, "Shoot, next time just say you want to sit in the back," and that night at work she was glowing: "I sat in one of the fancy booths!" We talked for a while about how much we liked the Touch and how we felt special to sit in back, and it occurs to me now that I didn't even ask what she ate.

Who cares? It'd be like asking Corky how that loop to Multnomah Falls was. I know how it was. And next time, I want to go.

Wait: None.
Seating: About 100, with tables, counter, booths, and fancy high-top booths.
Large groups? Not so much.
Portion size: More than enough.
Changes: They'll make whatever you want.
Coffee: Farmers Brothers.
Other drinks: Farmer Brothers tea, beer, and wine.
Feel-goods: "It's just a family restaurant."
Health options: Egg substitute available.
WiFi? No.

Gravy

New/Hip

Once new/cool, now establishment/cool

3957 N Mississippi Ave. (N/Inner)

503-287-8800

Tuesday through Friday, 7:30 a.m. to 3:00 p.m.; weekends, 8:00 a.m. to 3:00 p.m. Breakfast served all hours

$10–14 (all major cards)

———————◆ • ◆———————

I'm not sure when Gravy stopped being a place that was new and exciting just because of what and where it is.

It isn't that the place changed so much. It's still got that sort of relaxed vibe about it, which some folks call "funky" and others call "slow." The menu still offers a wide variety of down-home style choices, often with locally raised, organic ingredients. It's still so miserably crowded on weekends that waiting outside for up to 45 minutes is an accepted part of the experience, and other places on Mississippi Street are known as options to try "instead of waiting in line at Gravy" (see: Mississippi Station, FlavourSpot, Moxie RX).

Gravy set up shop back in March, 2004, when North Mississippi Street was just accelerating its fairly quick, and utterly inevitable, transformation from a neighborhood worried about abandoned homes and drug raids to one fighting over high-density housing and saving some diversity. You might say Gravy was to Mississippi sort of what Tin Shed was to Alberta: any good developer will tell you that one of the first things a neighborhood needs to attract younger, wealthier, whiter people is, along with art galleries, a "destination restaurant."

Enter Gravy, with its local organic ingredients, live piano music on weekends, modern art on the walls, a few tattoos on the staff, and food that is a kind of homage to old-school diners.

In fact, if there are gripes about Gravy, one is that the food is just that: basic breakfast food, not too exciting but in ridiculous portions. Honestly, if you can knock back a full order of the Brioche French Toast, I'd have you immediately tested for marijuana. When I do go to Gravy, it's often to get a hash or pork chops and eggs as a kind of long-term investment: buy breakfast, get stuffed, and walk out with dinner!

Still, there is a lot to be said for variety, and Gravy certainly delivers: numerous scrambles, hashes, omelets, meat-and-egg combinations, and griddle specialties. And if that isn't enough, there's a large "build your own" omelet section with vegetarian and vegan options. Also, the meals don't come just with potatoes; you can add bacon, sausage, ham, fruit, hashbrowns, or pancakes.

In a sense it's almost too much, and one can feel a little overwhelmed. Certainly, the weekends crowds are insane, but even during the week you may feel like the tables are pushed awfully close together. It's not a place to visit if you're looking for peace, quiet, and personal space. Or if you're impatient; complaints about slow and spotty service have been around since Gravy opened. My take has always been that the staff is just as overwhelmed as we diners sometimes are.

The décor might make you think the place is still evolving,

with its bare ceilings, exposed pipes, mismatched light fix-tures, a facade in front of the kitchen, a side of wood panel with a tile section implanted acting as a podium, and an old sideboard near the kitchen. But that's the (perhaps uninten-tional) theme: a work in progress that somehow got frozen in time when the place got so busy and popular there was no time to change. And it fits with the street as well as with the street's signature business, the nonprofit ReBuilding Center a few blocks down from Gravy.

Anyway, why should Gravy change? Even though you rarely hear it mentioned as one of the best places to eat break-fast in Portland, it's easily one of the most popular. I think it just quit being exciting to people, sort of like Mississippi Street itself. They're both cool, both good, both still grow-ing, and both completely accepted as an integral part of Portland.

Wait: Legendary on weekends; sometimes there's even a wait at lunchtime on weekdays. Very small area for waiting inside, with self-serve coffee.

Seating: About 30 at 9 half-booths, 12 at tables, plus a small counter.

Large groups? Maybe during the week, with some notice.

Portion size: Almost too much.

Changes: Within reason. **Coffee:** Seller Door.

Other drinks: Fresh orange juice, full bar.

Feel-goods: Many ingredients are local and organic.

Health options: Egg substitutes available, and build-your-own omelets give plenty of options.

WiFi? No.

Hands On Cafe

New/Classy/Mom and Pop
This is no student cafeteria!
8245 SW Barnes Road (SW/Outer)
503-297-1480
Brunch on Sunday only, 9:30 a.m. to 1:30 p.m.
$13–15 (cash and checks only)

———————————◆•◆———————————

Here's what I once knew about the Hands On Cafe: It's the
"student cafeteria" at the Oregon College of Art and Craft,
and it's really nice up there.

Here's what *Willamette Week* had to say:

> The first thing you need to know about this hid-
> den treasure is how to find it. Once there, feast
> upon healthy, original dishes like the "Wishing
> for Spring" fresh asparagus omelette ($9.75). You'll
> swear Joni Mitchell's *Blue* just hit record stores as
> you picnic among artisans' huts and lanky pines.

My snootiness alarm went wild upon reading that. But
one rainy February Sunday, for whatever reason, I said to my
artist girlfriend, "Honey, let's go check out that place at the
art school!" I had her at *art.*

First of all, as for getting there, all I can say is, use
Mapquest. Or call the cafe — they're very friendly and get
that call often.

We parked in a shaded lot and wandered down a path to
a low-slung building in which we found an art gallery, a gift
shop, and just the kind of "student cafeteria" you'd expect at
an art school in the West Hills: a little fireplace, some art
on the walls, jazz playing softly, flowers on the tables, and

 a room full of affluent-looking folks chatting amiably. It wasn't, in other words, the Mustang Cafe, which I used to haunt for chicken strips and pizza back at SMU.

The place must not be all that well known, because we arrived at 10:15 on a Sunday morning and there was exactly one couple waiting for a table—who promptly informed us about the community table in the back corner near the wide-open kitchen. A moment later we sat at that table, where we were instantly presented with a free plate of baked goodies and half a red grapefruit with candied ginger. The other couple there told us the wait is never more than 15 minutes, and the waitress said that in the summer, when tables are set up under the trees, rhododendrons, and azaleas, "there's hardly ever a wait."

By this time my snootiness alarm had silenced. The staff, made up of students and the owner's family, was friendly, sweet, and efficient. Well, they got Jenny at *art*, and they got me with a bite of our neighbor's grilled salmon cakes on corn, basil, and red pepper sauce topped with poached eggs and hollandaise sauce. It was served with tomato, arugula, and avocado relish and roasted potatoes.

There are always four items on the menu—when you see the size of the kitchen, you'll know why—and although the menu changes every one to three weeks, one item is always a pancake. When we visited, it was buttermilk cakes topped with winter fruit compote, crème anglaise, sweetened whipping cream, and toasted almonds. It came with scrambled eggs and a choice of sausage or bacon for $10.50. So you'll spend about $14 to eat at Hands On Cafe, but considering what all you get, it's a bargain. I'm told there's usually a pork dish as well, and the one I had was out of this world: sautéed tenderloin on a roasted red pepper and tomato sauce topped with pork demi-glaze sauce and served with two poached eggs, creamy polenta, shaved Parmesan, and greens with pancetta and mushrooms.

I ate every bit of it, and then I shamelessly swooped in on the rest of Jenny's pancakes, which had an earthy sweetness that must have come from the wheat—or maybe there was some sweet potato in the recipe. Either way, we made a joke about telling the waitress this should be the Hands Off Cafe, because I would have hurt anybody who tried to get those pancakes from me.

I think I'll go with "earthy sweetness" to describe the whole cafe, in fact.

Wait: Little to none, with a whole gift shop and gallery to explore.

Seating: About 60, all at tables, with lovely outdoor seating in summer. **Large groups?** Sure.

Portion size: Big.

Changes: Not so much: only four choices on the menu. You can split entreés for $4.

Coffee: San Francisco Bay.

Other drinks: Tea, juices, lemonade.

Feel-goods: None that they tout. Supporting students, maybe?

Health options: Ditto.

WiFi? Yes.

Hawthorne Cafe

New/Hip/Veggie

We can all agree: it's a happy place!

3354 SE Hawthorne Blvd. (SE/Hawthorne)

503-235-8286

Daily 7:30 a.m. to 2:30 p.m. Breakfast served all day.

$8–12 (cash, checks, all major cards)

It sure is fun getting people going about the Hawthorne Cafe. It looks like a harmless breakfast joint, with kind of a happy vibe that's a pure dose of Hawthorne's much-stereotyped hippie scene; there's even a place above it called Moonshadow, "serving the Portland pagan community since 1995" and the home of a local Druidic group. Seriously.

The Hawthorne is in a creaky old house with sloped floors, a glass-enclosed porch, wood blinds on the numerous windows, homey red-and-white tablecloths, hanging plants, flower boxes, even paintings of flowers on the cheery yellow walls. So it's a happy place. And it's kind of a hippie place.

I'll tell you what it's like: it's like the Grateful Dead of the local breakfast scene—and not just for its sunny, happy groove. Even folks who like it (myself included) would never describe it as particularly efficient. I was a huge fan of the Dead, too, and whenever people get going about the Dead, it's always the same conversation. One group says, "Oh, I *loved* those guys!" Another group says, "God, they were hardly even proficient musicians!" And the majority of people wouldn't recognize the Dead if they walked in the room, so they wonder, "What's the big deal about them either way?"

I always thought that the Dead was, at worst, a party band that didn't always succeed in knocking your socks off.

If you were into what they were putting down, and if they got it right, there was magic in the air. And sometimes they weren't so good. But I also recognized that even at the best Dead shows I ever went to, people were standing around thinking stuff like, "They're forgetting the words to their own songs!" Which they were, of course. And occasionally the staff at the Hawthorne might forget your order.

So back to breakfast. Here's a typical batch of notes from a trip to the Hawthorne: "pear crepe super-tasty, warm, and sweet . . . smoked-sturgeon Benedict interesting but not great . . . turkey wrap has a little spice to it, nice . . . sign near bathroom for a class called Wicca 101 . . . staff friendly and cute, not too efficient . . . homemade marionberry coffee cake like a big ol' slab of goodness. . . ."

See? Even somebody who's eaten breakfast in about 120 places in town couldn't tell you if the Hawthorne is consistently good. For the record, I never made the argument that the Dead was a particularly good band, either — just that it was, and is, my all-time favorite. And a lot of folks feel that way about the Hawthorne Cafe, which explains why it's been open and popular for so long. Of course, others will trash it thoroughly, but one online reviewer who suggested somebody new take over the place did admit the staff was "helpful and apologetic" (kind of like how most people consider Deadheads a harmless, goofy lot).

So the Hawthorne Cafe isn't a restaurant that gets

consistently high marks — or consistently low ones, for that matter. But it is a relaxed, happy place where you can get lots of veggie options (but not many vegan ones), wheat or buttermilk or daily-special pancakes, French toast, seven omelets, and a couple of Benedicts. You can also get some classic hippie-type fare like a bowl of granola with yogurt and fruit; a high-protein breakfast with oatmeal, 2 percent milk, peanut butter, yogurt, and fruit; and the Country Pancakes: walnut wheat cakes layered with peanut butter and topped with bananas, raisins, and hot syrup.

Looking for an amazing, life-changing performance every time? Skip the Hawthorne. And the Dead. Looking for a relaxed, friendly scene that does the basics pretty well, has fun, and doesn't take itself seriously? I recommend both.

Wait: Fairly long on weekends.
Seating: About 60 in several rooms all at tables, plus a patio.
Large groups? Yes.
Portion size: Decent.
Changes: Yes, and all omelets are available without potatoes or bread for $1 less.
Coffee: Kobos.
Other drinks: Espresso, fresh OJ, Stash Teas, plus House Blend of Fine Quality Tea.
Feel-goods: A certain pagan vibe, if you're into that.
Health options: Egg substitute available and several vegetarian options.
WiFi? No.

The Heathman Hotel

Classy

Old-fashioned fanciness downtown
1001 SW Broadway (Downtown)
503-790-7752
Daily 6:30 a.m. to 11:00 a.m. Weekend brunch menu with
lunch items from 9:00 a.m. to 2:00 p.m..
heathmanrestaurantandbar.com
$15–25 (all major cards)

———————◆•◆———————

A pair of waiters dressed in black and white descended upon
our table in a choreographed motion, revealing a wonderfully
presented Oregon Dungeness Crab Omelet and Brioche
French Toast. Jenny and I swapped a slightly startled glance
that said, "We're not at the Cricket Cafe anymore!"

The waiters returned and swooped in on my parents, lay-
ing down a Hickory Smoked Salmon Hash and an Eggs
Benedict with Smoked Pork Loin. Jenny and I leaned in to
admire, swapped another glance, then folded our napkins
onto our laps and sat up a little straighter.

Yes, we had performed a Portland breakfast cliché: we
waited for my folks to come to town before heading to the
Heathman. In part it was simple economics: the four entrées
sitting on our table went for a combined $57.85. Throw in
four cups of coffee (at $3.45 each!) and a reasonable tip, and
we had an $85 breakfast on our hands. I'm a freelance writer
and Jenny is a grad student; our budget is a lot more Cricket
than Heathman.

But it's also a cultural thing. My folks are pretty old-
school, and when traveling they are basically into two kinds
of meals: the local dive with color and the nice restaurant.

In other words, when in New Orleans they'll go to the back-alley joint where crawdads are served in a bucket and you wear a bib, but the next night they're going to Gallatoire's in the French Quarter.

So when breakfasting in Portland, they'll go with my friends and me to Beaterville, but the next day they need to get back their equilibrium with some white tablecloths, super-polite staff, a *New York Times*, and Reggiano-Parmigiano. So it was that I took Jenny and my parents (well, I drove) to the Heathman, the old-line hotel on Broadway with the Beefeater guys.

Portlanders are aware there's a restaurant in the hotel, especially on a night when there's a show at the Schnitz next door, but most of us, and certainly most of the crowd I run with, consider it a place for the rich and the out-of-town. And with good reason: it's pricey ($14.95 for corned beef hash, for example) and just a wee bit stuffy. A *Willamette Week* review lamented "a generic setting that harks back to the bad old days of anonymous hotel dining rooms." I just think of it as an old-fashioned fancy that keeps doing what it does because, well, it's always done that (since 1927, anyway) and because it works.

And although the dishes sound down-to-earth—omelets, Benedicts, hash, scrambles, French toast, waffles, pancakes—even on the menu you'll see the choices that set this place apart. In the amazing Hangtown Fry, for example, the eggs are "lightly folded with fried Willapa Bay oysters, peppers, onions, applewood-smoked bacon, and Reggiano-Parmigiano." Is it good? Hell yes. It ought to be, for $15.75.

Portland treats the Heathman with something like a reflex reaction. The average person who knows you're eating there will stiffen up a bit, put on some mock snobbery, and say, "Oh, really?" A dedicated foodie is likely to say it's just limping along on reputation. And the *WW* discussion of the Heathman's real-live French chef and the dinner menu is utterly typical of its rep in the media:

> Philippe Boulot's marriage of French-country and bistro cuisine with Northwest ingredients won him a James Beard Award in 2001. Sometimes it's easy to see why: A salad of peppery arugula and sweet Oregon berries, topped with a sachet of soft cheese, is a quiet little wow, as is an appetizer of chilled halibut over avocado-stuffed wontons.

I mean, what's a "sachet" and a "quiet little wow"? I can't imagine another Portland breakfast place being written about that way.

God bless the Heathman. If I ever get rich, I might become a regular.

Wait: Maybe a short one on weekends.
Seating: About 87, all at tables.
Large groups? With notice.
Portion size: Large—and lovely.
Changes: Within reason. **Coffee:** Fonté Roasters.
Other drinks: Espresso, Fonté tea, juices, cocktails.
Feel-goods: None they brag about.
Health options: Egg substitutes, and some vegetarian/vegan items.
WiFi? From the hotel, but it doesn't always reach the restaurant.

Helser's

Hip/New

Open, spacious, simple, casually elegant
1538 NE Alberta (NE/Alberta)
503-281-1477
Monday through Sunday, 7 a.m. to 3 p.m.; breakfast served all day
$9-12 with $4.50 portions available before 9 a.m. (Cash, Visa, MasterCard).

I went to Helser's once when I had been driving around Oregon for days, hosting a friend from Switzerland, staying in fancy hotels, and eating rich food. I was ready to settle back into my Portland routine and calm down, eat something simple and tasty. Manuela was still looking for a place to eat breakfast in America where she could get only what she wanted—pancakes and fruit—and not leave a meal's worth of feed behind. She said it made her feel guilty.

So we walked into Helser's, and I got Yukon gold potato hash, lightly seasoned, with poached eggs. Manuela asked about the pancakes, was told there were four to an order, asked if she could have only two, the waitress said absolutely, and she got a side of yogurt and fruit. Ate the whole thing. We spent $10 each. Perfect.

Another time I went to Helser's when I was heading out for a hike, and I wanted something filling but not too much so. I was there before 9 a.m. and got the single portion of smoked salmon Benedict—the fish moist and the sauce creamy. I paid $4.50 for it and didn't eat a thing during the hike. Perfect.

Another time I just wanted to feed my sweet tooth, so I walked over and got the full portion of the brioche French toast, sliced thick and soaked in vanilla cinnamon batter. I walked out with a little buzz working. Perfect. Everybody I know likes Helser's. It's either the Benedicts (they also come with local Zenner's ham or spinach, crimini mushrooms, and  tomatoes) or the French toast or the specials (one time it was maple breakfast bread pudding) or the warm pear and Havarti pie in an egg custard with crème fraîche.

The feel at Helser's is very simple, in a good way. It's borderline Zen. Wood tables, comfortably spaced from one another. Wood chairs that are wide and comfortable. Tall ceilings. Plenty of windows and light. A few flowers on the table. Some bamboo. Beige walls. Servers wearing black and white. Simple light fixtures. Soft jazz playing.

As for the food, the complaints I've heard boil down to two: they're trying to do too much or "I don't like how they do their (fill in the blank)." Usually, the latter complaint is focused on the Scotch eggs (hard-boiled eggs wrapped in bratwurst, lightly breaded and fried) or the Louisiana Hot Sausage Scramble (two eggs, fried onions, spicy smoked sausage wrapped in a tomato flour tortilla with Cheddar cheese and scallions) or the Dutch Baby, which is not as fluffy or as filling as at Zell's or the Original Pancake House.

Well, here's another way of looking at it: How many places in town have a Dutch Baby, Scotch Eggs, *and* three kinds of sausage? Russet potato pancakes *and* Yukon gold hash? And mushroom hash? And pepper bacon hash? And three Benedicts? And New York Steak and eggs? Absolutely, they are all over the map, and maybe they don't have the best-in-town of anything, but their average is darn high.

I'm biased, because I live about five blocks away and have a crush on half the wait staff. Consider that your disclaimer. All I know is that every time I go to Helser's I'm in the mood for something in particular, and they always have it. And if I get there before 9, I get it for $4.50, which might be the most sensible thing in town. Breakfast shouldn't hurt!

Wait: Up to 30 minutes on weekends.

Seating: Around 48, all tables.

Large groups? Yes, but might be a while.

Portion Size: Average, but smaller and cheaper before 9 a.m.

Changes/Substitutions: Easy

Coffee: Kobos, with French press available.

Other drinks: Kobos Loose Leaf Teas, Mimosas.

Feel-goods: Local meats; pure maple syrup for $1.25 extra.

Health options: Egg substitutes and meatless options for no charge.

WiFi? No.

Hollywood Burger Bar

Mom and Pop/Old School

Just grabbin' a bite before I head into town.
4211 NE Sandy Blvd. (NE/Hollywood)
503-288-8965
Monday through Friday 7:30 a.m. to 4 p.m. (breakfast until
11); Saturday 8 a.m. to 4 p.m. (breakfast until 1)
$6-9 (Cash and checks only)

———————◆———————

I sit on the little spin-around counter seat at the Hollywood
Burger Bar — there's a counter and about three tables,
total — and my knees hit the wall underneath. But since I
was about to eat breakfast for around six bucks, I didn't complain. What I thought was, I bet this place has been here a
long time. Folks used to be shorter, you see.

So I ask the guy behind the counter, who's already pouring a big mug of strong coffee, and he says "We've been here
17 years." Then he adds, "It's been the Burger Bar since 1954.
The place was built in the '20s, been serving food since the
'30s, before that it was a dry cleaner, before that it was a trolley stop."

A *trolley stop!* It all came together for me. The small seats.
The tiny kitchen. The church bells I heard as I walked in.
The pure simplicity of the menu, with names like "Breakfast
#1," "Breakfast #2," and "Breakfast #3." This used to be a little
hub of a little community.

Turns out two trolley lines ended here: the one that came
out Sandy (came out from Portland, that is, called the Rose
City Line) and the one that came up 39th. Back then, when
Sandy was Highway 30 heading out toward the Columbia
Gorge, what we now call the Hollywood District (named for

the theater, which was built in the '20s) was a little village on the edge of civilization, and folks would come in here to get a cup of coffee and a paper before hopping on the trolley to go into Portland.

Look around the neighborhood: Sam's Billiards has been there since 1962, Pal's Shanty since 1937, the Pagoda and the Mandarin since the '40s, Sylvia's since 1957, St. Michael's church since 1910, Paulsen's Pharmacy since 1918 (and they have an old-style soda fountain, too)!

This morning at the Burger Bar's counter we have a woman keeping a journal, a young guy waking up and stretching, an elderly couple being taken out by their middle-aged daughter, and a man and woman talking religion and politics. Three bus lines run by the door, and I wonder how much has really changed.

But perhaps you're wondering about the food. Well, I can tell you this: For me, it's all about the bacon. I don't put a lot of energy into being a food critic, since I'm no good at it, and besides, I have never noticed any correspondence between my tastes and a place's popularity. But I do like bacon. And I like it just so: crispy, but not so much that it snaps in my hand. Lean. Tasty, with some spice, but not chunks of black pepper. All this, and it should be shamelessly greasy.

In my world, the Burger Bar's bacon is perfect, and it has a nice story behind it.

See, the owner got his meats from the Fulton Meat Company, which was "down in the Fulton neighborhood." My companion nodded her head at the memory, and though I'd never heard of either, I am always charmed by neighborhoods, especially if there's a chance one was named for a meat company. Well, he says, Fulton got bought out by Sysco, and the whole thing went south. So he started shopping around.

How did he choose the meat company? "Turns out," he told us, "one of the guys we were looking at lives five blocks away from us, and that was pretty much it."

Perfect bacon, from the guy down the street, in an old trolley stop surrounded by long-time friends and neighbors. I love the Burger Bar.

Wait: Maybe on weekends
Seating: About 15 at the counter, maybe three other tables, about 24 seats total.
Large groups? See previous.
Portion Size: Reasonable.
Changes: Since the cook is 11 feet away, probably.
Coffee: Boyds Coffee.
Other drinks: Tea, and there's RC Cola signs all over the place; need I say more?
Feel-goods: You can see how clean the dishes are, because you're basically sitting on the dishwasher.
Health Options: Veggie burgers at lunchtime — and is RC healthy?
Wheelchair? Yes. **WiFi?** Hardly.

Hotcake House

Old School

Casual by day, circus by night
1002 SE Powell (SE/Inner)
503-236-7402
Breakfast served 24 hours
$7–12 (cash, Visa, MasterCard)

———————◆•◆———————

Saturday, 1:15 a.m. I haven't seen 1:15 a.m. since I quit drinking. I stumble out of the Crystal Ballroom, dazed. My ears are ringing, my back is stiff, my feet are throbbing, my head is pounding. It's finally time to go to the Hotcake House. Some things have to happen in the middle of the night.

I pull into the lot, see a few bikers, and watch as a drunk couple staggers to a car . . . that doesn't pull out. Well.

My God, there's a line! You're supposed to order, then get a table and wait. Several signs say No Holding Tables! There's a rent-a-cop who looks a little overwhelmed.

I get in line and look around: a lot of prom kids and another drunk couple; she's draped over him, asking if he remembers their first date. Zombie-looking dudes are coming out of the kitchen with steak and eggs, massive stacks of hotcakes, and piles of hashbrowns . . . at 1:30? I see a gaggle of black-clad teen boys in a booth, a couple of them with hoodies, plus a guy at a table telling two women about somebody screwin' him over. Every now and then he gets a little loud and profane, and the place gets quiet. The rent-a-cop looks nervous.

Are those three girls at the head of the line *still* ordering? I've been here 10 minutes already. My ears hurt.

An old guy halfway up the line waves at me, then points at me, then points at an empty table. What, am I supposed to sit down or something? Just then a crowd comes in. A woman in line is next to me now, and the old guy waves at me again, points at me, then points at her, then *licks his lips* and looks at

her. She and I exchange a nervous glance, and I look around for the rent-a-cop . . . who's disappeared.

The cashier is giving the three chicks a dumbfounded look. She isn't getting one word of whatever they're saying. I just realized one of the guys in a tux with a horrible red tie is not a guy.

It's now 1:35. I do some math: At 2:15 I'm either gonna be here, waiting for my food . . . or in bed after taking a shower. I bail. On the car radio, Tom Petty is singing "Breakdown," and I realize I shouldn't be awake at this hour.

ooooo

Thursday, 9:30 a.m. I walk in and go right up to the counter, where the specials, on sticky notes, are cinnamon rolls, Polish sausage, biscuits and gravy, and smoked pork chops. The menu, on a board under Peter and Cheree Welcome You to the Hotcake House, is a tour of Americana: steaks, eggs, ham, bacon, sausage, beef patties, country-fried steak, waffles, hotcakes, mined ham and eggs, corned beef hash. Pretty much everything is under $10. For $8.40, you can get three eggs with your choice of meat or corned beef hash *and* two cakes or hashbrowns or toast!

I order the blueberry waffle ($6.75), get some coffee from the glass pitcher, and grab a seat in a booth next to a guy who's singing along with Jimi Hendrix on the jukebox while playing Here Comes the Airplane to get his little daughter to eat. I see folks involved in friendly, multi-table conversations, I see pictures of the Little League teams the place sponsors, and it occurs to me that this is one of the very few places where I've seen blacks and whites eating breakfast together. The cashier has a gray ponytail and tie-dyed bell-bottoms on.

I'm pretty sure the waffle syrup is blueberry pie filling from a can, but the waiter topped the waffle with a whipped-cream heart. I decide that I prefer the Hotcake House's indulgent but friendly daytime persona a lot better than the crazy evenings, and I dig in.

Wait: Up to half an hour from about 10:00 p.m. to 3:00 a.m. on weekends.
Seating: Around 50, mostly in booths.
Large groups? During the day, sure.
Portion size: Look out!
Changes: Not much.
Coffee: Self-serve Farmer Brothers.
Other drinks: Juice, milk, sodas.
Feel-goods: Does the security guard count?
Health options: Eating someplace else.
WiFi? No.

J&M Café

New/Classy/Veggie

A place where you can take your parents – and pay!

537 SE Ash St. (SE/Inner)

503-230-0463

Monday through Friday 7:30 a.m. to 2 p.m., full breakfast until 11:30 plus some limited breakfast offerings until 2. Weekends, 8:00 a.m. to 2:00 p.m., breakfast all day

$8-12 (Cash and checks only, but there's an ATM in the lobby)

———◆•◆———

My parents grew up in Mississippi during the Depression and swore they'd leave poverty behind. Today, when they travel, they pick their restaurants from *Gourmet* and the *New York Times*.

So I was raised to appreciate spots like Paley's Place and Genoa and Alba Osteria; but my freelance-writer income is a bit more Beaterville than Morton's. Hence, I keep The List of Places I Want My Parents To Take Me To When They Visit.

There are two other lists. One is the Places My Parents Wouldn't Go To In A Million Years: Fullers Coffee Shop, Tosis, Johnny B's, and so on. And then there's the list J&M Café is on: Places I Would Take My Parents To. To get on this list, a place has to be clean, comfortable, serve good and interesting food, not cost too much, exhibit some class, and yet include a touch of what makes Portland the great, goofy city it is.

Here's the case for the J&M: It's in an industrial neighborhood, within eyeshot of empty buildings, a rehab center, and busy, grimy Grand Avenue. But as soon as you walk

in, you see high ceilings, wood floors, big windows, brick walls . . . and a restaurant design that could easily offer the most stylish of food. Nonthreatening modern art (just my parents' style) hangs on the wall, there's plenty of space between tables, and the clientele includes lots of families and young people.

And then there are the small-town Portland touches: self-serve coffee (Stumptown, of course) from an oddball collection of mugs hanging on a metal vine, water served in Mason jars, an old-world wood-fronted refrigerator, the restroom keys on a burger and a lizard, butcher paper and crayons on the tables.

At this point I can see my parents starting to worry that I've brought them to some wacky, hippie place with scary food. But the J&M's food is a step above your basic breakfast place. When I've been there, every dish brought a collective "Gosh" from us, just for its presentation.

One time my special was a scramble with black forest ham, shallots, zucchini, cherry tomatoes, fontina, and spinach pesto. The texture was perfect and the pesto had just the right amount of zing. Another special had roasted eggplant, pine nuts, green onion, fontina, and fresh artichoke salsa. A regular item is a tofu, garlic, spinach, and feta scramble.

Even J&M's take on the basics has a classy twist. The egg sandwich (the J&M Plate) has "natural" bacon with basted eggs, fontina, Cheddar, and Parmesan on a toasted English muffin. The Belgian waffle is made with cornmeal and is delightfully light.

The wait staff shows up, treats you well, takes your order, comes back with food, and otherwise pretty much leaves you alone. I've seen some online reviews that consider such service unfriendly, but I think of it as, "You have your food, coffee and water are self-serve, and if you need anything, we're right here."

Oh, and a basted egg apparently is poached and basted with the water, like you'd baste a turkey with drippings, so the egg cooks consistently. My friend Lori told me her mom did the same thing, but with bacon grease, and we were okay with J&M being a little healthier.

Somehow, the basted egg captured the whole thing for me. The J&M could have just poached it or fried it but did something that was simultaneously unique, effective, and healthy. Sipping my excellent, local coffee and looking around at all my nice fellow citizens enjoying a relaxed, tasty meal in pleasant surroundings, I kind of felt proud of Portland.

Wait: Up to 30 minutes after about 9:30 on weekends; there are a few padded benches to wait on inside, but no shelter from the elements if you're waiting outside
Seating: 60 or so, all at tables. **Large groups?** Yes.
Portion size: Medium. **Changes:** No problem.
Coffee: Stumptown.
Other drinks: Tazo Tea.
Feel-goods: Local, natural meats; wild-caught Pacific salmon; homemade Granola.
Health options: Some veggie options, and tofu can be subbed for eggs.
WiFi? No.

Jam on Hawthorne

New/Hip/Veggie

Clean, simple, basic, and sweet

2239 SE Hawthorne Blvd. (SE/Hawthorne)

503-234-4790

Monday through Thursday 7:30 a.m. to 3:00 p.m. Friday through Sunday 7:30 a.m. to 4:00 p.m. Breakfast available all day.

$8-12 (all major cards)

———————◆——◆———————

Billy Joel. That's what was playing when we ate at Jam on Hawthorne. Think for a moment about Billy Joel's career — not what you think of his music, but what he's known for. Basic, straight-ahead rock and roll, right? Enthusiastic, solid, not exactly other-worldly, and occasionally some ventures off into cheesy, overly sweet tunes (see "Billy the Kid" and "Uptown Girl").

By the end of a visit to Jam, you may think, as we did, that Billy Joel is the perfect musical accompaniment. The place is nice, colorful, not too crowded, and really good at one thing: sweets. You might say the lemon ricotta pancakes are Jam's "Piano Man." But I get ahead of myself.

The little corner of SE Hawthorne and 23rd Street has been a breakfast destination for years; Cafe Lena was the previous inhabitant, and Jam fits in the same groove. It's a place that locals walk to, even if folks from other parts of town might not know exactly where it is. To them it may be "the little place across from Grand Central Bakery and that produce place (Uncle Paul's)." This means the lines aren't too bad. Jam's colors are bright, the staff is young and cheerful, and it's a relaxed place and cozy, with just six booths and eight tables.

Just as Billy Joel burst onto the scene with "Piano Man," his best song ever, Jam leads with its signature namesake spreads, which are on the table before you order. Even disparaging reviews of the place say things like, "Don't go unless you just really like homemade jams." The *Portland Mercury* called them "spectacular," and the seasonal flavors I've seen include blueberry, strawberry-mango, and pear chai.

The other sweet signature dish is the lemon ricotta pancake, which The *Oregonian* featured in a pancake special feature: "With a drizzle of warm blueberry sauce, these 'cakes sound more like a haute dessert than a flapjack breakfast. But the citrus hit is subtle, the mild ricotta lends body to the batter and the house-made topping is vibrant with fruit. A sweet way to start your day."

My impression of Billy Joel's music has always been that he's kind of fun for a while, but the more I listen the less I like it. Likewise, my dining experiences at Jam have seemed to fade. The biscuits, though freshly baked, weren't too exciting; the salmon scramble and the hash seemed a little dry; and my chair was a little goofy. But the coffee was good, the service nice, the atmosphere relaxed, and the prices downright reasonable, so we weren't upset. We walked away saying things like, "Well, it wasn't the greatest breakfast ever, but I liked it." Besides, I'm a sucker for sweets, although I wasn't quite up to the Cinnamon Sugar French Toast or the wheat-free Vegan Oatmeal Blueberry Chai Pancake.

Jam also gets a stamp of approval from the veggie crowd. An Internet blog called "Stumptown Vegans" said Jam "know(s) what vegan is" and gave them credit for stocking Odwalla juices (plus a full bar with breakfast cocktails), local produce from Uncle Paul's across the street, and soy margarine (I wasn't aware it existed). Indeed, the veggie options do seem more interesting than most, including the much-appreciated build-your-own option. I also give credit for hashbrowns that are crispier and less greasy than many and how the Stumptown coffee is brewed: strong and smooth.

Jam has a lot of options and doesn't try to do too much, rather like Billy Joel had hits in three decades without having to go through some weird reinventing of himself. Although some musicians might dislike the word *formula*, in the restaurant business you need something to depend on. In Jam's case, being friendly and healthy, getting produce from the little stand across the street, and having two or three items that really stand out are enough to make it a nice little place for breakfast.

Wait: Mild on weekends.
Seating: About 60 at tables and booths.
Large groups? Not a problem if it's not busy.
Portion size: Decent. **Changes:** Sure.
Coffee: Stumptown.
Other drinks: Tea, Odwalla, cocktails.
Feel-goods: Produce from the place across the street,.
Health options: Good options for vegans and vegetarians.
WiFi? No.

Joe's Cellar

Old School

Victim-to-be of Pearl expansion?

1332 NW 21st. Ave. (NW)

503-223-2851

Weekdays 6:00 a.m. to 7:00 p.m.; weekends 7:00 a.m. to 5:00 p.m. Breakfast served until 5:00 p.m. in the cafe and until 7:00 p.m. in the bar.

$8–11 (Visa, MasterCard)

———————◆•◆———————

Sitting in front of me was a pile of bright yellow, eggy French toast and two pieces of limp bacon on a thick, white oval plate; butter in a paper cup; and coffee in a white mug. Across the room the waitress was working on a crossword puzzle. It was 8:15 a.m. on a rainy Wednesday, and we were the only two people in the place.

There was a Keno stand on the table and a vague cigarette smell in the air, and the walls had a mix of old-Portland black-and-whites and modern-art posters. A vase of fake flowers sat in the back corner.

I looked across the empty street and saw an abandoned building. There was a single shoe on the sidewalk. "What was that place?" I asked.

"An old truck company," the waitress said. "It's been closed a long time. Now they say it's gonna be part of the Pearl district."

Now, Joe's Cellar is at the corner of NW 21st Avenue and Overton Street—quite a few blocks from the Pearl. Still, I knew what she meant, and she wasn't confused on geography.

"Condos, huh?"

"Yep."

"Well, won't that be good for this place?"

She shrugged. "For a while. We'll get some of the construction workers."

She didn't have to say what would happen after that. When I suggested that Fuller's Coffee Shop has done pretty well right in the middle of the Pearl, she looked at me and said flatly, "I've never been to the Pearl district."

At that moment I realized I was eating an $8 full breakfast (two eggs, two slices of bacon, French toast, and coffee) on the edge of a cultural divide. Or maybe at the end of an era. Either way, Joe's may be the last of its breed in Northwest Portland.

Funny thing is, it wasn't even always here. Joe's is actually three buildings that were down by Union Station and were moved back in the '30s or so, then crammed together into the semi-landmark it is today. It's been a restaurant since 1941, and the upstairs (which the waitress says used to be, of course, a brothel) is now condemned.

Here's a funny note about the place: a goofy crowd that uses instruments to look for ghosts reported several "conscious entities" at Joe's, including "an ex-prostitute, a man who died in a fire here, a homeless man who is a wee bit mental, and a little wiener dog with a jingling collar." On a more earthly note, the investigator also arrived at a common conclusion: "The Biscuits & Gravy are to die for."

My waitress took me on a tour. We left the quiet cafe for a smaller back room she called the "adult room"; clearly, smoking was allowed in there. Then we went through another door—and into a completely different world. A whole *bar* was back there, with AC/DC cranking, conversation rolling, and about 25 people scattered around—at 8:30 in the morning! Apparently there's a happy hour from 7 to 11 a.m. for (one would hope) folks getting off the graveyard shift, and the reputation is that it's a friendly place with stiff drinks.

The prices in the cafe are decidedly not stiff. The special is likely to be an egg, a piece of sausage or bacon, and a pancake for $3.50, or a sausage and cheese omelet with potatoes and toast for $5.95. There's not much of that left in Northwest Portland.

While I was finishing breakfast, a nice car pulled up and a stylish lady wearing a leather jacket got out. The waitress and I both watched quietly as she went across 21st Avenue. I went back to my bacon and wondered if she knows about the ghosts at Joe's.

Wait: None.
Seating: One room with seven booths and a counter, seating about 40, another (smoking) with room for about 20.
Large groups? No. **Portion size:** Big. **Changes:** Sure.
Coffee: Farmer Bros. **Other drinks:** Hot cocoa, sodas, Bigelow tea, and one of those Sunshine milk dispensers.
Feel-goods: They'll probably remember your name.
Health options: Low carb items on the menu, cottage cheese and fruit substitutes for starches.
WiFi? No chance.

John Street Cafe

Mom and Pop/Old School

Come out and eat in our backyard!

8338 N Lombard (N/Outer)

503-247-1066

Wednesday through Friday, 7 a.m. to 11:00 a.m., lunch until
2:30; Saturday 7:30 a.m. to 12:00 p.m. Breakfast served until
11 on weekdays, noon on Saturday, and all day Sunday 7:30
to 2:30.

$8–12 (checks, Visa, MasterCard)

————————•————————

I was wrong several times about the John Street Cafe. First
I thought it was just the tiny, unadorned place you can see
from the street; I didn't know about the garden patio out
back. Then I thought that since it was in old-timey St. John's
it must have been there forever; it just opened about 10 years
ago. Another time I walked by on my way to Pattie's Home
Plate across the street (see page 235) and saw young couples
waiting in line reading the *New York Times*, so I thought
maybe it was a snooty hipster joint.

Wrong, wrong, wrong. It's the old Tabor Hill Cafe from
Hawthorne reborn in downtown St. Johns. The owners sold
the old place and moved north in 1997, and behind that ster-
ile-looking front is one of the warmest, most colorful outdoor seating areas in town. The food is more *Oregonian* than
New York Times, and there's hardly a whiff of snootiness
about the place.

The Breakfast Crew gathered there, about seven of us,
and some early scouts had secured a table out back. Walking
through the front room to the patio is like going through

an art museum and emerging in somebody's backyard. Before I knew it, the owner was pouring coffee while greeting by name two regulars among us, and we were  looking at a one-page menu with a major focus on omelets. A quick glance at the ingredients showed a whole lot more Cheddar, Swiss, and Monterey than Brie. The staff also calls hazelnuts filberts, like good Oregonians, and will give your kids Gumby dolls to play with.

Before we get to the food, here's a picture of the patio: a seating area with 10 or so picnic tables is ringed by beds of fuchsia, bleeding heart, columbine, geranium, creeping phlox, Japanese maple, and bamboo. Dogs, welcome on the patio, sit curled up beside picnic tables filled with families. An enormous fig tree looms overhead providing shade — and fruit in September.

The homey, simple feeling kept right on coming with the food. All the omelets come with oven-roasted red potatoes and wheat bread. The day's special was huckleberry-blueberry coffeecake, which had just the right balance of fluffy, moist, and crunchy. The bacon was sweet without being too mapley. The corned beef in a special hash had a little more zing to it than usual, and the leftovers were a meal in themselves. A spinach and bacon omelet had a hearty portion of greens as well as avocado, sour cream, and salsa. My friend Toni summarized her generous Shrimp Scramble: "Usually these things are egg-egg-egg-shrimp-egg-egg, but this one is more like egg-and-shrimp, egg-and-shrimp, egg-and-shrimp."

At first the prices seemed high — $6.50 for two eggs,

potatoes, and toast; $5.75 for just one black currant and filbert pancake. But that pancake was a telling example of what the cafe is up to: yes, it was just one, but it was dinner-plate size, thick, and perfectly cooked, with an almost-burned crust outside giving way to a light, fluffy inside made a little chunky by the nuts and sweet-chewy by the fruit. It was served with warm maple syrup, and we fought over it.

The John Street's signature dish is another example of its homey friendliness: oatmeal. It comes with milk and brown sugar plus your choice of dried raisins, currants, apricots, or cranberries, and chopped filberts or walnuts. If eating a nice bowl of cereal at a picnic table in a sunny garden sounds like, well, your bowl of oatmeal, then head to St. Johns Café and make your own first impressions.

Wait: Long on weekends after about 9:30, no cover outside.

Seating: About 40 inside and 50 outside, when sunny.

Large groups? More than six can be a hassle.

Portion size: Big.

Changes: None, but you can build your own omelet.

Coffee: Kobos.

Other drinks: Espresso, fresh orange juice, Kobos tea, hot cocoa, milk.

Feel-goods: Homemade cookies and truffles, banana breads, cheesecake, and Mimosas.

Health options: Omelets can be made with egg whites only for $1.

WiFi? No.

Johnny B's

Mom and Pop/Old School

Dad's cookin' and Mom's servin'!

1212 SE Hawthorne Blvd. (SE/Inner)

503-233-1848

Monday through Friday 6 a.m. to 2 p.m., then midnight Friday night all the way to 2:00 p.m. on Saturday. Then again midnight Saturday to 2:00 p.m. Sunday. Breakfast served all day. $7–10 ($5 minimum for Visa or MasterCard).

———————◆●◆———————

It doesn't get any more like a mom-and-pop breakfast than Johnny B's. Dad cooks it and Mom brings it out. On Saturdays their kids work. The family photo is on the menu. One time I showed up and a sign on the door said it was closed because they were feeling "under the weather."

It doesn't get much more down home than Johnny B's, either. The motto is "We're hooked on cookin'," and it's apparent they don't put much energy into anything else, other than making the place enjoyable. The decorations consist of red-and-white checkered curtains, white lights strung up over the windows, an aerial photo of the neighborhood . . . and that's about it. Tennis balls are on the bottoms of the chair legs so they don't scrape the checkered floor, and the high chair has socks on it.

You might think Johnny B's has been there a while, but it opened only in 2000. Before that it was a Winchell's Donuts, and I doubt the clientele has changed all that much. Johnny B's gets city workers on breaks, students in for slacker breakfasts, old guys in a corner commenting on somebody's new

haircut, a postal worker who comes in with a fruitcake and trades barbs with the cook.

At this point you may have an idea of what the food is like, and you're probably right. The hefty, oval-shaped plates brim with eggs, meat, golden hashbrowns, and French toast made with that big Texas toast and a dash of cinnamon. Plenty of meat options. Sweet yellow peppers in the Denver omelet. Water in red plastic cups. Farmer Brothers coffee, which my friend Julia, who normally likes two or three creams in her coffee, said needed only one. And, when you're done, there's candy and breath mints at the register.

Though it's fairly new, Johnny B's is probably the closest thing to a neighborhood hangout that Ladd's Addition has. And if there's a neighborhood that needs a breakfast hangout place, it's Ladd's Addition, a quiet cul-de-sac between two bustling neighborhoods. Johnny B's is like a quiet outpost on the fringes of Ladd's, out on the nutso border at the intersection of 12th Avenue and Hawthorne. Back behind the restaurant lay community rose gardens, a central traffic circle filled with rhododendrons, narrow streets lined with American elms, and a diagonal street pattern that dates back to 1891, when William S. Ladd, a Portland mayor, broke up his 126-acre farm into residential lots.

Johnny B's isn't the only breakfast place within walking distance of Ladd's. Junior's is over on SE 12th, and Genie's is down at Division. They both have more interesting (and expensive) food, but a classy old neighborhood like Ladd's seems best served by a place where the folks all know each other, the staff is family, and Special #7 is "Don't move my tables."

Then again, by the time you read this they might be gone. In the spring of 2007, Mom and Dad were saying that when their son graduates high school he might go to school in Hawaii, and if he does, they just might go with him. Seems like a perfectly reasonable, family-oriented decision — one that would fit perfectly with everything else going on at Johnny B's.

Wait: None.
Seating: About 40, all at tables.
Large groups? "Don't move my tables."
Portion Size: Solid.
Changes: Fine; a split plate is only 50 cents.
Coffee: Folgers, "just like at home."
Other drinks: Stash Tea.
Feel-goods: Um, the atmosphere?
Health Options: Limited vegetarian.
WiFi? No.

Junior's

Hip/Veggie

Kitschy, cozy, comfy, cramped, and cool

1742 SE 12th Avenue (SE/Inner)

(503) 467-4971

Hours: 8:00 a.m. to 2:30 p.m. weekdays; 8:00 a.m. to 3:00 p.m. weekends; breakfast always served

$10–13 (cash, checks; credit cards with a $0.75 fee)

To look at 29-year-old Audra Carmine, you might not think she owns a restaurant. She seems so nice and sweet, not haggard and nutty like many restaurant folks are. Yet since 2005 she has owned Junior's Cafe on SE 12th Avenue, for years one of Portland's favorite little breakfast joints.

You also wouldn't guess that she came through something like a revolution after taking over the restaurant. With her sunny demeanor, she tells stories of online reviews that made her cry and customers who got upset at every little change — even having to run off most of the staff from the previous ownership.

But things have settled down considerably at Junior's, and although there have been some subtle changes to the menu and crowd, it's still a friendly, popular place that will fill you up, not empty your wallet, and not rush you along at all.

Junior's is the first restaurant Carmine owned, though she worked for years at Dot's, the Clinton Street institution that spawned Junior's a decade ago. Still, she admits she had a lot to learn.

For example, there was the dedication of some customers. "People would call me over and be like, 'Why are the

zucchini chopped like this?'"
she says. "People have a huge
emotional attachment to this
restaurant."

And what were these radi-
cal changes? She tweaked
some of the classic dishes like
the Country Scramble (now
with mushrooms, sausage, flat
leaf parsley, Jack cheese, and
black pepper), the 12th Avenue
(zucchini, corn, green onions,

tomatoes, and Parmesan), and the Migas (green chiles, jala-
peño, sausage, and tortilla chips topped with salsa, cilantro,
and salty goat cheese). Several kinds of French toast replaced
the waffles and pancakes, and she brought in fresh herbs for
the first time. Crazy, huh?

The biggest change has been a greater emphasis on vegetarian and vegan options. *StumptownVegans.com* gave the
place high marks, especially the Superhero (sautéed tofu,
tomatoes, garden sausage, green onions, and spinach).

"We don't use any partially hydrogenated oils or corn
syrup," she says. "We use real ingredients, and we make
everything by hand. We try to use local providers and fresh
eggs, and I hand pick all the fruit, which is all organic."

I must admit, I was one of those old-time customers con-
cerned about the changes at Junior's. I miss the waffles, and
I'm a dedicated meat eater, but I loved the heaping Vegan
Potatoes, topped with mushrooms, corn, zucchini, and spicy
tofu sauce for $7. I also got two meals out of it. And being
a sucker for French toast, I liked that there were options: a

regular version, one topped with organic fruit, and another with yogurt, a whole chopped banana, and toasted almonds covered in honey. Of course there was also vegan French toast soaked in bananas, applesauce, and soy milk. There's still a relaxed, slightly goofy vibe to the place. About a dozen gilded mirrors adorn the walls, the booths are still a glittery gold, and the tiny bathroom is still a hallucinatory sea of graffiti.

For me, Junior's used to be a place I'd stumble to from an apartment down the street when I was hung over or still working on a buzz. I remember being impressed that staff applied butter to the toast with a paintbrush and often seemed to be as stoned as I was. Those days may be gone, in more ways than one, but Junior's is rolling right along with the times.

Wait: Long on weekends, with very little room inside or cover outside. **Seating:** About 50, all in booths.
Large groups? One booth could handle five or six.
Portion size: Reasonable, as are the prices.
Changes: Add veggies or cheese to any entree for $.50 or meat into any scramble or omelet for $1.50.
Coffee: Stumptown. **Other drinks:** Tao of Tea, Dragonfly Chai, juices, and lemonade.
Feel-goods: Most ingredients are locally grown or made and organic.
Health options: Plenty for vegetarians and vegans.
WiFi? No.

A version of this chapter first appeared at LivePDX.com.

Kenny and Zuke's Delicatessen

Hip/Old School

A big ol' slab of New York in Downtown Portland
1038 SW Stark Street (Downtown)
503-222-3354
Monday through Thursday 7:00 a.m. to 8:00 p.m.; Friday 7:00
a.m. to 9:00 p.m.; Saturday 8:00 a.m. to 9:00 p.m.; Sunday
8:00 a.m. to 8:00 p.m. Some breakfast options available all
day. Full breakfast menu served weekdays until 11:00 a.m.,
weekends until 2:00 p.m.
kennyandzukes.com
$14–18 (Visa, MasterCard, Discover, Checks)

I was amazed by Kenny and Zuke's even before I ate there. I
heard there was a good New York-style deli downtown, so I
went to check it out. Now, I was thinking about delis I had
gone to in New York; I recall they were about the size of my
college apartment, somewhat grimy, and filled with unpleas-
ant people but good food.

When I saw Kenny and Zuke's, I said to myself, "Holy
mackerel! *That's* the deli?" It's enormous, bright, clean, and
well ordered, and the people seem nice. It's like a palace
compared to my deli memories. And then I saw the menu,
a whopping four pages of options. The breakfast page alone
made my head spin. Pastrami and eggs; salami and eggs; lox,
eggs, and onions; three omelets (including, of course, pastrami, as well as the lox, cream cheese, and chives omelet);
pastrami hash; corned beef hash; salmon hash; a few
Benedicts; latkes; challah French toast; and maple granola.

But I've seen big breakfast menus. Kenny and Zuke's had

me at the sodas. Any place that has 13 root beers, 6 ginger ales, 7 cream sodas, 5 colas (including Mexican Coke and Pepsi, with real sugar), 5 diet sodas, 20 fruit sodas, 2 "Others" (including Yoo Hoo!) and 11 "Premium and Rare Sodas" from places like Germany and Jackson Hole, Wyoming . . . well, like I said, think palace more than deli. What I think is, I better go hiking on Saturday 'cause I'm getting some pastrami and a Premium Soda on Friday!

Ah, you ask, but is it all good? Well, yes. How good depends on whom you ask—and it seems like everybody in town has an opinion. Kenny and Zuke's exists at the rare intersection of deli culture, big-time restaurant culture, and foodie culture. This means some folks get really worked up about the place, generally in a positive way.

The fact that in June 2008 there were 82 pages (more than 1,600 comments) about the place on *PortlandFood.org* isn't just because the Zuke of Kenny and Zuke's is Nick Zukin, the Web site's host. Folks are genuinely nuts about the place, and they get into conversations ranging from how much to trim the pastrami to whether it's worth being open late at night.

And it's not just that Web site. Just about every blog in town has heaped praise on the place, usually along the lines of "This is the closest thing to real New York pastrami and bagels you'll ever find in Portland." The *Oregonian* said of the Reuben (lunch service starts at 11, by the way), "You'll name your firstborn after it." *Willamette Week* hailed it as downtown coming full circle after an old Jewish neighborhood was destroyed to make way for the Portland State campus and called it "downtown PDX's first truly egalitarian new restaurant in decades," whatever that means. A writer for *Seattle Magazine* ate there three times in 24 hours. Even Matt Groenig, Portland native and creator of *The Simpsons*, dropped off a sketch of Homer saying "Mmmm, Kenny and Zuke's!"

Sure, it seems a little exorbitant. I mean, it's a *deli*, right? The prices, surprisingly, are not really high. The Smoked Salmon Benedict is $12.75, and for $8.50 you get more challah French toast than a person should be able to eat. I usually go for the pastrami hash with two eggs ($10.50), and for breakfast at home the next day I have the leftovers with a couple of eggs.

Whether Kenny and Zuke's is "authentic" is entirely up to you. It's sure as heck impressive, and I recommend you check it out for yourself.

Wait: A bit on weekends, with little room inside.
Seating: About 80, all inside.
Large groups? Yes.
Portion size: Outrageous.
Changes: "Substitute a bagel for a buck."
Coffee: Stumptown.
Other drinks: Numi Tea, milk, fresh orange juice, and a wide world of sodas.
Feel-goods: Kenny and Zuke buy local beef and make their bagels.
Health options: Come on, it's a deli!
WiFi? No.

Kornblatt's

Old School

"Would do just fine in New York"

628 NW 23rd Ave. (NW)

503-242-0055

Monday through Friday 7:00 a.m. to 8:00 p.m., weekends 7:30 a.m. to 9:00 p.m. Breakfast served all day.

kornblatts.com

$10–15 (all major cards)

———————◆●◆———————

Whenever a place has a location for its theme — like Kornblatt's calling itself a New York Style Delicatessen — I have a system to test that assertion. I call it the Memphis Barbecue Test, and it goes like this: Since I am from Memphis and love barbecue, I ask myself how a particular barbecue place would do if it were in Memphis. So to apply this test to Kornblatt's, which humbly asserts it has the finest deli food west of the Hudson River, I invited David, a Jew who grew up in New Jersey, and Rich, who grew up on Long Island, to have breakfast with me.

I had always thought the décor might be a bit too New York: the autographs from Derek Jeter and Alex Rodriguez, the poster of the 1955 Dodgers, the picture of the guys eating their lunches on the beam high over the city.

On the plus side, I once had a wonderfully spastic waiter who kept calling me "my friend," sang loudly along with Frank Sinatra on "Chicago," and stepped outside for a smoke while saying he was "going out to lower my life expectancy." So the place can have a particular kind of energy, which seems entirely typical for a New York Style Delicatessen. I also appreciate that the place has a glossary of deli items, including egg cream, phosphates, blintz, kasha vaniskes, knish, nosh, kishka, kugel, lox, matzo balls, matzo brie, rugelach, pastrami, and latkes.

And although the portions are Big Apple-size, I always the corned beef was good but not as "punch-you-in-the-mouth" tasty as some places make it. The hollandaise seemed to lack a little zing. Hence, my invitation to David and Rich.

Rich immediately said that on appearance alone, Kornblatt's would easily fit in Great Neck, where apparently there's a large Jewish population. And David said he'd been coming here for years. So it was looking like a pass on my test already. David got the Eggs Bageldict, and the waiter repeated the line from the menu: "If you say it, we'll make it." I asked if he's required to say that, and he just smiled wryly and said, "No, I'm just being a shit."

The Bageldict is a Benedict with mild pastrami and hollandaise on a bagel of your choice. David agreed the sauce was a little light, but he also cleaned his plate, and since my girlfriend was along, nobody made any off-color jokes.

I got a full order of blintzes (four for $10.75), and if the ones in New York are any better than these, I might have to move. They were light and delicious, served with sour cream and blueberry and strawberry preserves. It's best to get them if you're splitting your friend's savory dish, and in my case I was trading them out for chunks of a mushroom-onion omelet, a massive but mildly flavored corned beef hash, and David's (ahem) dish.

The menu has nine omelets, ranging from basic options to, I assume, New York staples: sautéed chicken livers and onions, lox and onions, lox and cream cheese, and the Famous Mixed Deli, which is made with salami, corned beef, and pastrami and served pancake style. (Take my word: plan on taking a nap after that one!)

If that's not New York or Jewish enough for you, you can also get Matzo Brie (scrambled eggs with matzo balls) or French toast with homemade challah, and practice your pronunciation of *challah*. And for dessert some kugel, a jumbo eclair, or some New York Cheesecake. Might make you want to go home and sing along with Sinatra, too.

Wait: A little on weekends.
Seating: About 45, at tables and half-booths, up to 60 total when outside seating is available.
Large groups? More than eight might be tough.
Portion size: Big.
Changes: Not much, but they'll make smaller portions of hash for $1.25 less.
Coffee: Allan Brothers.
Other drinks: Espresso, soda, egg cream, hot chocolate, phosphates, seltzer.
Feel-goods: You don't have to deal with too many real New Yorkers.
Health options: Wrong place.
WiFi? No.

Laurelthirst Public House

New/Old School/Veggie

A Portland bar that serves Portland breakfast
2958 NE Glisan St. (NE/Hollywood)
503-232-1504
Breakfast served daily 9:00 a.m. to 3:00 p.m.
mysite.verizon.net/res8u18i/laurelthirstpublichouse
$8–13 (Visa, MasterCard, Discover, no checks)

———◆●◆———

A bar that serves breakfast. There's an exciting concept, right? You may be wondering if they're scooping powdered eggs out of a box and microwaving pancakes. I did, when my friend Amy K would invite me to go with her.

But first allow me to introduce you to Amy K. She is a charming and very hard-working person who recently bought (and is thoroughly renovating) a big, old house not far from "the Thirst." She works very hard, and then she relaxes very hard. When she finally got me to have breakfast at her favorite place, we couldn't schedule it before 10, and she was planning to spend the rest of the day watching the NFL playoffs.

Now, let's move on. It's a drizzly Sunday at 10:15 a.m., and Amy and I just sat in a booth at the Laurelthirst. About one in four tables is occupied (on a Sunday, no less), but Amy tells me it gets busy later. Later than 10:15! One of the most tired clichés in breakfast writing is that a place has "great hangover food." But sitting there in the Laurelthirst, with its dark red brick walls, the goofy bar décor (like old bikes up on the wall), the red leather booths, the smoking room in back with the pool table, and the possibility of getting a microbrew

with my scramble, I thought that this might actually be a place where hungover breakfast eaters start tying the next one on.

Although the feel of the place reminds me of a neighborhood jazz club in New Orleans, the Laurelthirst is pure Portland, with a mostly countrified music scene and a hip young staff who occasionally generate complaints about moving a little slowly. A *Portland Mercury* review said it had a "perma-stoned feeling."

The food really is better than you may think. Did you expect, for example, a bar that's famous for a cheap and heaping pile of vegan pancakes? They're made with buttermilk, too, and you can add bananas, strawberries, blueberries, or walnuts for just 50 cents per cake. No matter how you do them, they're a fluffy, filling delight—but for some reason they aren't available on weekends. You can get the basic-style French toast (traditional or vegan) anytime, though.

The rest of the menu reflects, as the *Mercury* review put it, "a real understanding of simplicity in breakfast food." I would add that the prices are reasonable (omelets max out at $8.50), and the Thirst also gets credit for offering a choice of the same ingredients in an omelet or a scramble. You'll have eight pairs of those options, as well as the Basic Breakfast (two eggs, a side, and toast) for $4.50; add bacon, sausage, or veggie sausage and it's $6.50.

The most renowned special is a massive breakfast burrito, with two scrambled eggs, Jack cheese, veggie beans, red or green salsa, sour cream, and home fries ($7.50); add chorizo, turkey chili, sausage, or veggie sausage for another dollar. (There's also a vegan burrito with tofu and avocado for $7.50.) The biscuits are excellent, with meat or veggie gravy.

With all this working-class breakfast fare, and folks starting to shuffle in and order beers, I was a little surprised to see a mimosa ($6), though it is served in a pint glass. Amy K agreed, saying "This is *so* not a mimosa place," then adding with a friendly wink, "and you would be berated for ordering one."

That was my last and best impression of breakfast at the Laurelthirst: comfy like a neighborhood bar, but better than you'd expect and refusing to take itself too seriously.

Wait: Maybe a little on weekends starting around 11:00.

Seating: About 70 in the main room, at tables, booths, and a bar; another (smoking) room is in back.

Large groups? Yes, but if you have seven or more they'll put you on the same check with 18 percent tip

Portion size: Not huge, other than the pancakes, but cheap.

Changes: Yes; it's $.50–$1 for substitutions, limit one per order.

Coffee: Stumptown.

Other drinks: Beer and Wine, juice, soda, Stash tea, mimosas.

Feel-goods: They make their own veggie sausage.

Health options: Plenty here for the vegetarian and vegan; tofu and egg whites available as well.

WiFi? No.

Marco's Cafe

Classy

Because a village needs its own restaurant
7910 SW 35th Ave. (SW/Inner)
503-245-0199
Weekdays 7:00 a.m. to 9:00 p.m.; Saturday 8:00 a.m. to 9:00
p.m.; Sunday 8:00 a.m. to 2:00 p.m. Breakfast served all day.
marcoscafe.com
$12–16 (all major cards, local checks)

––––––––––––◆●◆––––––––––––

Since the cafe's own Web site says the owners want the place
to "remain primarily a 'neighborhood cafe,' . . . for local
neighbors, merchants and visitors," it's important to consider
that neighborhood and how Marco's fits in.

Multnomah Village really does have a small-town feel to
it, and I've always thought that, like any small town, it has
subtle class divisions. I don't mean animosities—the Village
is hardly a place with class tension—but in the breakfast
scene. The working-class Village has the Fat City Cafe,
where old guys sit at the counter talking city politics and
there's an item on the menu called the Fat City Sizzle.

Now consider Marco's, where the last time I visited, the
specials (written on etched glass just inside the door) were a
tomato-basil eggs Benedict and an asparagus, bacon, tomato,
and spinach scramble in fennel-butter topped with Asiago.
Well. And then there's that Web site: the most-developed of
any place in this book, and if you click on "Our Chef" you'll
see a picture of Maurice in a tuxedo and you can read about
his work experience in Laguna Beach and Switzerland; he's
also fluent in both French and Spanish!

Okay, before my prejudices from growing up among rich white suburbanites start to show too much, let's pause for a moment and be reminded that Marco's has been a wildly popular restaurant since 1983, and there are some reasons for it. The food is always good, the folks are friendly, the place is clean, and the prices aren't bad for some pretty classy food.

But it is very much a Southwest Portland place: a while back Marco tried to open one on NE Fremont Street and it flopped. And although I like to make some fun, I also agree with the *Oregonian*: "Marco's manages to be both nouveau and down-home at the same time."

I dragged my usual Fat City gang of fellas over there one time, and after all the jokes about whether they'll let us in and I sure hope I don't drool on these nice tablecloths, etc., we chose among six omelets, eight egg dishes, and a dozen specialties ranging from blintzes to roast beef hash to bagels and lox. Everything had a legitimate, expert touch to it: a light but sturdy hollandaise on two Benedicts; a perfect mix of Italian sausage, sweet peppers, tomato, onion, herbs, and Asiago in the Mediterranean omelet; the yummy fresh fruit atop the brioche French toast.

We were impressed and satisfied, as I always have been at Marco's. And whenever the food or feel starts to get just a bit snooty, I see the Franz bread, the packets of Freezer Jam, the regulars, and all the accommodations for kids, and I feel a little more at home. I do still giggle at some of the goofier touches, like the collection of umbrellas hanging from the ceiling and the quotes painted on the wall: "One cannot think well, love well, sleep well, if one has not dined well," said Virginia Woolf, whom I'm certain no one has ever read. And "All happiness depends upon a leisurely breakfast," said John Gunther, whom I'm certain no one has ever heard of.

I can make up a breakfast quote too: "Since today is all we have, what better way to get started than with a fine breakfast with good friends?" Maybe they'll put *that* up on a wall someday!

Wait: Pretty long on weekends, with a small space inside and some cover outside.

Seating: About 80 at tables plus one small counter.

Large groups? Yes, but they say no separate checks.

Portion size: Reasonable.

Changes: Within reason; fruit cup instead of potatoes add $1.25; muffin, croissant, or bagel instead of toast add $.50.

Coffee: Equal Exchange (organic, fair trade).

Other drinks: Espresso, fresh juices, specialty coffee drinks.

Feel-goods: Solar hot water, local naturally grazed beef, local organic herbs and mushrooms, hormone-free milk.

Health options: Good options for vegetarians, egg substitutes available.

WiFi? No.

Meriwether's

New/Weekend/Classy
A good place, aiming for greatness
2601 NW Vaughn (NW)
Phone: 503-228-1250
Brunch served Saturday and Sunday 8:00 a.m. to 3:00 p.m.
meriwethersnw.com
$15–20 (all major cards)

A common theme among people's reactions to Meriwether's is, "This really should be one of the great restaurants in town." Some people think it is, but many go on to say, "Too bad it isn't." Meriwether's looks great, it's in a great spot, the menu is amazing, and the patio out back is as nice a place as you can find in Portland to eat breakfast. The vibe coming from Meriwether's is that it aims to be a Real Restaurant; sometimes that comes off as attitude, sometimes as aspiration, sometimes as a business plan. But it certainly doesn't lack ambition.

The location has hosted a few restaurants over the years, and everybody seems to be pulling for the current one. The Breakfast Crew was suitably impressed by the exterior—a charming old house near Forest Park—and wowed by the amount of money obviously invested.

Then we were told that even though we had four of our five people we couldn't be seated yet. Since everybody was sitting out back, we stood in the completely empty restaurant waiting for our fifth member. And *then* when he showed up we went to the patio, which was half full, and were put at a table for four, two of us crammed onto one corner. Hmmm. Sure seemed like staff could have pulled over another table.

In the online world of restaurant reviews, the Meriwther's story went like this: It opened, had promise, but suffered from terrible service and inconsistent food. Then came its presumed hero, Tommy Habetz.

Ever heard of him? From Gotham Building Tavern fame? Well, join me and the 99 percent of Portlanders who haven't. But among the serious restaurant people, this was news. As the *Oregonian* put it in 2007, "Meriwether's was never on the radar of Portland's serious eaters, but with the coming of talented chef Tommy Habetz the restaurant is beginning to ride high again . . . knowing and dedicated diners are gradually coming back." That mostly positive review went on to say that Habetz "leans to classics . . . but he can riff on convention, as when he substitutes watercress and roasted pork belly for a traditional salad of frisee and lardons."

Just as this book went to press, Habetz left Meriwether's. But my point is the same: I have no clue what frisee and lardons might be. In fact, there are things on Meriwether's menu (confit, frizzled onions, basil *pistou*) that I can't identify. And this is precisely what fascinates me: It's a place where Serious Dining and Portland Breakfast intersect.

My crew was certainly impressed, and we had a fine time. Jerry, a musician, loved the musical selection. We all loved the patio, which is adorned with wrought iron, heat lamps, copper piping to hang canvas in cooler weather, bamboo fencing, fuschias, hydrangias, hostas, and a fountain. And it's a *big* patio, with three separate areas to it, one covered.

We had eggs Benedict with country ham and red-eye gravy ($14), which I suppose constituted "riffing on convention" since it didn't have hollandaise; Fried Chicken and Waffles with sage butter, apple-wood smoked bacon, and pure maple syrup ($14), which was good; and Pork Confit Hash with Yukon gold potatoes, garlic, spring onions, and frisee. We made fun of one another for not knowing what confit and frisee were, even when they were on our plates, but we liked the dish. The Rustic French Toast with mascarpone and rhubarb compote was also impressive, even though I don't care for rhubarb.

I think the same food served in a lesser location would somehow seem more impressive (and probably cost less). Regular food in this setting would drive the place out of business, pronto. Instead, it's a beautiful and impressive place with great outdoor seating and, well, pretty darn good food. So let's hope it makes it.

Wait: Not bad.
Seating: Abundant.
Large groups? With notice.
Portion size: Smallish for the price.
Changes: Within reason.
Coffee: Kobos.
Other drinks: Espresso, cocktails, champagne, juices, hot chocolate.
Feel-goods: It even has its own farm. And it has a full parking lot West of the building.
Health options: Egg whites for omeletes, substitute fresh fruit for potatoes ($2), salads on the brunch menu.
WiFi? No.

Milo's City Cafe

New/Hip/Old School
If New York was down-home...
1325 NE Broadway Ave. (NE/Broadway)
503-288-6456
Breakfast served Monday through Friday, 6:30 to 11:00 (full breakfast menu) then a fair portion of the menu during the lunch until 2:30 p.m.; Saturday and Sunday 7:30 a.m. to 2:30 p.m. Full breakfast all day.
miloscitycafe.com
$10–15 (Checks and all cards).

———————◆•◆———————

My friend Bob and I love getting together for breakfast early on weekdays. Sometimes we meet with the fellas down at Fat City Cafe for a boisterous round of shit-talking, and sometimes it's just the two of us, talking writing and politics and perhaps a few personal things before he goes to the insurance company and I go home to chase pennies as a freelance writer. We're professionals, slackers, creative folks, and old buddies.

For these occasions, Milo's is our default choice. It's kind of like Bob and me: professional in that it's clean and has excellent food, slackerly in that it's not a problem hanging out for a while, and friendly in that we always have the same waiter and often see somebody we know.

To dig where Milo's stands in the Portland breakfast pantheon, you'd first have to get a handle on Northeast Broadway itself. What *is* the character of that street? Hawthorne is hippie, 23rd Avenue is shopping, Alberta is a little wacky, Broadway is . . . what? You've got your Elmer's Flag and

Banner, Dollar Store, and tanning booths *and* your Peet's-
Grand Central-McMenamins
corner at 15th, a dozen kinds of
food, both discount and high-
end shopping, old-time places
like Helen Bernhard's Bakery
a few blocks away from a sushi
chain. It's like a neighborhood
place and a mini-downtown.
And in breakfast terms, you've

got your blue-collar Village Inn, your happy-wicker-gay
Cadillac Cafe, and good ol' Milo's.

Milo's is not a down-home place, mind you. The décor is
sort of a sleek, stylish New York kind of thing, but the feel
is both efficient like a serious restaurant and relaxed like a
neighborhood place. The menu doesn't make you say Wow,
though the portions and preparation might. Six omelets
and six Benedicts feature veggies, pepper bacon, Italian
and chorizo sausage, ham, and smoked salmon, and the
Benedicts also offer petite tenderloin and crab cake options.
Four hashes include pepper-bacon, smoked salmon, and
corned beef. Vegetarians need not run away, however. In
addition to a veggie option on all of the above, there's granola, oatmeal, waffles, and French toast.

But Milo's makes its name on the meat dishes, which
speaks to their sophisticated simplicity. The overall theory is simple. One of the owners, Loren Skogland, told the
Portland Business Journal in 2002, "I buy really good ingredients and I don't screw them up." The article also said that the
Skoglands, long-time restaurant folk, "opened Milo's in part

so they could control their own hours and schedules, and chose the location, within a few minutes of their Alameda home and the grade school, in order to better juggle all the demands on their time."

All the kids have menu items named for them, and the vibe continues with Jeremy's Peanut Butter and Chocolate Waffle plus Peanut Butter and Jelly Stuffed French Toast, which is basically a big, gooey PB&J sandwich on sourdough French toast.

And such is Milo's: unpretentious and impressive at the same time, with a subtle dash of family and friendly. The same *Journal* article quoted Caprial Pence, co-owner of Caprial's Bistro in Southeast Portland and veteran host of TV cooking shows, "They do really nice food — nothing earth-shattering in terms of being innovative, but sometimes really nice food is earth-shattering by itself."

Indeed.

Wait: Long on weekends, covered benches outside.
Seating: About 60, at tables and booths.
Large Groups? Yes, with advance notice.
Portion size: Big.
Changes: Yes.
Coffee: Boyds.
Other drinks: Tea, sparkling water, hot chocolate, juices, beer, wine and full bar for cocktails.
Feel-goods: Nothing in particular.
Health options: Some veggie options; no-cholesterol eggs or egg whites $1 extra.
WiFi? No.

Mississippi Station

New/Classy

Hidden gem, or neglected stone?

3943 N Mississippi (N/Inner)

503-517-5751

Breakfast Served 10:00 a.m. to 3:00 p.m. weekdays; 8:00 a.m.
to 3:00 p.m. weekends, with expanded menu.

mississippistation.com

$11–15 (all major cards)

———————◆●◆———————

I keep hearing the same three things about Mississippi
Station: it's nice, it's changed recently, and hardly anybody
ever goes there. This goes all the way back to when my friend
Cheryl, who lives in the neighborhood, called me excitedly
to say she had found this great place on Mississippi Street.
By the time she convinced me to go, she said it had changed
a little, and she didn't like it as much.

Flash forward a year or so, and I read about it again
on a blog called Breakfast in Portland, which said, "Have
you stood in line waiting to get into Gravy on Mississippi?
. . . Well next time just take a little walk down the street to
Mississippi Station. . . . there has never been a wait when I've
been there." The blogger went on to complain that the place
had recently changed coffees, but otherwise she loved it.

So here's the thing: If a place is in the middle of a happening neighborhood like Mississippi and there's no line,
what does that mean, exactly? That nobody knows about it?
That it's not very good? In the case of Mississippi Station,
maybe it's just that nobody's ever seen the patio out back,
a distinct advantage over its better-known neighbor. Based

on my food comparisons, the only reasons to wait in line for Gravy when Mississippi Station is right down the street (unless it's changed again since I wrote this, of course) is that you get a little bigger portion and more variety at Gravy.

I took my friend Robin to Mississippi Station, and as soon as we walked in, we felt comfortable. It was a chilly day, and the fireplace was going as was an open brick oven, but the look and feel of the place was also comforting, with wood and brass and chandeliers and candles. On a wall was a big, gaudy mural of a 1950s-looking couple, and over the back door a Thai goddess. And an old-timey dresser served as a sideboard.

This décor reminded me of something a chef at another restaurant once told me about Mississippi Station: "They can't seem to decide what they want to be."

He was actually talking about the menu, but "undecided" might seem, for you as it did for me and Robin, like a place with plenty of options. There are scrambles with thick-sliced pepper bacon, chicken apple sausage, honey cured ham, prusciutto, and just "ham." There are also vegetarian scrambles: a spinach-feta and a mushroom-Roma tomato-Swiss. There are two standard Benedicts (Canadian bacon and spinach-tomato) and two more interesting ones (bacon-tomato-avocado and Portobello mushroom with truffle hollandaise sauce).

The "From the Griddle" section included malted buttermilk pancakes (with optional berries) and something called

Bread Pudding French Toast. I say it's "called" that because we couldn't find anything about it that resembled bread pudding. It wasn't moist or overly sweet, didn't have raisins in it, and was encased in a golden crust. It was good (in fact, we thought all the food was just "good"), but it wasn't bread pudding—all in all, another check in the "what is this place up to?" column.

I'll say this: In my whole research project, this place had possibly my most favorite potatoes. And since the blogger at Portland Hamburgers said he loved the fries, I'd say Mississippi Station is good at potatoes. And the patio out back is wonderful.

So maybe Mississippi Station doesn't "know what they want to be," and maybe the décor combines a few too many things (Robin and I called it "funky hip industrial"). But there's a lot to be said for a good breakfast place in a cool neighborhood with no lines on the weekend.

Wait: None.

Seating: About 40 at tables plus a small bar; also a really nice patio which seats about 70 people. Limited indoor waiting area.

Large groups? Definitely, with notice. Recommend reservations during the summer for parties over 6.

Portion size: Reasonable. **Changes:** Within reason.

Coffee: Stumptown.

Other drinks: Numi Tea, juices, sodas, cocktails.

Feel-goods: None that they brag about.

Health options: Limited vegetarian options.

WiFi? No.

Mother's Bistro

Classy

Somehow both dressy and faded
212 SW Stark St. (Downtown)
503-464-1122
Breakfast served Tuesday through Friday 7:00 a.m. to 2:30
p.m., weekends 9:00 a.m. to 2:30 p.m.
mothersbistro.com
$12–15 (all major cards)

———————————◆—●—◆———————————

If this place was called anything *other* than Mother's, I'd
say the name was wrong. As soon as you walk in, you feel
that combination of dress-up, old faded comfort, and class
we associate with Mom. At least I do, but I was raised by
a Mississippi native descended from French stock, so when
I saw gilded mirrors, white curtains, built-in cabinets, and
chandeliers, I felt right at home.

I ate at Mother's once with my friend Alice, who spent
10 years in Mississippi, and she said the same thing: kind of
an Old South-French feel. It's by no means modern, and in
places it seems like it could use a little dusting. But so can
my mom's house.

We were seated by a white-clothed hostess who indicated
our table with that upturned hand I associate with people
who've been trained in politeness, and when I looked around
I got another dose of that grown-up feel: there were women
in heels and men in suits! I'd always wondered where the
Downtown business crowd eats breakfast, and here they
were, bathed in the light of tall windows while Billy Holliday
crooned through the speakers. And the people were quiet!
Were they on their best behavior too?

By now you may be think-
ing that the food is expensive
and fancy. It is a little higher
than in some places, but not
all. On one visit I managed
to spend $20 with tip, but
most entrées range from $8
to $11. Alice and I shared a
French press coffee for $4.50
and got three cups out of it.
The low cost end is organic

oatmeal for $5.50 (add raisins, bananas, pecans, or walnuts for
$1) and the high is the House-Cured Lox Platter for $12.95.

What lies between is some down-home stuff. At lunch
and dinner, Mother's is known for comfort food like meat-
loaf, macaroni and cheese, and chicken and dumplings. But
there's also an international flavor as well; a message on the
menu from the owner explains that she's after an international sense of Mom (pierogi, ravioli, green curry), and every
month there's a Mother of the Month (M.O.M.) featured in
the menu with her story and some of her dishes.

Breakfast doesn't veer too far away, with a mushroom
omelet, a prosciutto-garlic-basil-provolone scramble called
Mike's Special, sausage and biscuits, and all your favorite
Northwest must-haves: wild salmon hash, tofu scramble,
and challah French toast. I had the French toast as a side
instead of the potatoes (the substitute was no worries and I
think they charged me $1), and I thought it was great: a lit-
tle crunch on the outside, nice and soft on the inside. Alice
had a portobella-spinach-Asiago scramble that was perfectly
done. And yes, we cleaned our plates.

The international flavor shows up in a Greek frittata

(spinach, garlic, sundried tomatoes, feta, and kalamata olives) and migas, a yummy Mexican treat of eggs, corn tortilla, Jack cheese, onions, and peppers topped with salsa and sour cream.

I've always found the food at Mother's to be basic, tasty, and well done. It's never innovative or eye-popping, and I suspect we're paying another dollar or two per entrée for all that ambience and the seeming abundance of staff (otherwise, why is migas $8.95?). I know foodies who think it's dull and younger folks who think it's stuffy, but Mother's seems to be full all the time, and it can't be just tourists and the suit crowd.

Wait: Quite long on weekends, with some indoor seating available.

Seating: Around 200, all inside and at tables.

Large groups? Yes, but they request you make a reservations

Portion size: Large.

Changes: Easy, but there might be a small charge.

Coffee: Stumptown Drip and rotating blend for the French Press.

Other drinks: Harney and Sons tea, mimosas and other cocktails, house-infused vodkas with seasonal fruits.

Feel-goods: The menu says Mother's is "committed to making your meal a warm, fuzzy experience."

Health options: Egg whites available (for $1.50) and vegetarians have several options.

WiFi? Not at the table, child!

Moxie Rx

Weekend/Hip/Veggie

A wholesome picnic in the middle of town
At the corner of N Mississippi and N Shaver (N/Inner)
503-285-0701
Friday through Monday 9:00 a.m.-ish to 4pm-ish
moxierx.blogspot.com
$6–8 (cash only)

━━━━━━━━◆●◆━━━━━━━━

Let's see how many images of Americana we can bring in: the road trip, the picnic, the woman in an apron making biscuits, the neighborhood folks getting together, the traveling salesman whipping out "elixirs." It's all here at Moxie, which is generally known as "that little cart on Mississippi Street, next to the Fresh Pot."

Yes, the little cart in the lot next to the old drugstore, which of course is now a coffee shop. And right there you have a perfect condensation of what can make Portland so cool: we turn old drugstores into coffee shops, and we make fantastic, healthy food in carts. And the woman making the whole thing work, the one in the apron, came up from California and has tattoos all over her arms.

But the whole scene going on in Portland these days is, for the most part, a return to a simpler lifestyle: local ingredients, neighborhood joints, and grassroots development. Moxie shows all these influences, starting with its appearance. It's a 1964 Kenskill trailer with picnic tables and a small counter. The vibe says having friends over to eat in the backyard, with touches like the dirty dish bin sitting on a chair and furniture apparently from thrift stores. A review on *pdxguide. com* called it "Strawberry Shortcake meets Ani DiFranco."

Willamette Week pitched in with "Betty Crocker-meets-Pee Wee's Playhouse-at-a-flea-market." But there are also tablecloths and flowers adding some style, and the food . . . well, it ain't what you might think of with "cart food."

For drinks you can choose up to three fruits (grapefruit, banana, orange, lime, lemon, berries, apple) to have them juiced, or you can get an Elixir: the Healthy Glow is pineapple, cucumber, ginger, and apple; the Three Bee Boom is apple, royal jelly, bee pollen, and lemon; and the Iron Punch is carrot, beet, celery, and spiralina. One step up the nutritional scale are the Remedies: the Morning Glory (banana, berry, orange, and granola), the Rx (banana, almond butter, dates), and the Mexicali (mango, lime, coconut, milk, and lemon).

Can you feel that old-fashioned healthy vibe going through your body? Well, now it's time to eat. Just let these dishes kind of roll over you, and imagine eating them at a picnic.

The Buckwheat Belgian Waffle with banana, yogurt, and syrup. My friend Jane said it was cooked perfectly; you should also know she said this with simultaneous happiness and awe as well as a glance back toward the camper. Her look said, "This dish came from *that* trailer?"

Cheddar biscuit with herbed egg and applewood-smoked bacon or smoked salmon. Probably Moxie's calling card, this biscuit had the perfect biscuit texture, just the right blend of herbs, and wonderful thin-sliced salmon. The Swell: a fried egg sandwich with prosciutto, provolone, roasted peppers, and basil on ciabatta. Everything was just the right texture and mix of tastes. Sunrise Special: greens and fried eggs, yellow peppers, vinaigrette, and tomato chutney. Couldn't tell you how it tasted because the person who ate it didn't utter a syllable while devouring every bite of it.

I should tell you that the menu changes with the season (and sometimes with the day), but even that is a nod toward an earthy healthiness. And Moxie is known for sometimes just not being open (check the Web site for sporadic updates). And get some baked goods to go. I've seen or heard of almond-plum scones, raspberry crumb muffins, pignoli cookies, and shortbread.

By this point chances are you'll be feeling like such a Portlander you'll probably want to go out and advocate for the rights of bicyclists, protest the Iraq war, or get into a debate about how Mississippi Street should look in five years. And why not? Just by eating at Moxie's you've already gotten a perfectly Portland start to your day.

Wait: Gets a bit long.
Seating: Two picnic tables and about eight at counters; some cover.
Large groups? Sure, but you'll order one at a time.
Portion size: Small, but so are the prices.
Changes: No.
Coffee: From the Fresh Pot next door.
Other drinks: Serious fruit elixirs.
Feel-goods: Ingredients are almost all local and organic.
Health options: The whole place is about as healthy as you can get. **WiFi?** Same as the coffee, but no plug-ins.

My Father's Place

Hip/Old School

A greasy, grimy favorite

523 SE Grand Ave. (SE/Inner)

503-235-5494

Daily from 6:00 a.m. to 2:30 a.m. Breakfast served all the time.

$7–10 (Visa, MasterCard, no checks)

What I love about My Father's Place is that even people who like it — and most people seem to love it — use words like *greasy* and *sticky* and *dive* to describe it. I looked on the Internet for comments, and I found two types: longtime customers who love the place, and plenty of references in *Willamette Week* to either meeting rock bands there or getting drinks that "err on the side of windshield-wiper fluid."

As for the food, consider what the author of the Portland Hamburgers blog said about the burger: "This is a fill-er-up, soak up the alcohol, hangover cure-all, grease bomb that comes cheap. It's not going to win any awards, but it does put a brick back in your belly. They also have a colon clogger, the My Father's Place Special Burger with bacon, ham, 2 cheeses, and an egg."

The breakfast menu's answer to that is the Country Benedict, which is a biscuit split open with a slab of sausage laid on top, two fried eggs on top of that, and sausage gravy all over it. It ain't subtle. It comes with hashbrowns, and my waiter asked if I wanted regular or O'Brien Potatoes, which are hashbrowns with grilled onions and peppers. I said O'Brien, and out they came: a regular slab of hashbrowns with grilled onions and peppers just tossed on top!

That kind of no-nonsense nothing-fancy touch is what My Father's Place is all about, as was my waiter's remark when he dropped the gut bomb on the table: "There you go," he said with a smile. "Now you won't have to eat again all day!" And he was right. I sat there and read the paper and slowly gorged myself, trying to figure out if the yelling coming out of the kitchen was happy or angry. (I think it was happy.) I also enjoyed a waiter's repeated cry to the cooks, "Can I get some more gravy on this, please?"

It's a big place, with three rooms: one for the restaurant and a bar, one traditional barroom, and a third with pool tables and pinball machines. It is, according to various commenters, the kind of place where bikers and hipsters might drink together in peace. At any rate, strangers are treated kindly and fed thoroughly. Once I was supposed to meet my friend Jane there, and I spaced it for some reason, so she reported back to me, "I think I was the only other female in the place besides the waitress, who was chipper and efficient. Old guys with caps and their newspapers, and everyone seemed to know each other's names. Motif/decor was like someone cleaned out the grandparents' attic. Neil Young for ambiance music."

Perhaps you're getting the picture by now. It's a bar — a

big, friendly, smoky, regulars-filled bar — that serves big, cheap, greasy breakfasts. The menu is huge and covers all the bases, and everything is less than $8. As for the décor, *Willamette Week* agreed with Jane: "It feels like someone raided grandma's memory chest and grandpa's tool chest." Among the items you may notice on the walls are an iron, tea kettles, tin horns, pictures of FDR, airplane liquor bottles, and cast-iron skillets.

Hanging out at My Father's Place is like taking a break from the modern world. What cracks me up is that it's practically right across the street from Next Adventure, that hub of outdoorsy, Gore Tex-wearing, hiking and climbing go-getters. The easy stereotype is that probably nobody from one place ever visits the other — though I know this isn't true because both Jane and I shopped there after breakfast.

What I do know is that if some tree-hugger strolled in wearing the latest in fancy raingear and lightweight sandals, all that the folks at My Father's Place would do is say howdy, sit 'em down, and fill 'em up.

Wait: None.
Seating: About 115 total between the restaurant area, all in booths and the bar (smoking and non-smoking seating available.) **Large groups?** Maybe at the bar.
Portion size: Look out! **Changes:** Sure.
Coffee: By the Bean Coffee.
Other drinks: Well, it's a bar . . .
Feel-goods: Well, it's a bar . . .
Health options: Someplace else.
WiFi? Yeah, right.

Niki's

Old School/Mom and Pop

Stop in, on your way through
736 SE Grand (SE/Inner)
503-232-7777
Daily 6:30 a.m. to 3:30 p.m.; breakfast served only until 11:30
$7–11 (all major cards, no checks)

———————◆●◆———————

Somehow, Niki's always has the feel of folks just passing through, even though it's been in the same place since 1972. It's almost certain, if you've been in Portland a while, that you've seen the place; when you're sitting at the light on SE Morrison waiting to get onto the Morrison Bridge going downtown, it's there on your right, with gold bricks and a spiffy new awning. The #15 bus stops right in front of it too.

This geographic setting could contribute to the traveler's feel. It could also be the neighborhood, which is a semi-industrial transition zone between residential Southeast and urban Downtown. Niki's is surrounded by places to store your stuff, used office furniture stores, a few folks on the street, and, of course, lots of traffic. And in the big-picture view of Portland planning, the whole area is considered the Next Big Thing. One day they'll probably find the needed billions to bury I-5, and what is now known as the "Central Eastside Industrial District" will probably get a much catchier name.

In fact, transition is already visible from Niki's, with the East Bank Saloon across one street and a runner's clothing shop across the other. But inside, change happens slowly. You're likely to hear diners at the counter on a first-name

basis with the staff and older folks speaking Greek in corner booths; the place is owned by a Greek family, and the waitress once told me, "Dad used to work here." It's hard to imagine Niki's has changed a lot since it opened, from the food (fundamental American diner breakfast) to the mountain mural, ceramic figurines, beer steins, and faux roof over the kitchen.

I took my friend Jan there once, and after she slid into the brown booth and sipped from the white mug with the black rim, she closed her eyes in restrained ecstasy and purred, "Mmmm, coffee shop coffee." She got the French toast—big and thick, made the old-school way on Texas toast—and I had the Fresh Spinach Omelet with scallions and a heap of feta cheese that gave it a creamy texture. (There's also a Greek omelet with feta, tomato, scallions, and black olives, but most of the Greek influence shows up at lunch, with Greek baked chicken, Greek salad, homemade hummus, and baklava.)

Jan decided the food was "institutional, but good," and we both agreed a city needs places like this: honest, working-class restaurants with consistent cooking and expert, friendly staff. As trucks rumbled and a pack of brightly colored bikers whizzed by, I spread Kraft grape jam on my sourdough toast, Jan smothered her abundant French toast with maple syrup from a glass pitcher with one of those pull-back metal tops, and we enjoyed casual breakfast conversation. My hash browns were the big-slice variety with no seasoning, and my toast was sourdough wedges on a side plate.

I recognized a sales guy from my old insurance job, but I didn't say hi because he looked like he'd chosen the place for some peace and quiet. I heard a waitress ask somebody, "How's the knee?" I saw a sign offering iced coffee, and Jan and I both wondered how long it's been since iced coffee was new and exciting enough to hang a sign about it. Jan asked me what I thought nonsmoking had done to Niki's, and I said all I know is that you'd never ask a question like that about, say, Francis up on Alberta Street.

When I got home and looked for Niki's on the Internet, all I found were a few travel sites calling it a "comfy commuter's stop," and I saw that the Elder Resource Alliance has its Second Thursday Social there every month. I guess the rest of us are usually too rushed to stop in.

Wait: None.
Seating: 10 booths plus a counter and a big second room, seating for about 80.
Large groups? Yes, and the side room can be rented for seriously large groups.
Portion size: Solid.
Changes: Sure.
Coffee: Boyds.
Other drinks: Espresso, orange juice, hot chocolate.
Feel-goods: The staff will probably remember you.
Health options: Nothing in particular.
WiFi? No.

Old Wives' Tales

New/Veggie/Kiddie

Veggie-family-wholesome goes mainstream
1300 E Burnside (E Burnside)
503-238-0470
Sunday through Thursday 8 a.m. to 9 p.m.; Friday and
Saturday 8 a.m. to 10 p.m. Breakfast served all the time.
oldwivestalesrestaurant.com
$12–15 (All major cards, checks)

When it comes to rating what the public thinks of a restaurant, it's best to approach it the way figure skating is judged: throw out the highest and lowest scores, then average what's left.

In the case of Old Wives' Tales, that venerable veggie-friendly, family-friendly mainstay at the goofy intersection of Burnside and Sandy, what you have left is this: A place with lots of room, a kids' play area, a quiet room in the back, a soup and salad bar that's host to a very famous Hungarian mushroom soup, a massive menu filled with wholesome cooking, dozens of vegetarian and vegan options, and food that everybody agrees is neither cutting edge nor fancy.

Even folks who like Old Wives' Tales, and there are plenty of them, use words like "predictable" and "old-fashioned." Folks who don't like it say it lacks flavor, is overpriced, and has all the charm of a Denny's. Vegetarians and vegans seem to appreciate the diversity of choices but think the food is often better elsewhere. Do with all of that what you will.

I dined there once with the Play Group, five moms and six kids who go out once a week. When I arrived early and told the host what was coming, he said, "Great!" He actually seemed excited, then put us in a big room next to the kids' playroom, all the while telling me how wonderful it is to get the kids out for a wholesome meal. With quilts on the wall, wood tables and chairs all around, and several kids already playing in the playroom, the place did feel homey.

It is also big. If you're looking for something cozy and charming, this isn't it. If, on the other hand, there's a dozen of you or you're dining with kids, Old Wives' Tales was made for you. Also, if you like peace and quiet, make your way to the Classical Music Dining Room in back, past the restrooms.

My take on the food is the same as the place: it's just the kind of stuff a bunch of old wives would come up with. They'd want the kids to have space and the grownups to have peace, they'd want to use healthy ingredients but not necessarily get it straight from local farmers (too pricey), and they'd try to cater to everybody's tastes and dietary restrictions. They also wouldn't try to impress anyone with their fine cooking. For example, the Play Group was excited to see Moroccan Oatmeal on the menu; it has raisins, dates, apricots, cinnamon, coriander, and turmeric, and it's served with milk or soymilk and brown sugar or maple syrup. Then, when the oatmeal came, the somewhat-Yuppie moms declared it "a bit hippie," further explained to mean that it wasn't very exciting but sure sounded good: a common refrain from OWT's detractors.

I had a mushroom omelet topped with a denser version of the famous soup. It certainly didn't lack flavor; it was punch-you-in-the-face mushroomy and very heavy, about as subtle as a train. If you like mushrooms, you'll love it, but you still might have a hard time finishing it. I had the yam side (other options are scone, muffin, roasted potatoes, toast, fresh tomato slices, steamed veggies, and fresh fruit) and got exactly that: yams, with no other obvious flavoring.

The Play Group gave points on the kiddie stuff: a large menu in the $1–4 range for standards like mac and cheese, applesauce, and a PB&J sandwich. "Someone gets it," one mom said.

When we were done, there was some sticker shock (I spent $14.50 with tip) as well as agreement there had been no real Wow dish, except maybe the pancake with a mountain of whipped cream and fresh strawberries. So although I don't give ratings to restaurants, it's safe to say that if it were in the Olympics, Old Wives' Tales would finish and get polite applause, but probably not a medal.

Wait: Not bad; they also take reservations.
Seating: About 170.
Large groups? Absolutely.
Portion size: Medium.
Changes: Within reason.
Coffee: Portland Roasting, Organic.
Other drinks: Tazo and Stash Teas, espresso, beer and wine.
Feel-goods: Natural chicken and wild seafood.
Health options: They can handle any dietary restriction you can imagine.
WiFi? No.

Original Pancake House

Old School

It's like Mickey Mantle is still hitting homers
8601 SW 24th Ave. (SW/Inner)
503-246-9007
Wednesday through Sunday, 7 a.m. to 3 p.m.
originalpancakehouse.com
$15–20 (cash and checks only)

———◆———●———◆———

Maybe it's the tiny wooden booths. Or the community table. Or the regulars who, when the place opens, have a newspaper and their favorite dish waiting on their tables. Or the traditional, shared misery of waiting in the lobby. Or heck, maybe it's the waitresses in the little pink skirts.

All I know is I'm in love with the Original Pancake House, and I'm not alone. I also know that it's not of this era. It's like the *Prairie Home Companion* of Portland breakfasts, with its old-world charm that steadfastly refuses modern trends like credit cards and good coffee. Just ask folks about it sometime; you'll either get a crinkled nose and a comment such as, "What, wait all that time and pay all that money for *pancakes?*" Or, you'll get kind of a warm-glow smile and a story about eating there with Grandpa.

Maybe it is the prices; pancakes and coffee will set you back about $15 with a tip. But these aren't your ordinary pancakes (warning: highly biased remarks ahead). For one thing, there are 14 kinds: buttermilk, buckwheat, potato, sourdough flapjacks (pause here while I enjoy a warm glow), Swedish, blueberry, bacon, banana, Hawaiian, Georgia pecan, coconut, and wheat germ. There are also pigs in a blanket, sourdough French toast, strawberry waffles, Danish Kijafa Cherry

Crepes, and the twin signatures, the Apple Pancake (a steaming mass of Granny Smith apples and cinnamon glaze) and the Dutch Baby (a baked bowl shape of eggy pancake pleasure with whipped butter, lemon, and powdered sugar).

Plenty of other options are on the menu — another half-dozen waffles and types of meat, seven omelets, oatmeal, cream of wheat — but that's like saying *A Prairie Home Companion* has comedy sketches and musical guests. Does anyone even remember those things? I don't, and I love that show.

What I remember about trips to the Pancake House is bumping into people I know in the lobby while we're waiting, or having to scrunch to get into a booth, or getting all excited if we get the one in the back right corner with the view of all the rhododendrons, or flipping through the little specials cards that remind me of Monopoly cards. My friend Craig and I consider it a special occasion to go there, mainly because of the prices. But that adds a certain flair to the occasion: we're deciding where to go, then the Pancake House comes up, and we get all excited, like a couple of little kids.

Deciding what to have is an excruciating ordeal for me, because half my mouth is filled with sweet teeth, and to pick one kind of pancake is to eliminate so many others. I usually put myself through the tortures of the damned, my head spinning with visions of pecans and powdered sugar, crispy Swedish edges and sweet lingonberries, the hearty simplicity of the buckwheat . . . and then I always get the sourdough flapjacks, which are so sweet I catch a buzz off them. Throw in a side of bacon, coffee, and a tip, and I've had myself a $20 smilefest.

That's a lot, I don't deny it. I am also thoroughly biased and consider $20 worth it every now and then. And the OPH is a chain, the only one in this book. But the one on Barbur is the *original* Original Pancake House, opened in 1953. From there, a chain of some 100 places has blossomed across the country. And none other than the James Beard Foundation gave it an America's Regional Classics award. You can argue with me and thousands of other Portlanders if you'd like, but I don't see how you can disagree with James Beard. Or the sourdough flapjacks.

Wait: Nearly constant, and up to 45 minutes on weekends.
Seating: About 80, at tables (one community) and some booths. **Large groups?** No.
Portion size: Decent. **Changes:** No.
Coffee: A "special blend."
Other drinks: Hot chocolate, tea, and, believe it or not, buttermilk and Postum!
Feel-goods: The Web site says it uses "93 score butter, pure 36% whipping cream, fresh grade AA eggs, hard wheat unbleached flour, and our own recipe sourdough starter."
Health options: You don't have to eat it all.
WiFi? No.

Overlook Restaurant

Old School

Working classy
1332 N Skidmore (N/Inner)
503-288-0880
5 a.m. to 9 p.m. daily. Breakfast served all day.
$7–10 (all major cards, no checks, ATM on site)

The first thing I heard about the Overlook was that it was "a place for contractors and alcoholics." Considering that this remark came from a good friend who's a contractor and a recovering alcoholic, it wasn't an insult—though it hardly captures everything the Overlook is about.

When I took a job slinging packages for FedEx on Swan Island, I found out that the late-night crew regularly sent out for chicken-fried steak from the Overlook. Since we were making about $10 an hour part-time, heavy emphasis was on qualities such as filling, cheap, and convenient.

When I got around to checking out the breakfast, two people from the Breakfast Crew showed up: Tom, who said he "used to go there when I was a contractor," and R, another recovering alcoholic. Coincidence? Well, it was also the only time in the research for this book—almost 150 breakfasts over two years—that professional basketball was ever discussed. The Overlook is a bedrock, working class, fill-you-up restaurant with staff who are total pros, more food options than just about any place in town, and the ability to handle kids and large groups. And you can damn near kill yourself with food for $10.

I walked in and saw one of those classic dessert cases right inside the door, and more were stretched out behind the bar like trophy cases. Some of the desserts were a foot high! I counted 11 cakes, 8 pies, 2 puddings, and a custard. We sat down at a table with brown and white coffee mugs, and above us were a Keno screen and a high-definition TV showing Fox News (this ain't your lefty Portland).

And the menu! One online reviewer joked that it had won several literary awards. Eggs Benedict, eight omelets (including taco), eight farm-style breakfasts and eight "specialties." Pancakes, plain and Belgian waffles, and four kinds of French toast. Two versions of steak and eggs are $8.65 (top sirloin) and $9.65 (NY Steak), including toast, jam, and pancakes or hash browns. And heck, for $1.95 they'll cover anything with their sausage gravy, thick with big chunks of sausage in it.

I could go on. In fact, I think I will. The Grand Slam ($7.75) is two each of pancakes, eggs, sausage, and bacon. The cinnamon roll French toast special comes with two sausages, bacon, and eggs for $7.75. The waffle special comes with two eggs, two sausage links, and two bacon strips for $6.50. And right below the biscuits and gravy and the cinnamon roll, a small box says simply, "Danish, $2.25."

Tom, for old times' sake, was wearing a Carhart shirt and ordered the Monte Cristo: a triple decker French toast sandwich with grilled ham, cheese, and egg that came with a serrated steak knife stuck through it. We called it the Sandwich of Death. I got the cinnamon roll French toast, which was just a mess of sweetness I could barely finish. R got the half-order of biscuits and gravy and marveled that anyone would ever eat the whole one.

We talked sports and jobs and women, just three dudes having a filling breakfast. Other diners were families, older couples, businesspeople with notebooks, somebody who may have slept outside the night before, and some kids from the University of Portland who looked like they were on an anthropological field trip. And, yes, some contractors.

Don't miss the lounge, by the way. I was there at 9 a.m. and the waiter was serving a couple of highballs to two guys watching golf on one of the many televisions. The lounge is lifted straight from the 1960s — and I don't mean the hippie 1960s, either. I'm talking about caged-in gas fireplaces with seats branching out from them, wood paneling, green seats, slot machines, and faux stained-glass windows.

So, my first report on the Overlook wasn't all wrong or all right. What I'd call the Overlook is a comfy, filling cross-section of America.

Wait: Maybe a little on weekends.
Seating: About 80 at tables, booths, and a counter.
Large groups? No problem.
Portion size: Massive.
Changes: Limited, none on the specialties.
Coffee: Boyds.
Other drinks: Stash tea, milkshakes, cocktails in the bar.
Feel-goods: Uh, no.
Health options: Egg substitute available.
WiFi? No.

Pambiche

New/Hip/Weekend

Music! Colors! Options!

2811 NE Glisan (NE/Broadway)

503-233-0511

Weekdays 7 a.m. to 11 a.m. and weekends 7 a.m. to 2 p.m.

pambiche.com

$12–16 (Visa, MasterCard, cash)

The bright Caribbean colors are here. The music is here. The voodoo priestess is here with her cigar. But why is the sun shining?

Yes, as of spring 2007 Pambiche branched into brunch. The place whose Cuban fare and style got it named *Willamette Week's* 2002 co-Restaurant of the Year just had to get in on Portland's morning action. (They even open at the decidedly un-Portland hour of 7 a.m.)

And it isn't a token offering, either. The menu offers three stuffed pages that cover nine *entremés* (sweet bread starters), ten *bebidas* and *platos de desayuno*, six *sanwiches*, and four tortillas, which the menu explains is a word that, outside Mexico, means an omelet or frittata. So you're always learning something at Pambiche, as well.

With the colors around you, the strong, rich café Cubano in your veins, and all the options before you, the excitement is palpable. Throw in a $5 sampler basket of those sweet treats, and you're off and running. The best of them is the fruit-filled and sugar-coated *empanaditas*, which on any day may have mango, guava and cheese, pineapple, papaya, or *dulce de leche*. And we also fought over the *pan de toronja* (grapefruit pound

cake). Just *saying* the rest of them gets you worked up: semi-sweet coconut bread with ginger and pineapple, cream muffins with chunks of mango, sweet potato spiced cake with guarapo icing, sweet bread filled with peanuts and baked in caramel.

Now on a roll (no pun intended), we welcomed our main courses. Although the Spanish names sound exotic, what you're often getting is a Cuban twist on something you're used to seeing: Huevos Cubano, for example, is a couple of fried eggs with rice, black beans, avocado, and a side of yummy, sweet fried plantains. The *bistec* is an onion-smothered Cuban steak and eggs. The *torrejas con frutas* is advertised as "Cuban toast," and among Portland's many takes on French toast, what makes this one stand out is the crunchiness of the bread and the ridiculously sweet sugar cane syrup.

In fact, Pambiche's strengths seem to be in it sweets. Granted, I am a sugar hound, but even among my friends there was more excitement for the bread basket, the mango milk shake, and the dessert counter than for most of the main dishes.

Interesting and traditionally Cuban dishes also abound. *Pisto manchego* is a pile of Chorizo, smoked ham, creole pork, shrimp, potatoes, asparagus, pimentos, and petit pois with an olive oil sofrito sauce. (A similar, meatless version, the *revoltillo a la jardinera*, features roasted peppers—but it's darn near the only option for vegetarians.) The *tamal en hoja* (creole pork in red sauce, encased in corn, yucca, and plantain masa) was a favorite as well.

If anything, our group thought that the main dishes, although tasty, didn't live up to their original promise. No single dish blew our minds, several were strikingly similar to one another in makeup and taste, and most lacked the zing we had anticipated. Chalk it up, perhaps, to sensory overload or to overhyped, sugar-fueled expectations. Maybe the American palette is more accustomed to the boom of rock and roll than the smooth rhythms of rumba.

Or maybe Pambiche is still searching for its morning groove; if so, it certainly isn't far off.

Wait: Not bad, with plenty of cover outside.
Seating: About 50 inside, tables with heat lamps outside.
Large groups? Get there early.
Portion size: *Grande!*
Changes: Within reason.
Coffee: Their own special blend, company name not disclosed, but it's like being plugged into a car battery.
Other drinks: Fabulous fruit smoothies and shakes, espresso, fruit juices, and sugar cane lemonade.
Feel-goods: None in particular.
Health options: Lots of meat? Low on carbs?
WiFi? No.

Paradox Cafe

Hip/Veggie

The hippies took over the diner!
3439 SE Belmont Ave. (SE/Belmont)
503-232-7508
Weekdays 8 a.m. to 9:00 p.m.; Saturday 8 a.m. to 9:30 p.m.;
Sunday 8 a.m. to 3 p.m. (hours change seasonally) Breakfast
served at all times.
paradoxorganiccafe.com
$8-11 (all major cards)

I might be a pig. I might be a backward-thinking Tennessee
hillbilly. And yet I have traveled the world, seen several
dozen Dead shows, smoked more than my share of grass,
lean way left politically, and think of myself as sensitive and
open-minded. Can I be both of these people?

Is this what they call a paradox?

These are the things I think of as I eat vegan biscuits and
almond gravy at the Paradox Café—but it started before
that. I went to the Web site and found the café's philoso-
phy: "wholesome common meals at a fair price . . . seasonal
organic produce, organic grains, local and organic tofu and
tempeh, free range eggs and hormone free meats . . . local co-
ops . . . breads, sauces and desserts are mostly dairy and egg
free . . . maple or fructose for our sweeteners." This sounds
wonderful, I thought.

The site, at the time, didn't list hours or what forms of
payment accepted. And when I called to ask, the person answering had to check on the hours. My inner hippie said, "Go with the flow," but my 40-year-old grump set

off a stoner alert. When we got there, I dug the neighborhood feel, the '60s-diner look, the Formica tables, the parquet floor, the egg-shaped light fixtures, and the blue booths—then I sat in a booth and got poked in the ass by a spring. Now, is that quirky or something that ought to be fixed?

The place opened in 1993, and although I wasn't in Portland then, I suspect it was one of the first mostly vegetarian places in town. As the *Willamette Week* has said, "Customers learned to expect a little grease here, a little filth there (but) cheap and easy comfort food." A friend is familiar with the "Vegetarian Community," and she tells me that the community "bailed" on the Paradox because of the grease and filth. I also suspect this process accelerated when the original owner founded the more upscale Vita Café on Alberta Street, and generally when other vegan-vegetarian places opened around town.

As for the food, perhaps I'm not the person to ask: I refer you to the disclaimer I gave some moments before. I tried the vegan sausage patty and found it dry; I wished it had meat and fat in it. I tried the potatoes and liked them a lot; they were crunchy on the outside, soft inside, and lightly seasoned. I tried the vegan corn cakes and found them mealy. I had the French toast, which is made with sourdough bread and dipped in an egg-free mixture of fruit juices, and I thought they should have soaked it more, though the citrusy taste worked well. I had the waffle, with oats in it, and thought it was good—and that they shouldn't try to make waffles healthy with stuff like oats. I read the back of the menu and appreciated somebody explaining what *tempeh* is.

One friend had the biscuits and gravy and declared it warm, filling, and almost without taste. Another had the breakfast burrito (tofu, cauliflower, broccoli, cabbage, brown rice, whole wheat tortilla, carrots, and kale, all well cooked without added flavoring) and it was tasty. We also thought it wasn't breakfast, because it didn't have eggs and sausage in it. But, as I say, I might be a pig.

I'm not a foodie, but I can tell you this: I ate at the Paradox with five people, asked them all what they thought of the food, and every one of them shrugged. So maybe we're all pigs. Or maybe vegetarian food is kind of dull. Or maybe the Paradox is just a little neighborhood place with a lot of healthy food that isn't trying to impress anybody.

Wait: Medium on weekends
Seating: About 40 in tables and booths
Large groups? No more than 6, I think
Portion Size: Moderate
Changes/Substitutions: Menu says "Substitutions $1"
Coffee: Stumptown
Other drinks: Large variety of natural juices and sodas
Feel-goods: Local ingredients, free-range eggs, hormone-free meats, seasonal produce
Health Options: Many dishes are vegan, vegetarian, dairy-free, etc.
WiFi? No

Pattie's Homeplate Cafe

Mom and Pop/Old School

1947, downtown, somewhere in America

8501 N. Lombard St. (N/Outer)

Monday through Friday 7am to 6pm, Saturday, 8 a.m. to 6 p.m. Sunday 9 a.m. to 3 p.m. Breakfast served all the time.

503-289-7285

$6–8 (Checks, Visa, MasterCard)

————————◆•◆————————

I used to go by this place on the #75 bus all the time on my way to play disc golf in Pier Park. I would see tables outside and read something about a soda fountain, and I'd think "Man, I need to go there." Problem was, I couldn't catch the name of the place. In fact, now that I've eaten there, I *still* don't really know what the name of it is. But I know what people call it. And if you think that's the same thing, you don't know small-town America.

Folks call it Pattie's, because Pattie owns it, runs it, and generally occupies it. She was there when I was, sitting at a table with some regulars. It's Pattie's place. It might officially be called Pattie's Home Plate Cafe . . . but if you ask the old-timers in St. Johns, they'll tell you it's just Pattie's place.

I didn't know all this when I decided to check it out. I looked around on the Web for breakfast places on North Lombard Street, and I wound up at the John Street Cafe, on the other side of the street—and in another decade. The John Street is white tablecloths, the *New York Times*, flowers, original art, and sour buttermilk pancakes. All well and good—and *not* what I was looking for that morning.

So I walked across the street, and when I entered Pattie's, four guys at the counter stopped talking, looked up at me,

gave me the head-to-toe, then went back to their coffee. I felt like I was on the road!

Pattie's is in the middle of "downtown St. Johns," and when you walk in, you couldn't be further away from what many people think of as Portland: jogging paths, urban planning, peace marches, lattes, and so on. Some of the folks in Pattie's look like they "make it down to Portland" only once a year or so and couldn't imagine why they'd go any more than that.

Whole families were coming in, three generations at a time. Men with canes. Women in slippers. People speaking Spanish. A referee in uniform, people asking which game he was working today. Camouflage hats, flannel shirts, and Cat Diesel baseball caps.

The food is precisely what you would expect, and then some. Contemplate the words "home plate cafe" and "lunchbox." I sat at a table with a laminated Coke tablecloth and had scrambled eggs with ham, hashbrowns (the grilled strip variety), crisp bacon, and pancakes. I ordered orange juice and got a bottle of Langers. I asked for maple syrup and got a bottle of Aunt Jemima.

The food was good, filling, and not pricey. While I ate, I watched the waitress greet people with lines like "Well, it's a regular family reunion in here today!" I watched the guy behind the counter cook while trading barbs with the old guys. I looked at the store in back and saw wigs, yarn, picture frames, bird feeders, costumes (in March), costume jewelry, fish lures, plastic flowers, you name it.

My favorite moment was when a Young Portland Couple came in. He had a thin figure, sideburns, and thick-rimmed glasses. She had matching workout clothes, a bike helmet, and a newspaper. They looked at each other briefly, and so did everybody else. They surveyed the scene, made a loop through the store, talked in hushed tones near the toy section, then casually strolled out—and across the street, I'm sure. Probably rather wait in line at the John Street than cross the cultural divide.

They don't know what they missed.

Wait: Can't imagine.
Seating: 30ish with booths, tables, a counter and some outside seating.
Large groups? Sure!
Portion Size: Decent.
Changes/Substitutions: Easy.
Coffee: Standard.
Other drinks: Juice by the bottle.
Feel-goods: The folks.
Health Options: Juice in bottles!
WiFi? Heck no.

Petite Provence

Weekend/Classy

"Our waiter is from Marseilles, and he's hot!"

4834 S.E. Division St. (SE/Division). They also plan a location on NE Alberta for 2008.

503-233-1121

Breakfast served Monday through Saturday, 7:00 a.m. to 8:30 p.m. (breakfast until 2); Sunday 7:00 a.m. to 2:00 p.m.

$8–13 (all major cards)

———————◆●◀———————

"I would go 10 miles for these pastries; they're better than sex."

I won't divulge the name of the person who uttered that remark (her boyfriend might read this), but I will say it was typical of the Breakfast Crew's trip to Petite Provence. It was Beth who let me know that our waiter was from Marseilles, then added "and he's hot!"

Yes, things got a little saucy for us at the fancy French place on Division Street. In fact, every reaction I've read or heard goes something like this: "I saw this place on Division, and I couldn't believe it was there in the middle of that dingy neighborhood, so I went in, and . . . Oh My God! I had one of the best [whatever]s of my life, the place was lovely, and my server was really cute and had a French accent."

People just seem to be in love with this place. Consider what the *Portland Tribune* had to say: "The perfect croissants are so light they nearly float; the buttery layers puff up against the flaky crunchy crust. . . . and it's hard to get out of there without a pound cake, pumpernickel baguette or cutely decorated meringue." *Willamette Week* slipped past love and into lust, calling the *croque monsieur* sandwich

"almost pornographic . . .
oozing with Gruyère, butter
and creamy béchamel."

All the pastry delights
will be waiting for you right
inside the door, as will a very
French scene: a cute person
addressing you, gilded mirrors, gold leaf, Impressionist
art, lantern-style light fixtures, and of course the fleur-
de-lis motif all over the walls and tables. We found the staff
to be, in addition to cute, brisk but not rude, although the
Tribune's writer was also smitten by the "authentically snarky
French- speaking staff" and their "silky accents."

But it's still an American place, with its come-as-you-are
dress code (it's so Portland to be in baseball caps and shorts
amid all this fanciness), reasonable prices, and large portions
on the big menu. At the low end is the House Breakfast
(baguette, croissant, juice, jam, and butter) for $7.95 and the
Day Breaker, which is two eggs, choice of bacon or sausage,
potato cakes with parsley, toast or muffin, orange juice, and
coffee for $7.50, or $8 if you throw in a pastry.

The menu includes three hashes: corned beef, salmon
(with smoked and cured salmon and a lemon dill sauce), and
Latin (chorizo, onions, cilantro, and sour cream); notable
omelets include the open-faced Colette and a blue cheese-
shrimp. For sweets, the multigrain pancakes come with
banana-pecan sauce, and the French toast is studded with
berries. Crepes are available during the week only.

The items we ate almost sent us into lovers' tangles. The
Petite Provence Omelet with chorizo was perfectly light and

fluffy despite being loaded with sausage; the hollandaise on the Benedicts wasn't gooey like it is in a lot of places, but "light with some bite," as someone chuckled. (I'm telling you, there was a *vibe* at our table!) My friend Cheryl had pancakes with a crème brûlé sauce that tasted like honeysuckle and had the consistency of eggnog; I shamelessly dipped my multigrain pancakes in it, and when I wanted more I started lightly stroking Cheryl's arm.

By then, Cheryl's boyfriend was giving me a look. On the way out, Beth said something to the hottie from Marseilles, and I pursued my own passions: a run past the pastry counter for something to go. Hmmm, shall it be the cheese brioche, the almond brioche, the chocolate croissant, the Napoleon, the meringue cookie, the mousse cake, the orange éclair. . . .

Beth wasn't the only one getting a crush at Petite Provence.

Wait: Long on weekends after about 9:00 and sometimes even during the week.
Seating: About 30 at table, plus two window counters.
Large groups? With notice.
Portion size: Big.
Changes: Yes.
Coffee: Mossa Samilia Coffee.
Other drinks: Espresso drinks, Italian Soda, Lemonade, Beer and Wine.
Feel-goods: You can flirt with French cuties.
Health options: C'mon – it's French!
WiFi? No.

Pine State Biscuits

Old School/Mom and Pop

Y'all come visit and have some biscuits!
3640 SE Belmont (SE/Belmont)
503-236-3346
7:00 a.m. to 2:00 p.m. Tuesday through Sunday
pinestatebiscuits.com
$8–10 (Visa, MasterCard)

When you're talking to Kevin Atchley, one of the owners of Pine State Biscuits, it's clear that he's a restaurant guy through and through. He politely gives credit to previous mentors, compliments all his vendors, and lovingly describes the eight-month process he and his partners went through with their "chef and foodie" friends to get just the right biscuit recipe. And then he'll drop something like this on you: "See that cabinet over the door, how it's facin' the kitchen? We're gonna put a TV set in there, and y'all ain't gonna know we're watchin' ACC basketball!"

Yes, Atchley is just as much a North Carolinian as he is a Portland foodie, and now he and his partners — Brian Snyder and Walt Alexander, all Pine State transplants and NC State Wolfpack fans — have given the Portland breakfast scene something it never had before: a genuine biscuit kitchen. "We all miss North Carolina breakfasts — biscuits, gravies, grits, and the like — and we figured we owed it to ourselves to open a place that was an homage to the type of food we grew up with," he says. Then he adds another fine southern twist: "The food is what kept us going home, along with family."

Take this mix of old-style southern goodness and modern restaurant professionalism, throw in some Portland foodie sensibility, and you have Pine State Biscuits. Using only the freshest local ingredients, often straight from the farm, Pine State built a following at the Portland Farmers Market with golden Creamtop Buttermilk Biscuits served with sausage or mushroom gravy, thick-cut bacon, fried chicken, eggs, grits, and preserves.

Such was this following that within two weeks of the "soft" opening, Pine State was already doing the same amount of business as at the market: about 500 biscuits daily; but as Atchley says, "now we won't run out."

So, what's in this fabulous biscuit, anyway? Of course, Atchley won't tell. But he will say there's no shortening at all. There is some butter, but all the flakiness comes, he says, entirely from baking technique. "We decided to do something a little more health oriented. We use very, very fresh ingredients, all perishable and sourced as close to home as possible. The inspiration is from North Carolina, but the ingredients are all from right around the greater Portland area."

The tiny green place is perfectly positioned to take advantage of Belmont's neighborhood feel as well as its commuter crowd. Atchley says he also hopes Pine State will become "a place where southerners would all come back together under the guise of trying to rediscover they food they grew up with." In fact, while he was talking with this Memphis native, a woman from a neighboring table said she was from Clarksville, Tennessee, "and these are some great biscuits!"

To further tempt us, Atchley offers sweet tea and Cheerwine (a super-sweet cherry soda from North Carolina), and he occasionally features country ham. "When all the true-blood North Carolinians come in and visit with us," Atchley says, "the first thing they say is, 'When are y'all gonna do country ham?'"

Country ham is a heavily salted, cured bacon Atchley admits is an acquired taste; what he has, on occasion, is ham from Johnson County, North Carolina, which has about 40 percent the usual salt content of a "real" country ham. "It's more of a domestic prosciutto," he says. Still, to many Portlanders it will seem awfully salty; that, of course, is what the sweet tea is for.

Plans call for an expansion into classic southern lunch fare like "meat and threes," blue plates, and shrimp and grits—and if you don't know what any of that stuff is, or you don't know the significance of ACC basketball, y'all just need to git on down to Pine State and visit with them nice folks!

Wait: Long on weekends.
Seating: About 20 at tables and a small counter.
Large groups? No.
Portion size: Bigger than you'd think.
Changes: Limited.
Coffee: Stumptown.
Other drinks: Sweet tea and Cheerwine soda, hand-crafted chocolate milk made by a local chocolatier.
Feel-goods: Everything's local and fresh.
Health options: Does "no shortening in the biscuits" count?
WiFi? No.

A version of this chapter first appeared at LivePDX.com

Podnah's Pit

Old School/Weekend

Git yer Texas on!
1469 NE Prescott St. (NE/Alberta)
503-281-3700
Breakfast served weekends 9:00 a.m. to 1:00 p.m.
podnahspit.com
$9–12 (all major cards)

━━━━━━━━◆●◆━━━━━━━━

Podnah's Pit doesn't look like much, inside or out. And the menu, especially at breakfast, is as simple and to-the-point as the décor is. But the depth of feeling Podnah's Pit elicits from folks around Portland conveys what it is: a serious attempt to capture the simple, profound magic of Texas-style barbecue.

Podnah's doesn't actually serve barbecue at breakfast, but here the emphasis is as much on *Texas* as on *barbecue,* and besides, barbecue isn't just a style of cooking or a sauce; it's a state of mind and a way of life. Like Podnah's Pit, it is utterly non-ornamental and is entirely about substance. I once experienced a slightly teary moment of peace at a Formica table, sipping iced tea and chewing a piece of brisket while Dolly Parton sang "Smoky Mountain Memories."

I'm not alone in this experience. Among the volumes of positive comments about Podnah's on the Internet, the one must-read is the Food Dude's rapturous soliloquy at *PortlandFoodandDrink.com*. In describing childhood summers in Maypearl, Texas, he wove together images of hay bales, ceiling fans, raising a calf, losing his virginity, a living room he wasn't allowed to use, "impossibly red tomatoes," and watching his grandmother make "perfect chocolate pies with a meringue that always cried a little; she said they were angel's tears." It's the best thing he's written for his immensely popular Web site, and he went on to heap praise on Podnah's. (It turns out, in fact, that the owner of Podnah's is from Maypearl.)

When word got out the menu had expanded to include weekend breakfast, the foodies celebrated—and hoped it wouldn't get overrun. No worries as of this writing. While throngs of people wait a few blocks up at the Alberta Street palaces, Junior Brown and Merle Haggard are singing down at Podnah's and folks are digging into some down-home Texas vittles.

There are no pancakes or waffles, but there's plenty of food—until the kitchen runs out. You can get biscuits and gravy for $5.50; add a couple of eggs for another $1.50. Or you can get just a biscuit with jam for $2.25 (or 3 for $6). The biscuits are, according to the *Oregonian*, "the best biscuits in town—at once buttery, tall, flaky and tender, with a subtle crispness around the edges." You can get them with grits, ham, and two eggs for $8.50, which, in fact, I recommend.

A little further up the fanciness scale is a yummy smoked trout hash ($7.50, or $9 with two eggs), and more basic is a burrito with potatoes, egg, and cheese for $5. If you get it, add chorizo for another $1.50 and plan on taking a nap soon afterward. The house-made salsa is available on the burrito, too, and isn't to be missed.

There will also be the occasional pot of *menudo* (a spicy soup) and maybe some *kolaches,* Czech fruit-filled pastries that for some odd reason are huge in Texas. The town of Caldwell, Texas, has the Kolache Festival every year, and Fayetteville calls itself the Kolache Capital of Texas. Kolaches, as well as other specials like pork belly, are likely to show up on the "Out Of" board, so I suggest you arrive early for breakfast.

Even now, sitting at my computer, I think back to a particular feeling I had at Podnah's Pit. It was early on a Saturday morning and my friend Steve and I were in for a filling meal before doing some work. I was having the hash, and Steve was happily working on a burrito. We weren't talking much, because there wasn't much to say, and when Tony Joe White started singing "Polk Salad Annie," Steve half-closed his eyes, stopped chewing for a second, dropped his head a little, and started groovin'. I slouched a little deeper into my chair, felt the warmth radiating from my stomach, reached for some more tea, and let myself drift down south for a spell.

Wait: None that I've seen.
Seating: About 30 all at tables, and sometimes a few tables outside. **Large groups?** No.
Portion size: Solid.
Changes: Not so much.
Coffee: Stumptown.
Other drinks: Orange juice, mimosas, and red beer (Tecate beer mixed with tomato juice).
Feel-goods: It's all smoked in-house.
Health options: Uh, no.
WiFi? No.

Porto Terra

Classy

*Not **quite** what it seems*

830 SW 6th Ave. (Downtown)

503-944-1090

Breakfast served weekdays 6:30 a.m. to 11:00 a.m.; weekends 7:00 a.m. to 11:00 a.m.

portoterra.com

$15–20 (all major cards)

———————◆•◆———————

Maybe this sounds familiar: you're downtown near Pioneer Square and you see this fancy-looking restaurant called Porto Terra, which is Italian for "port" and "land." It's an impressive-looking place, and peering through the windows you'll see candles, a fireplace, and beautiful people eating at beautiful tables.

Did you know it serves breakfast? I didn't. So I looked it up on the Internet and started reading about "the warmth of Northern Italy" and "creative Tuscan cuisine prepared with passion. . . . Every dish handcrafted with authentic ingredients imported from Italy." It even listed an executive chef!

Eager to see what Tuscans might eat for breakfast, I invited Jennifer, a recent graduate of the Western Culinary Institute and a dedicated foodie, to join me. Like me, she didn't know the place served breakfast, and she was as excited as I was.

I got there early, and the first people I saw were a flight attendant, some businessmen with briefcases, and an older couple with a map of Portland and a copy of *USA Today*. The waitress brought me a mug that said "Breakfast!" in bright letters, and something started to dawn on me: This is not

a Tuscan restaurant — at least, not at breakfast. I looked around some more and realized it's a Hilton Hotel restaurant.

Jennifer showed up and whispered a hello. I asked why she was whispering, and she said the place felt like a library — which, come to think it, was also true. We started perusing the large menu. Pancakes are $10.95. Waffles are $11.95. The Frittata di Porto Terra ("Hey, I found some Italian!") with sausage, marinara sauce, and mozzarella was $12.95. So it's not a cheap restaurant, either.

We turned our eyes to the décor. It's a big, corporate-looking place, with metal sculptures, track lights, and shelves filled with wine bottles, some of them the really big bottles you only see sitting empty on shelves. There is, I suppose, a Tuscan theme to the place, but in the morning it consists mainly of paintings of tomato, garlic, and eggplant.

Otherwise, it's a pretty straightforward breakfast menu: a couple of frittatas and a breakfast panini (listed under "Tuscan Specialties"), seven "American Classics" like a Benedict and a few omelets, and a griddle section with pancakes, waffles, and challah French toast (a noted Tuscan favorite, I assume). The cheapest item in all those sections was $10.95.

Jennifer and I were, I think, trying to be positive and polite. But when we were about five bites into the meal, I asked what she thought, and she said the potatoes "could have been cooked a little more." In retrospect, that's when the thing started going wrong. Truth is, I was thinking the marinara in my frittata might have come from a can, and when I said so, she countered that she certainly had better Benedicts. Then I noticed the little packets of Smuckers jam. I held one up to her and said, "Smuckers? Really? When a side of toast is $4.25?"

Pretty soon we were both making various smart-aleck remarks about $4 orange juice (even more than Bluehour) and our goofy little "Breakfast!" mugs. In truth, I think we were a little embarrassed. Well, I was. I had invited a serious foodie to a $21 breakfast that we probably could have made at home. At 7 that morning she had listed her status on Facebook as "going to breakfast at Porto Terra. Didn't even know they served breakfast. We'll see!" By 11:30 it was "Jennifer has a stomach ache. Not the best breakfast in town. Oops!"

Yeah, what she said.

Wait: None.
Seating: About 90, all at tables.
Large groups? With notice.
Portion size: Small for the price.
Changes: Within reason.
Coffee: Viennese Dark Roast.
Other drinks: Espresso, juices, hot chocolate, tea.
Feel-goods: The view is nice.
Health options: None that is bragged about.
WiFi? No.

Prescott Cafe

Mom and Pop/Old School

Home cookin' in a place from the 40s — literally
6205 NE Prescott St., Portland (NE/Outer)
7 a.m. to 2 p.m. weekdays, 6 a.m. to 2 p.m. weekends; breakfast always available
503-287-8495
$8-10 (Cash and checks— but they've got a cool old-timey register!)

————————◆•————————

When Jean and I got to the Prescott Cafe and sat down, the first thing I read on the menu was, "We use real butter, real cheese, and fresh grated real potatoes." And I thought, As opposed to what? And then I remembered shopping at New Seasons Market, feeling overwhelmed by the French, Portuguese, and English Gruyères and Camemberts and what-the-hell-ever . . . so now I'm thinking the message of the Prescott Café is, "That ain't real cheese—and neither is that soy stuff. We use *Cheddar*. Like from Tillamook."

In fact, the whole place says, "We don't mess around – sit down, relax, and we'll go back and cook you some food."

The Prescott has white lace curtains, every version of Trivial Pursuit cards on the table, the specials written on an RC Cola chalkboard, items like a 2x2 (eggs and pancakes) and Pig in a Blanket and corned beef hash and a *six-egg* omelet. It's the United States of Generica, straight out of black-and-white television, cash only, and served quick with a smile.

We were greeted with exciting news: fresh razor clams today! And what do you do with them? "We bread 'em, put

'em on the grill, and serve 'em with hashbrowns and eggs." Well, of course you do.

I wondered what a place like the Bijou Café would do with razor clams: probably have them in a scramble with wild mushrooms and fresh basil for $11.95. And that's fine — sometimes you want to be impressed. Other times you want to be fed and you want the waitress to bring you a pair of gigantic tasty biscuits and say, "You want honey, honey?"

While we were testing each other's trivia knowledge, I noticed a picture of the place from the 1940s, back when it was just one room. The waitress said it used to be called Mary's Fine Dining. She turned to a guy sitting alone in a booth and said, "Bill (not his real name), did you used to eat here back in the '40s?" He looked like he could have fed his kids here back then, and his response of "No, I'm only 40!" drew a laugh from several tables. I noticed I was the only guy in the room under 60 and not wearing a plaid shirt.

The menu had things like linguiça (a kind of sausage) and eggs and three-egg omelets with shrimp or crab or otherwise-unspecified "seafood." See a pattern? Eggs and meat and potatoes. The Working Man's Feed is three eggs, meat, hashbrowns, biscuits, and gravy. Strawberry waffles when strawberries are in season, which is something I admire. You aren't supposed to have strawberries in January.

Is the food good? Well, that depends on what you like. Jean said she liked it because it's what she grew up with. My fried eggs were perfectly round and still had little pockets of butter and grease on them—literally just like mom used to make. My hash may have came from a big can. The huge blueberry pancakes came with a slowly dissolving pile of whipped butter and squeeze bottles of maple and blueberry syrups.

The point is this: I didn't see one thing I couldn't have made at home. And that either is, or isn't, the point. The Prescott Café is not the kind of place that knocks your socks off with its subtle or stylish flavors or presentations. It's the kind of place where you relax, feel at home, and eat.

Wait: Never seen one.
Seating: About 50 with tables and booths.
Large groups? With some notice.
Portion Size: You're good 'til dinner.
Changes: You bet, hon.
Coffee: Old school.
Other drinks: Tea.
Feel-goods: Real cheese!
Health Options: Some vegetarian items. And real potatoes!
WiFi? Check back in 20 years.

Rose's Restaurant and Bakery

Old School

A Portland tradition or a lesser replica?

Address: 838 NW 23rd Ave (this is one of several locations in Portland and Vancouver, 5 total, hours vary by location. See website for details.)

503-222-5292

Hours: Breakfast served weekdays 8:00 a.m. to noon; weekends 8:00 a.m. to 2:00 p.m.

rosesrestaurant.net

$10–15 (payment)

───────────◆───────────

When long-time Portlanders talk about Rose's, their eyes almost mist. It was a legend on NW 23rd Avenue starting in 1956 when Rose Natfalin founded it. Seems like everybody has a story about eating at Rose's: first bite of corned beef or first date, or, in the case of former Senator Mark Hatfield, the site where he proposed to his wife. That was the "old" Rose's. When these long-time Portlanders talk about the "new" Rose's, misty eyes often turn to crinkled noses.

I can't speak to the old Rose's because I moved to Portland after it had closed. As for the new Rose's, what it looks like to me is a quiet, friendly place that serves a deli-style breakfast: kosher salami omelets; scrambles with lox, corned beef, or smoked salmon hash; cinnamon roll French toast; and blintzes. I find none of it to be exceptional in any way, though the prices seem to be inflated a bit by the location.

In a bigger sense, what Rose's looks like to me is a brand somebody is trying to take global. Its reputation was forged as a neighborhood place where a lady named Rose made deli-

style dishes from scratch and created a family-style atmosphere where everyone ate well and had fun. Rose retired in 1967, the place closed in 1993, and everybody agrees it was a sad thing.

By then, Rose's was owned by a former attorney and restaurant developer. After closing the original, he decided to keep the brand alive by trying express versions in malls. Then he got a new partner, an entrepreneur with a background in high-tech ventures, and they developed a new business plan, as stated in the *Portland Business Journal:* "(develop) Rose's as a growing regional chain . . . open as many as eight restaurants and lounges between Seattle and the California border. Eventually, the duo want to expand Rose's to the East Coast."

Remember the lady making stuff from scratch? Seems long gone, doesn't it? It's not necessarily a bad thing; nothing wrong with guys making money. And the *Journal* reported that, as of late 2005, revenues were up tenfold. They even got a plug in *USA Today,* so at least the marketing seems to be effective.

Before I get to what the community seems to think of the new Rose's on NW 23rd (not exactly its original location, by the way), I'll tell you ahead of time that I don't see what all the (mostly negative) fuss is about. It's not the best food on the street, but it seems to stay open and there's rarely a wait.

Of course, it may be there's no wait because a lot of people can't stand the place. A reviewer for *Willamette Week,* after paying homage to the old Rose's, went on to trash the new one with lines like "there was no evidence that an actual chicken had come anywhere near the insipid (chicken soup)" and the "meat loaf looked like that mysterious 'Swiss steak' they used to serve at the school cafeteria." Well.

Over on *CitySearch*, you'll see a majority of comments like "pretty good for what it is," "Worst food and service for the money in Portland," "nothing more than greasy spoon," "Nothing special," "famous name, average food," "Greasy average rueben and dry cake," and "You can only ride on your old Portland reputation for so long."

One other reviewer suggested the same thing I would: forget about the past and judge the place on its own merits.

In the back of the store on 23rd, there's a Rose's sign hanging in a corner. I asked the waitress if that was the original sign from the old place, and she said no, it's a replica one-fourth the size of the original.

A lesser replica, hanging over the whole scene, not as prominent or bright as it once was, but still there. Seems about right to me.

Wait: Not much.
Seating: About 60, all at tables.
Large groups? Yes.
Portion size: Reasonable.
Changes: Within reason.
Coffee: Portland Roasting.
Other drinks: Stash tea, espresso, Italian Sodas.
Feel-goods: None that they claim.
Health options: At a deli?
WiFi? No.

Roux

Weekend/Classy

Over the top — as it should be
1700 N Killingsworth (N/Inner)
503-285-1200
Brunch served Sunday 9:00 a.m. to 2:00 p.m.
rouxrestaurant.us
$12–17 (all major cards, local checks)

———————◆——•——◆———————

At some point during the madness of our trip to Roux, Denise came over to my part of our large table, practically grabbed me, and yelled, "It's too much!"

Denise was not complaining. She was smiling broadly, with a half-mad look in her eye, and after she issued her summary, she went back to her seat and kept eating. Roux is a New Orleans place in volume, taste, price, and indulgence, so "too much" is just about right.

Roux doesn't look like much, especially from the outside. Its setting on North Killingsworth hardly screams "fancy." Inside, it's all earth tones, wood tables, large photos of fruit, and Mason jars on a shelf. Rumor had it the founders spent $750,000 on the place and had such fancy restaurants as Zefiro, Wildwood, Genoa, and Bluehour on their resumes. So they were aiming high from the start.

From our more pedestrian perspective, Roux passed the class test right away. Cheryl informed me that her teapot with loose tea came with a dish for the strainer, which is her personal litmus test; the drinkers in our crowd were blown away by the two dozen cocktails and 50-plus wines; and I had a crush on both our waitresses, who did a terrific job with our big group.

With the music blar-
ing above the din (Roux
is quite loud when it's
full), a big community of
friends around me, and
such debauchery as the
Fried Oyster and Bacon
Benedict on the menu, I simply let go and let the good times
roll. Somebody got some oysters on the half shell (yikes! $20
per dozen), somebody else got a few plates of beignets ($7 for
3, with apple butter or strawberry coulis), and Patrick and I
decided to go for broke and got the French Quarter Brunch.
It's a four-course journey that runs $25 per person but only
$30 for two.

First up on the French Quarter were seasonal fruits and a
basket of warm breads. Bouncing among mango, pineapple,
and red grapefruit on the one hand and a scone, corn muffin, and buttermilk biscuit with warm blueberry preserves
on the other got my juices going. Patrick was working on a
huge Bloody Mary.

Our next course was a choice between oysters on the half
shell and shrimp fritters, and since somebody else already
had oysters, we got the fritters. They were cooked perfectly,
seared on the outside and just a little gooey on the inside,
with green peppers giving them some kick.

On a normal day, at that point I would have been filled
up. However, other folks from the Crew started bringing me
samples of what they were having, and things got fuzzy. I got
a taste of a French omelet with Gruyère and fresh herbs that
was amazingly light, like a soufflé. Hickory-smoked bacon
went by, and it might be my favorite bacon of all I've written
about in this book. A smoked trout hash with horseradish

crème fraîche was divine. I *think* somebody gave me some French toast with caramelized bananas, whipped cream, and cane syrup, but I can't be sure.

Oh, yes . . . Patrick and I had a third course: a choice of Benedicts (smoked pork or oyster-bacon) or any omelet. We got the oyster-bacon Benedict because, really, how often can you do such a thing? It was absurdly good, and I was starting to feel absurdly stuffed. Fortunately, the last course was *just* some beignets, warm and sugary and served with apple butter. I knocked back about my seventh cup of coffee, and we all tried to take stock.

We decided that American portions of French food is a perfect summation of what New Orleans is all about. Somebody used the phrase "gut bomb" and, like Denise, wasn't complaining. I asked for other words, and out came "loud, big, family, community, rich food, over the top, crazy, too expensive," and, finally, "just right."

Wait: A little long after about 10:00 a.m.
Seating: About 100.
Large groups? Yes, with reservations.
Portion size: A little nuts.
Changes: Within reason.
Coffee: Caffe Vita and Community Coffee (New Orleans brand with chicory).
Other drinks: Cocktails, wine, espresso, juices.
Feel-goods: You might think you're in New Orleans.
Health options: You don't really have to eat it all.
WiFi? No.

Salty's

Weekend/Buffet/Classy

Seafood extravaganza with a view
3839 NE Marine Drive (NE/Outer)
503-808-1998
Saturday 9:00 a.m. to 1:00 p.m. (Sunday until 2:00 p.m.) Food
is still out until about 3:00. Reservations strongly suggested.
saltys.com/portland
$34.95 all-you-can-eat buffet includes bottomless mimosa
and other beverages, though Espresso drinks are a la carte.
Buffet prices for kids under 12: it is $1.50 per year of age for
children 12 and under. (all major cards)

◆━━━━●━━━━◆

Big. That's what Salty's is, and big is what you'll get: a big
time, a big belly, a big bill, a big marketing plan, and a big
view. The weekend brunch at Salty's can hardly be called
breakfast, although breakfast items are in abundance (along
with everything else). An experience is what it is.

You drive past the yacht clubs and the Portland airport to
a big building on the shore of the Columbia River. You offer
your car to the valet service (free, but you should tip). You
walk into a buzzing scene of staff greeting you and running
around with trays of food, and people surrounding buffet
tables looking like animals released to the feed trough.

The place feels like a factory, but it borders on elegant.
It's also very structured. Our young waiter greeted us immediately and offered beverages. When two friends joined us
unexpectedly, he said the same things, word for word. Salty's
also has a newsletter, chef blogs on its Web site, brochures
touting its being named Nation's Best Sunday Brunch by
MSN-Citysearch.com, and live music three nights a week.

As for the scene, you'll see old folks dressed up, entire families, and young people shuffling in wearing sweatpants. It doesn't matter; it's all about stuffing a pile of food down your gullet — most of it from the ocean. Here's the list of what was being served when I took my sweetie for a Valentine's meal. (And by the way, when I reserved the table they asked what we were celebrating, and lo and behold we got a corner spot upstairs by the window, with two balloons tied to the table.)

Offerings for the day: Peel & Eat Prawns, Dungeness Crab, Salmon Lox, Seafood Ceviche, Clams & Mussels, Fresh Oysters Shucked to Order, Omelettes, Crêpes, Pastas Made to Order, Belgian Waffles, Fresh Fruit, Vegetables & Cheese Trays, Array of Seasonal Salads, Bacon & Sausage, Country Potatoes, Biscuits & Gravy, Teriyaki Salmon, Prime Rib & Baked Ham, Salty's World-Famous Seafood Chowder, Coffee, Juice, Soda, Tea, Desserts Made from Scratch, Apple Dumplings, Breakfast Breads & Pastries, and a Fountain of Cascading Liquid Chocolate.

Kind of overwhelming, isn't it? Well, you should *see* it!

And yes, there *is* the Fountain of Cascading Liquid Chocolate. You haven't been indulgent until you're standing with a heaping plate of food in one hand, holding your marshmallow or strawberry under four feet of molten chocolate with the other hand, and giggling like an eight-year-old.

The quality of the food is helped immensely by two factors. One is the idea that, if you want, you can load plate after plate with crab legs and oysters on the half shell, certainly a $35 deal all at once. The other factor is, of course, the bottomless mimosas or champagne.

What I'm trying to say is that nothing at Salty's will be the best version you've ever had. But it would be hard to cook that stuff ahead of time, feed hundreds of people, and have it taste consistently excellent. (I read one online review that said the food was "about on par with a nice hotel banquet.")

Just a couple of days before we went to Salty's, Jenny and I stopped at a little market in Florence on the way to the coast, spent about $15 on a cooked Dungeness crab and a side of garlic butter, and ate the whole thing on a blanket at Sunset Beach. That we will remember as a wonderful meal in a romantic setting. Salty's, I think, we will recall as an over-the-top, special-occasion spectacle with good friends, very friendly service, a comfortable setting, and a fantastic view.

Wait: Almost none if you make a reservation.
Seating: A multitude. **Large groups?** Absolutely.
Portion size: Whatever you can carry. **Changes:** No.
Coffee: Boyds.
Other drinks: Espresso (a la carte), Bottomless mimosas, champagne, and juices.
Feel-goods: You don't have to eat for about two days afterward.
Health options: In a place with a four-foot chocolate waterfall?
WiFi? No.

Sanborn's

New/Classy

Real cooking, real casual
3200 SE Milwaukie (SE/Inner)
503-963-8000
Wednesday through Sunday 8:00 a.m. to 2:00 p.m.
sanbornsbreakfast.com
$10–16 (Visa, MasterCard, no checks)

———————◆•◆———————

At some point in this town—at least, if you're researching breakfast places—your mind starts to fill up. You reject new information the same way you'd wave off a short stack when you're already loaded down with an omelet.

So it was when a friend named Robb said I needed to check out this place called Sanborn's. Actually, what he said was, "It's the *shizzle* for breakfast." This made me doubt Robb's credibility, as did the place's location at SE Powell and Milwaukie. Hardly an area one associates with fine dining.

Undeterred, I headed down there, and as soon as I walked in I remembered how foolish geography-based restaurant reviews are. I was confronted with a classy-looking place that also seemed completely casual, and best of all, no line whatsoever at 10:00 a.m. on a Saturday. In fact, a little Internet research revealed that hardly a word has ever been written about the place: one glowing review in *Willamette Week*, to be exact.

Ah, the mysteries of Portland breakfast.

While waiting for Robb, I realized that another guy was waiting for Robb too. He turned out to be Derek, who told me this was just about the only place he comes for brunch.

Derek is also a pretty serious restaurant person; he
posts regularly on *port-*
landfood.org, and when the
subject of best burger in
Portland came up, he said

"Castagna" in a tone similar to a guy saying water flows
downhill. I mean, *of course* it's Castagna!

So I figured we had a pretty serious restaurant person on
our hands, and he loves Sanborn's. And indeed, how does
this sound? You slide into a comfy booth in a spacious, nat-
ural-light restaurant. A pleasant waitress (one is the owner's daughter who runs the front-of-house staff) brings you a
French press of coffee (that's a $5.99 option; a regular cup is
$1.99) and hands you a menu fill of delicious-sounding meals
at perfectly reasonable prices, with half orders available on
everything except potatoes.

It's heavy on baked goodies, with two waffles, sourdough
French toast, and five kinds of pancakes ranging from $6.29
to $8.49: buttermilk; buckwheat; sourdough (from a genuine
1847 Oregon Trail starter); blueberry with powdered sugar
and blueberry compote; and potato with diced green onion
and egg, served with sour cream or house-made applesauce.
Then you cruise over to the Specialties section of the menu,
and see the German Pancake with whipped butter, lemon,
and powdered sugar; the Apple Pancake with sliced apples
caramelized in sugar and cinnamon; seasonal pancakes; and
the Mango Pancake with sliced mango caramelized with
sugar, ginger, lemon, and orange peel.

Stop and read that last dish again. This place is a serious
restaurant!

Anyway, I would be reporting on said pancakes, but Derek told me the chorizo is excellent and the omelets are like nothing I'd ever had, so I promptly went to the Build-Your-Own Omelet section (any two ingredients in a three-egg omelet for $10.99, another $0.89 for more ingredients) and got one with chorizo, feta, and peppers. There were 15 other ingredients to choose from, and you can get the same deal in a scramble for $9.29.

What came out was as surprising as the rest of the place: a massive omelet in which the eggs had been whipped, then stuffed with the ingredients, folded over, and baked. I was stunned. And soon I was stuffed. The potatoes, as the *Willamette Week* and Derek both noted, needed some work, but everything else I saw and tasted was amazing.

Sanborn's is also casual and friendly (and even a little odd: for some reason, every price ends with a 9). And it's not crowded. And it's at Powell and Milwaukie. Who knew?

Wait: A little on weekends.
Seating: 60 at tables and booths.
Large groups? Yes, but notice would delay the wait.
Portion size: Heapin'.
Changes: Within reason; also, half orders are available on the pancakes. **Coffee:** Bridgetown.
Other drinks: French Press Mocha (!) and teas, individual teas, hot cider, and seven juices.
Feel-goods: None that is touted.
Health options: Egg substitute or whites available on omelets and scrambles. Veggie sausage available as an option.
WiFi? No.

Screen Door

Weekend/New/Classy

Southern soul meets Northwest style

2337 East Burnside St. (E Burnside)

503-542-0880

Brunch served weekends only, 9 a.m. to 2:30 p.m.

screendoorrestaurant.com

$14–18 (all major cards, checks)

————————◆•◆————————

I was all ready to make fun of the Screen Door. I'm from the South, you see, and when a restaurant outside the South calls itself Southern, I tend to load up the Sarcasm Cannon. Waiting for my friends at the Screen Door, I saw Swiss Chard and Bacon Frittata, Goat Cheese Scramble with Roasted Red Peppers, and Bananas Foster French Toast on the specials board; good luck finding any of *that* in the South, I thought.

The atmosphere didn't exactly say down-home, either. If I brought my Mississippi grandparents in, they would say, "Oh, we're eating fancy!" There was wine on the shelves and modern art on the walls instead of checkered tablecloths or an actual screen door. Looking for a word to describe the atmosphere, the Breakfast Crew wavered between "minimalist" and "nuveau rustic."

So it's not a Southern place, in the stereotypical sense. It's a Portland restaurant with a Southern theme. And, as it turned out, that was just fine with all of us.

Who says Southern food has to be from the 1950s? Who says it has to be greasy or boiled beyond recognition? If people from Louisiana want to settle in Portland and open a place committed to using fresh, local, organic ingredients, I say more power to them.

Still, the Sarcasm Cannon almost went off when I saw something called Garden Grits, with spinach, grilled tomatoes, onions, and provolone, and Farm Grits with ham, poached eggs, and provolone. That's not how you do grits! I thought.

I emailed this news to some of the prime Southern ladies in my life. They forwarded it to various friends and cousins from Maryland to Mississippi. Here are some of the actual responses:

My mom, Marjorie, in Memphis: "Well child, I just can't imagine all these names they thought up for grits! Cheese grits is a standard brunch dish here, but with cheddar, for Pete's sake! If I ordered regular grits — which a menu would never need to say, cause grits is grits — I would just put a heap'a butter on it. Mercy!"

My sister-in-law, Lela, in Memphis: "Having been born in Alabama, raised in Tennessee and schooled in New Orleans, I've yet to meet the self-respecting grit that would interact with Provolone."

My sister, Lucy, in Maryland: "Provolone is great on a turkey sandwich but definitely NOT on grits. I may have left the true south but there are just some things you don't fergit." (Yes, she typed *fergit*, but she was going for the effect. I think.)

Dee, a family friend in Atlanta: "All that gussied up grits on the menu is just for those poor Northwesterners who don't know any better."

So the South didn't exactly rise up in favor of this grits

thing, nor for the Screen Door's Praline Bacon, which is very sweet and covered with pecans. And I didn't have the heart to tell the ladies about the Tofu Hash.

But I had to e-mail everyone back and say, "I hate to tell y'all, but this place was *good*, and the regular side grits have Cheddar in them." Indeed, the Breakfast Crew was entirely impressed, from my Crabcake Benedict to the waffle smothered in fruit and whipped cream to the Alabama Scramble with ham, green onions, and pimiento cheese. The menu is full up (as my grandma would have said) with modern twists on old faves: a mushroom omelet with morels and fontina cheese, Brioche Vanilla Bean French Toast, a puff pastry filled with eggs, caramelized onions, fontina, tomato, and thyme cream.

Two objections come through in most of the Crew's reactions to the Screen Door: the place is way too loud, and it feels a little overpriced. I told the Southern ladies the dinner menu included hush puppies at $5.75 and fried chicken for $14.75; their responses were unprintable.

I don't think there are too many places in the South like the Screen Door. But I think maybe that's the South's loss.

Wait: Mild on weekends after 9:30; no cover outside and a small area inside.
Seating: About 100 inside, with several picnic tables outside.
Large groups? Yes. **Portion size:** Large. **Changes:** Easy.
Coffee: Stumptown
Other drinks: Fresh juices and a wide range of cocktails.
Feel-goods: Produce and meats from local vendors.
Health options: Organic ingredients.
WiFi? No.

Seasons and Regions

Weekend

It's all about the fish

6660 SW Capitol Hwy. (SW/Outer)

503-244-6400

Breakfast served weekends 9 a.m. to 2 p.m. Lunch is available at same time.

seasonsandregions.com

$12–16 (all major cards)

————————◆————————

Seasons and Regions is a restaurant that practically nobody in the Portland breakfast scene has ever heard of. For one thing, it's on SW Capitol Highway, hardly the center of our culinary world, and it's not even in the Hillsdale stretch of road we know. It's across from the Mittleman Jewish Community Center. Since breakfast is served only on weekends, it's hardly the signature offering. If you were to drive by you would probably think, Gee, it looks like an old Dairy Queen or something. And that's precisely what it was; the drive-through window is still there, in fact.

So what is served? One word: Seafood. Even on the weekend brunch menu, the bounty of the sea dominates. The Vera Cruz Omelet has fresh Oregon bay shrimp, salsa fresca, bell peppers, onions, pepperjack cheese, and sour cream. There's Crab Cake Benedict, Nova Scotia Benedict with house-smoked salmon, and Hangtown Fry with fried Willapa Bay oysters, eggs, bacon, spinach, and mushrooms topped with freshly grated Parmesan. There's Smoked Salmon Hash, Smoked Salmon Scramble, and the all-out Tillamook Scramble: three eggs scrambled with salmon, bay shrimp, halibut, mushrooms, onions, spinach, tomatoes, and Tillamook Cheddar. The prices are downright reasonable as well: the Tillamook Scramble is only $8.90.

Seasons comes off as a kind of semi-serious place. And that's not a slight: the Web site boasts "Fresh Northwest seafood and shellfish, transformed into world class creations and served by friends." Many of the patrons are local regulars. There's a full bar, and the food falls somewhere between diner and cutting edge: both down-home stuff like the Chorizo Breakfast Burrito and a strawberry waffle, and Mornay sauce (on the Florentine Benedict and Northwest Omelet). Just about everything comes with rosemary potatoes (crispy outside, soft inside); light, fluffy rosemary scones; or both.

As you may imagine, a former Dairy Queen is not exactly an architectural or interior must-see. I happened to eat there with three women (not braggin', just sayin'), and they said it "looks like a dude decorated it." I would have called it casual and friendly, especially for a seafood place, but they had a point. Trivial Pursuit cards were on the unfinished wood tables along with salt and pepper shakers in the form of slot machines. Grapevine-shaped lights hung from a black ceiling that said "evening dinner," but the yellow walls said, "daytime cheery." Faux picture windows "looked out" at lovely scenes that were not SW Capitol Highway. A year-round outside seating area is covered by a tent and has overhead heaters. It's a nice touch, but my friends were less than impressed by its appearance.

Turns out that not only did two dudes, in fact, decorate Seasons and Regions; they actually did all the renovation work and still own it. They met while working at McCormick's Fish House & Bar in Beaverton, and the folks who aren't too impressed by Seasons would say it's just a local version of that chain. (Critics might also say that the "served by friends" on the Web site means the service isn't always hyper-efficient.) In a 2002 *Portland Business Journal* story, the owners said they aim for a wide breadth of options based on what's currently available, so you'll see a revolving menu and different specials depending on the time of year.

The women and I enjoyed our meal, especially because we didn't have to wait at all on a Saturday morning. Seasons and Regions seems to put more effort into dinners, but there's a lot to be said for a down-home laid-back breakfast place with fresh seafood and just a hint of fanciness without being over-the-top expensive.

Wait: Perhaps a little on weekends.
Seating: About 75 inside at tables and booths plus a covered, heated patio.
Large groups? Better outside.
Portion Size: Solid.
Changes: Easy.
Coffee: Seattle's Best.
Other drinks: Kobos Espresso, mimosas, bloody marys.
Feel-goods: Most ingredients are fresh and local.
Health Options: Egg substitutes available, Gluten Free and Vegetarian menu now available.
WiFi? No.

Simpatica Dining Hall

Weekend/New/Classy

A serious place—and seriously good

828 SE Ash St. (SE/Inner)

503-235-1600

Brunch served Sunday, 9 a.m. to 2 p.m.

simpaticacatering.com

$12–16 (Visa, MasterCard, checks)

———◆•◆———

Most of us operate in the normal world of restaurants: They have signs outside, they post their menus, and they serve food that's dependable and familiar. But there's another world of restaurants: It's a parallel universe of experimentation and innovation, and it's on a higher plane, like the New York fashion world is to the local mall. Most of us eat in the mall; the Serious Food People eat in New York.

Simpatica Dining Hall is of the Serious Food World, and it was born in a Portland restaurant movement that is simultaneously innovative and old-fashioned: family-style suppers featuring the creations of highly trained chefs and made from local ingredients. It started as invitation-only suppers among friends served in backyards or local restaurants. Three of the guys (two are owners of Viande, a specialty meat company) created a catering company that eventually started hosting events in the basement of the long-lost Pine Street Theater. This is Simpatica, where reservations-only fixed-menu dinners are served a couple of nights a week with brunch on Sundays.

Among the Serious Food People, it's considered the best brunch in town. It won that honor "by a landslide" on

portlandfoodanddrink.com, Portland's biggest and best restaurant blog. Still, you sort of have to know where it is. A small line forms outside the non-descript building (with only a small sandwich board outside an otherwise unsigned door announcing its presence) just before 9 every Sunday morning, with people doing crosswords and reading magazines to kill time. Seating is still family-style, so if you're a party of two, you'll be seated across from each other and next to another party. This leads to much cross-party conversation and menu discussion.

Despite the mildly underground vibe, it is a very serious restaurant; in fact, *Bon Appetit* named Simpatica one of the Top 10 hot new restaurants in the US for 2006. But neither the prices nor the attitude is worrisome. And, keeping to the "old is new" spirit that makes family dining from local farmers something revolutionary, the menu at Simpatica is really just all your breakfast favorites done very, very well. I had French toast, for example, with a smoky orange marmalade and chantilly cream. At one point I was wiping up a combination of real maple syrup, cream, and marmalade with a piece of bacon, and I officially reached both the top of both the fat intake scale and, not coincidentally, the pleasure scale. Another time I had a crab cake Benedict, and after one bite actually felt sad that it would have to end.

Other offerings I have seen on the ever-changing menu include a classic Eggs Benedict with ham; crepes filled with butternut squash or bacon, asparagus, and crème fraîche; an andouille and prosciutto hash; and lunch items like a much-raved-about cheeseburger and a Philly cheese steak sandwich. All the meats are outstanding, as you would expect from guys who own a meat company; vegetarians will probably have to stick to the sweet stuff.

We counted four servers who stopped by our table at some point, all efficient and thoroughly knowledgeable about the entire menu. Substitutions were easy, and when other friends happened in and joined us, their orders were taken and somehow the food all arrived together.

Simpatica is really something, an accessible intersection between the Serious Food World and the world of regular-folks breakfasts. Among the many pleasures of living in Portland, one has to count the existence of young chefs like those who run Simpatica. They are serious about their food, not only its quality but also its role in the community of bringing people together, connecting diners with local producers, and constantly raising the bar on how good things can be.

Wait: Can get long; get there when it opens if you're in a hurry. **Seating:** About 52, all at tables.
Large groups? Tough. Reservations for parties of 8 or larger, maxed out at 20-25 people for groups.
Portion size: Decent.
Changes: Easy.
Coffee: Stumptown.
Other drinks: Tazo and Numi tea, cocktails.
Feel-goods: Everything is local.
Health options: Not much for the vegetarians.
WiFi? No.

Skyline Restaurant

Old School

Where "old" and "greasy" are compliments

1313 NW Skyline Blvd. (NW)

503-292-6727

Daily 8:00 a.m. to 9:00 p.m.; breakfast served until 11:00 a.m.

$9–13 (cash only, but there's an ATM)

Although it's not a breakfast item, let's consider a dessert served at the Skyline Restaurant: pie milkshakes. It's just what it sounds like: milk, ice cream, and a chunk of pie—banana cream, coconut cream, Dutch apple, chocolate peanut butter, pecan, lemon, pumpkin, or S'mores—all blended. That's in addition to other milkshake flavors that, when I ate there, included white chocolate raspberry, strawberry lemon, vanilla nut, peppermint crunch, red hot, and chocolate marshmallow.

I would say "They don't do it like that anymore," but I'm not sure "they" ever did. What I do know, at least from reading about the area, is that there used to be drive-in burger and shake joints out in the country, back before folks even knew the terms "unleaded gas" and "trans fats." And somehow one of them, the Skyline, survived.

Since 1935, when it was called the Speck, the Skyline has been slinging fare that people now affectionately call diner food. I've read online reviews from people who ate there in 1968 and in 2007 and swear the place hadn't changed. Even its mostly forested view probably hasn't changed a lot. But now Skyline fries in transfat-free oil.

Inside, the feel is more kiddie than *Happy Days*. There are kids' drawings on the back page of the menus and all

over the walls, teddy
bears everywhere, and
for Valentines Day a
painting in the window
featured two cherubs in
love with a hamburger.

There also remains a sense of being on the road, especially
when you have to step outside and around back to use the
restroom.

It's funny to compare the Skyline with some of the old-
timey-themed places. The Skyline doesn't put old 45s or pictures of Elvis (whom it predates!) or pink Cadillacs on the
walls. Food writer Jim Dixon called the dining room "a war-
ren of roomy booths and a few small tables [with] wood paneling, acoustic tile ceiling, and those Jetson-y light fixtures
from the days of Sputnik."

As for the food, it's the kind of place whose fans use the
word *greasy* as a compliment. The most common positive
reaction to the Skyline is a combination of sentiment and
indulgence. The place seems best known for burgers. Dixon
wondered, "Who still toasts and butters the bun?" James
Beard called them some of the best he'd had—back in the
1950s. What I wonder is, Who else still serves buttermilk as
a beverage?

Breakfast ranges from the healthy (granola with yogurt
for $3.25 or Cream of Wheat with brown sugar for around
$2.95) to the old-school, like a hamburger steak with two
eggs and hashbrowns, toast, or pancakes ($9.25). I'm guessing
that the NW Breakfast Burrito came along sometime since
the founding, though Biscuits and Gravy, Chicken Fried
Steak, Pork Chop and Eggs, and the six-egg Giant Omelet
have probably choked three generations of arteries. And yes,

I said six-egg omelet—but there's a three-egg version, too, and you can build your own version of either.

Naturally, in a place that serves pie milkshakes your sweet tooth won't be ignored. Basic pancakes ($6.75) and the Specialty Cakes (blueberry, fresh banana, or chocolate chip, all $7.25) can come with two eggs, or strawberries or blackberries and whipped cream, for a little extra. The French toast ($6.95) is abundant, highly eggy, and loaded with cinnamon.

I was born when the place was already 30 years old, so I can't get into the sentiment stuff. But I do know that sometimes I really crave the Skyline when Portland seems a bit too modern and full of itself and I just want to sit in a booth, eat something that's bad for me, and watch the world drive by.

Wait: Perhaps on weekends.

Seating: About 50 at tables and booths.

Large groups? No.

Portion size: Heapin'.

Changes: Lots of add-ons available, and I'm sure most requests are handled.

Coffee: Boyds.

Other drinks: Milkshakes, sodas, three kinds of lemonade, specialty-flavored milkshakes, peach and marionberry iced tea, floats, pie milkshakes, regular milkshakes, sodas, buttermilk (!).

Feel-goods: You can tell your grandparents you had the same food.

Health options: Sugar-free syrup is available.

WiFi? Heck no.

Stepping Stone Cafe

Hip/Mom and Pop

*Northwest Portland really **does** have a neighborhood place!*

2390 NW Quimby (NW)

503-222-1132

Monday and Tuesday 6:00 a.m. to 2:00 p.m., Wednesday and Thursday 6:00 a.m. to 10:00 p.m., Friday 6 a.m. to 3:00 a.m., Saturday 7:30 a.m. to 3 a.m., Sunday 7:30 a.m. to 10:00 p.m. Breakfast served all hours.

steppingstonecafe.com

$10–14 (all major cards)

———————◆•◆———————

My first apartment in Portland was on NW Quimby Street, back in 1996. I had just stumbled into town from a fishing season in Alaska, and I knew exactly one person in the whole city; unlike me, he had a job. So, on one of my first lonely mornings, I started walking toward NW 23rd Avenue, the only street I knew. On the way I passed a little corner diner with five people sitting in it.

My first thought was that I shouldn't go in because it looked like a place where the neighborhood's real people eat and I didn't know anybody. Better to go down to safe, touristy 23rd. But I heard laughter come out the door and smelled bacon, so I couldn't resist.

I walked into the Stepping Stone Cafe and immediately found myself taking, and then giving, a bunch of crap from the guy working there. I was fresh off a fishing boat, more than capable in such pursuits, and immediately fit in. For the next six months, until my fishing money ran out and I had to move to a hovel in Southeast, I ate at the Stepping Stone several times a week, and the legendary, cranky

staffer became something of a friend — until one day, according to published reports, he relapsed into his drug habit and was banned from the premises.

Those were different times, and today the Stepping Stone is friendlier, although the official motto, You Eat Here Because We Let You, harks back to the days when a thick skin and sense of humor helped as much as a big appetite did. A few years back the owners opened for late-night dinners, then made it an all-day place, then *renovated* it — I was shocked and worried — but all they really did was clean up, paint, add some nice awnings, and move the dishwasher back into the kitchen.

Now I live in Northwest again, and the Stepping Stone still feels like my local place. Yes, even "fashionable" Northwest has a little neighborhood diner. It's not like any other place in the neighborhood — not flashy like Meriweather's, or sophisticated like Besaw's, or faux sentimental like Rose's. It's just a diner and has been for more than 50 years, since the block across the street (now townhouses) hosted a garage for the streetcar.

The menu is probably similar to what the old streetcar guys ate: chicken-fried steak, ham, Tillamook Cheddar, five scrambles, and a dozen omelets, although they probably didn't have sundried tomato basil chicken sausage or an omelet with spinach, portabella, feta, and artichoke. Yes, "the Stone" has gone a little upscale, and the menu has expanded to include three kinds of French toast, Belgian waffles, and cheese blintzes. The cinnamon sweet roll is still insane (they used to joke that if you eat 10, you get a free angioplasty), and now it's been sliced up for French toast.

There's still a slight edge of funkiness about the place, like the (sometimes dismembered) action-hero dolls that move up and down when the doors open, and the chain-pull toilet in the men's room, where a Help Wanted sign has hung for years. But it's also extremely down-home, with checkered tablecloths, red vinyl chairs, immensely charming booths, and pictures of friends (called "Stepping Stoners") on the wall.

Some modern art went up with the new paint, but there's not a hint of pretension. You won't see high-heeled ladies sipping mimosas; more likely a musician just waking up and doing a crossword or, God bless him, some hungover kid in a corner booth staring blankly into his coffee.

I'm not that kid anymore, but I still feel at home at the Stepping Stone. And now that it's become entirely cruelty-free, you can too.

Wait: Medium on weekends, almost entirely outside.
Seating: Around 40 in booths, tables, and a counter.
Large groups? No. **Portion size:** Solid.
Changes: Plenty of options, sometimes with a small charge.
Coffee: Portland Roasting special blend.
Other drinks: Cocktails, espresso, great milkshakes, hot chocolate.
Feel-goods: Nothing jumps out.
Health options: Not much beyond fruit and cottage cheese available.
WiFi? No.

Tin Shed Garden Café

New/Hip/Veggie

These hippies are kind of grown up — and they can cook!
1438 NE Alberta St., Portland (NE/Alberta)
503-288-6966
All week 7 a.m. to 10:00 p.m.; Breakfast available every day until 3.
$11-13 (Cash, Visa, MasterCard).

———————◆•◆———————

Mushroom-rosemary gravy. Somehow that wraps up the Tin Shed perfectly — that, plus when the weather's nice there are so many people waiting out front and drinking self-serve coffee that they put up benches so people could share newspapers with one another.

In fact, when you travel east from MLK Boulevard, the first major indication you have arrived on the Alberta Scene is about 35 people milling around outside the Tin Shed. And the Shed is a perfect intro to the Scene. It's popular, inventive, and works very well, on its own terms.

Once you get inside — and it may be an hour on weekends — the feel that's always struck me is Grown-up Hippie, or, as a fellow former Southerner put it, "Kinda weird, but good." He was referring to the brie and green apples on top of his Sweet Chix scramble (with chicken-apple sausage, sweet onion, basil, and roasted red peppers). But he might as well have been talking about the light fixtures with forks on them, the artwork that features people in various skeletal stages, or even some of the people eating breakfast. The crowd is Alberta Arts + late-rising horn-rimmed hipster + just-bought-a-house young adult, all watched by curious

pseudo-tourists from other parts of town coming over to check out the galleries and shops.

The Tin Shed is a monument to what has happened on Alberta. As late as the mid-'90s, Alberta was a place that showed up on the local news every month or so—with police lights flashing. But it was cheap to live there, so artists moved in. Then they opened coffee shops and galleries, and people came over to browse. When the Pearl District started First Thursday, Alberta responded with Last Thursday. Eventually, restaurants like Chez What and Bernie's Southern Bistro opened, and then people started noticing all the cheap, older houses around the neighborhood.

Flash forward a few years; upper-middle-class white folks are sitting in the Tin Shed's garden patio eating French toast made with sweet-potato cinnamon bread; scrambles with portabella mushrooms, sun-dried tomatoes, spinach, and goat cheese; and the Tim Curry: tofu, roasted garlic, yams, zucchini, mushrooms, and sweet onion in a coconut-curry sauce served over a bed of spinach and topped with toasted peanuts, raisins, and avocado.

Kinda weird. Also damn good.

And the Shed has cilantro-jalapeño crème fraîche, but they also have solid, down-to-earth stuff like biscuits and gravy, done very well. And that's the word of *two* former Southerners. The biscuits are crunchy around the edges, fluffy in the middle, and, if you prefer, they also have apple wood-smoked bacon gravy.

And then there's the potato cake. It's what the place is known for, and as a signature it's an appropriate choice. The Shed potato cake is somewhere between hashbrowns and potato pancake—golden brown outside, soft in the middle, semi-mashed and semi-stringy—and served by the hundreds each day, either as a side with sour cream and green onions or underneath a scramble with bacon and eggs and Cheddar, or sausage and gravy, or spicy sausage, peppers, onion, and eggs. Mmmm.

In other words, the signature potato cake is just right, and it's got variety, and it's unique, and folks love it, "kinda weird" or not. And that's all you need to know about the Tin Shed.

Wait: Bad on weekends, mostly outside, but with free coffee. **Seating:** 25 inside, 20 outside in a patio with fireplace, plus the garden area for another 25 during summer months.
Large groups? One big table seats 8.
Portion Size: Medium-big.
Changes: With some small charges.
Coffee: Their own "Tin Shed Blend" from Portland Roasters. **Other drinks:** Numi tea, espresso, cocktails.
Feel-goods: Free-range eggs, and for a small fee you can get pure maple syrup.
Health Options: vegetarian, vegan, egg whites, tofu.
WiFi? No.

Toast

New/Mom and Pop

One man's quest, a neighborhood's gain

5222 SE 52nd Ave. (SE/Outer)

503-774-1020

Brunch served Wednesday through Sunday 8:00 a.m. to 2:00 p.m.

toastthepossibilities.com

$9–13 (cash and all major cards)

———————◆———————

The way Donald Kotler sees it, every neighborhood needs a great breakfast place. So when he and some old restaurant friends wanted to open a place, it made sense to do breakfast in his own Woodstock neighborhood. Apparently, the neighborhood agreed: when Kotler opened Toast in August 2007, a 45-minute line lasted for two hours. The little place, which gave in to local suggestions to serve dinner four nights a week, has been hopping ever since.

"From the beginning we wanted to have a nice, neighborhood restaurant," Kotler says. "Eighty percent of the people who eat and work here live in the neighborhood."

Kotler's other goal was to keep it simple—on the menu and in the space. "We wanted to take food and bring it back to its simplest form, not over-processing food or covering it with overly lemony hollandaise sauces, but letting the true flavors of the food stand out on their own."

Toast's appearance is also clean and simple, with bamboo tables and comfortable chairs. The room's history is a little more interesting: it used to be Bad Ass Video, purveyor of porn, and the name lives on in the Bad Ass Sandwich (fried eggs, cured pork belly, and shaved Gouda on toast served with a potato *rosti* for $8.00).

One more thing about the space ties in with Kotler's plan for the food: Toast is *small*—what you can see is all there is—meaning food can't be kept for very long. So everything is fresh, and much of it (like jams, peppers, baked goods, and sausage) are made in-house. He's even got some herbs growing out back.

"We wanted to bring fresher ingredients to the table," he says, "like eggs that are no more than five days old instead of the ones at the supermarket that are five weeks old."

A lot of the food is from local farmers and vendors (ask to see a list of suppliers), and Kotler has created a menu that is, as he puts it, more brunch than breakfast. You can get a burger at 8:00 a.m., for example. And there's beer and half a dozen cocktails. You'll find granola (called Hippies Use Front Door) and oatmeal, and a sweet onion tart called the Occasional Hedonist, with a poached egg, fresh herbs, and a light béarnaise sauce. You can get steak and eggs, a Benedict with chard and house-made sausage, and a chicken breast with eggs over easy.

Portions and prices (all less than $10.00, except for the steak) are quite reasonable, and everything I've had was tasty—never flashy, never awe-inspiring, but there's a lot to be said for fresh ingredients cooked well. And the vibe, as you might expect from such a local place, is extremely welcoming and friendly. I'm also a sucker for any place that welcomes you with a little scone: the day I was there, it was cinnamon and raisin.

There's even a dash of goofiness. The daily blue plate special (served on a blue plate) is often a mystery Chef's Choice. "It changes every day, and sometimes we don't even tell people what it is. We just say if you like food cooked a certain way, or if you have food allergies, this probably isn't the dish for you. It's our way of having a little bit of fun. One day it was a beef hash with poached eggs, and we sold out," Kotler says.

Otherwise, Toast is wide open not only to changes ("we want to be a restaurant that says yes, " says Kotler) but also to suggestions: at first there was no bacon on the menu, but enough diners said they wanted it that there's now nitrate-free bacon.

What else would you expect from your little neighborhood brunch place?

Wait: Can get long on weekends.

Seating: About 32, with a few seats at a counter and summer seating outside.

Large groups? Probably should call ahead.

Portion size: Smallish but enough.

Changes: Wide open.

Coffee: Courier.

Other drinks: Beer, wine, cocktails, juice, and juice drinks.

Feel-goods: Everything's fresh and local, organic and natural.

Health options: The pork is nitrate-free. Tofu is on the menu and can be prepared to taste.

WiFi? No.

A version of this chapter originally appeared on LivePDX.com

Tom's Restaurant

Old School

A bit of small-town America in the big city
3871 SE Division (SE/Division)
503-233-3739
Monday through Saturday 7:00 a.m. 9:30 p.m., Sunday 7:30 a.m. 9:30 p.m. Most Breakfast items served all day. Some dishes available only until 2:00 p.m.
$9–13 (Visa, MasterCard, Debit)

———————————◆•◆———————————

Here's a little story that has nothing, or maybe everything, to do with Tom's. It's the story I pull out whenever the topic is small towns.

Back in 1991 I hiked a bunch of miles on the Appalachian Trail. One day during a break, I was having the Trail Burger at the Trail Cafe in Hot Springs, North Carolina—a town of a few hundred where the A.T. goes right down the middle of Main Street. At the table next to me were two old-timers wearing tractor-related baseball caps, and when a car drove down the street, the two of them stopped talking and watched it. The car made a left turn down one of the few streets in town, and one old-timer said to the other, "Now, where's *he* goin'?"

The funny thing is, I told that story to somebody a while back, and the very next day I was eating breakfast at Tom's Restaurant with my friend Trisa. We were catching up on mutual friends and old times when she looked out the window at the traffic on SE 39th and saw her sister making a left turn! I guess that could have happened anywhere, but the fact that it happened at Tom's seems somehow to fit the place perfectly.

Chances are you know exactly what kind of place Tom's is, even if you've never been there. They are in the blood of Americans, even if some folks wouldn't walk into such a place. They go by names like Diner and Family Restaurant, and they serve cheap, basic fare to long-time regulars and new folks alike. They also tend to have customers and wait staff that stick around for decades.

Tom's has all of that as well as the type of menu you'd expect: biscuits and gravy, waffles with strawberries and whipped cream, omelets that hover around $7 (only the Feta and the Taco with beef, Cheddar, salsa, and sour cream are different from any other place), and Breakfast Nos. 1 through 7 that mix various combinations of meats, eggs, pancakes, toast, and hashbrowns. There's also French toast, pancakes, a couple of items for the kids, juices, and fruits, and generally a special or two for less than $4. And the other side of the business is a sports bar where you can shoot pool and watch the games on TV.

What's funny about Tom's is reading people's reactions to it on the various Internet sites. (And for what it's worth, I doubt that many of Tom's regulars write reviews online.) I often wonder if all these reviewers are eating in the same restaurant. I've seen one that said Tom's has the best gyros in town (seems a stretch) but admitted, "It isn't the prettiest place to eat." Another complained about bad cooking but admitted the service was prompt and "the waitress was super nice." Yet another included such words as *puke* and *gag* and *icky poo* three times . . . but liked it for people watching.

Do you feel like you're seeing Tom's from completely different angles? And do you feel like you've seen Tom's a million times while driving by but have never gone in? And do you feel like you don't even need to? It's not fine dining, but sometimes you just want to feel like you're in a small town somewhere, taking a break for a cheap, casual meal.

Wait: Perhaps on the weekends.

Seating: About 75 in booths and at a counter.

Large groups? No.

Portion size: Big.

Changes: Ingredients can be added to omelets for $.35 to $.75.

Coffee: Boyds.

Other drinks: Juices, tea, hot chocolate, milk, pop, full bar.

Feel-goods: Not much in the food, but the waitress will treat you like family.

Health options: You don't *have* to get the homemade cinnamon roll.

WiFi? No.

Tosis

Old School

Not of the Portland you probably know
6120 NE Sandy Blvd. (NE/Hollywood)
503-284-4942
Hours: 6 a.m. to 9 p.m., 7 days a week, except Saturdays 7-9.
Breakfast all day.
$7–10 (Visa, MasterCard)

———————◆———————

Ah, Tosis. I confess a deep love for this place, which just about everybody I know has driven past and wondered about and not one has ever been in. And that's too bad, because for most people I know in Portland, a breakfast at Tosis would be like visiting another world.

Here's one reason: Tosis, family owned with wait staff whose service is probably measured in decades, is a place where the church crowd goes. It may be the only place in this book that can make such a claim. I don't go to church, but my Southern soul is profoundly soothed by the sight of a restaurant full of well-dressed old people eating after services are over.

Another reason: On several occasions I've been in Tosis when an older guy walked through the door, and a nearby table full of similarly old guys erupted into calls like, "Why, they'll let anybody in here" and "Oh, look out, here comes trouble."

But the biggest reason Tosis is dear to my heart is captured perfectly in the person of my dear friend Craig: fisherman, guide, author, French toast connoisseur, lover of old-school coffee, and occasional grouch. Craig used to live

 near Tosis and got me to go there because it had, he said, plain coffee, great French toast, and rude service. He turned out to be right on two counts: the service is actually quite nice, but if staffers are having a bad day or you're on their nerves for some reason, they're honest enough not to pretend otherwise.

At Tosis, you can sit and talk with your friends, or mind your own business, or work a crossword, or read the paper, or get in and out in about 20 minutes. You cannot sip a latte and surf the Internet. Tosis has fake flowers, coat racks, Formica tables, and cheesy paintings — in short, all the decorative charm of a cheap motel. And God bless the diners and cheap motels!

To Craig, who I can picture slumped in a booth going on about his daughter or fishing the Klamath Basin or theology or Frank Zappa, the appeal of Tosis is captured perfectly in its French toast, which, he wants the world the know, is perfect. But to understand that, you must understand that when I tell Craig about having French toast made with challah or brioche, or I regale him with tales of caramelized bananas at Roux or chopped pecans at the Cadillac, he usually rolls his eyes and lets out an obscene, cranky version of "Man, that stuff ain't French toast!" By French toast Craig means white bread that's been soaked to yellow in egg and milk and *perhaps* a little vanilla, then fried, covered in powdered sugar, and served six or eight pieces on a heavy, white oval plate, with a plastic pitcher of maple syrup, a mug of plain coffee, and a bowl full of creamers. Then leave him the hell alone unless he runs out of java.

I have been served nearly stale bread at Tosis, eaten meaty omelets with what looked like Kraft Singles mixed up in them, and seen people with beer and cigarettes playing video poker at 9:30 a.m.. Once, in my notes I described the food as "fishing cabin fare," and by God, sometimes a man needs to go to the fishing cabin. There are times when I just want my breakfast hot, quick, and cheap. Give me crisp bacon, mashed-style hashbrowns, fried eggs, sourdough toast, and some packs of Smucker's, and I'm a happy dude.

If you worked at it or tipped really well (which you should), you could probably manage to spend $10, though it would defeat much of the purpose of going there.

That purpose, it seems to me, is to strip away all the pretense that so often comes with food these days, hit the reset button, relax, and just go have some damn breakfast.

Wait: Maybe around noon on Sunday.
Seating: 100 or so, at tables and booths.
Large groups? Not so much.
Portion size: Decent.
Changes: Sure, but ask nicely.
Coffee: Boyds.
Other drinks: Iced tea, juices, soda.
Feel-goods: It's cheap!
Health options: Someplace else.
WiFi? If they ever get it, Craig and I will stop going.

Trébol

New/Weekend/Classy

Monumental Modern Mexican
4835 N Albina (N/Inner)
503-517-9347
Brunch served Sunday 11:00 a.m. to 2:00 p.m.
trebolpdx.com
$13–17 (all major cards)

———————◆•◆———————

One thing you should know about Trébol is that it is a very serious restaurant. I don't mean it isn't fun; I mean that the phrase "Mexican Brunch," although accurate, doesn't begin to describe what the place is about.

Everything about it says "more than a place to eat." The space is impressive, with high ceilings, big windows, and massive mirrors on the walls. The Web site, which includes Mexican rock music and impressive, flashy graphics, touts Trébol's state-of-the-art composting, oil recycling, eco-friendly cleaning products, and relationships with local farmers. There's also a list of upcoming events: the Tour of Tequila, for example (75 kinds) and Santo Sundays, when you can watch cheesy Mexican adventure films featuring a pro wrestler named Santo (with his mask on) who fights bad guys and saves people. It's even weirder than it sounds.

The menu seems much more predictable, at least at first glance. Names like Soup of the Day, Shrimp Cocktail, Guacamole, Chorizo with Egg, Tamale with Fried Egg, Flautas, and a Torta of the Day don't spin your head. Other items, like Chilaquiles (a soupy egg dish with fried tortillas) or Grilled Quail with Peanut Mole, hint at greater Mexican ambitions.

And it's those greater ambitions that really set Trébol apart. It's the kind of place I enjoy but don't go to often, so my opinion may be meaningless. In fact, I doubted my own opinion within 24 hours of eating there. And that's because my friends and I enjoyed the  food and had a great time, then I went online to read reviews and quickly decided that many reviewers and foodies, all of whom know and care more about food than I do, don't like Trébol as much as we did.

To the Breakfast Crew, it's an impressive place with fun-loving staff and great food that, we had to confess, seemed a little expensive ($8 for organic guacamole?). I had the Torta, with a cornmeal pita topped with layers of black beans, grilled flank steak, greens, cheese, and a spicy sauce that on first bite was a blow to my senses but then settled in wonderfully. I loved it, even if it seemed small for $10 and didn't come with anything else.

The rest of the Crew had nothing but praise for the Huevos Rancheros, the vegetarian Posole soup, and the tamale; the same was true for the Bloody Maria, made with tequila and house pickles on the side. Some things seemed odd to us. For example, one of the Santo movies was on, so we'd occasionally look up at the big TV screen over the bar—and a TV over the bar is a little weird on its own in a serious restaurant—and we'd see Santo talking with scantily clad women, overly dramatic young men, people in space suits, another wrestler in a blue mask, and so on.

A comment card came with the bill, which doesn't happen often, and our water had been served in a green bottle that looked like it may have once held wine or olive oil. Not offensive or problematic, but these things did cause us to pause and ponder. So did the owner/chef's announcement that Trébol had been named one of the 10 Best Mexican Places in the U.S. by *Bon Appetite*. I thought, Really? How does someone even come to such a conclusion?

At any rate, local reviewers are more mixed. The *Mercury* said it was "inconsistent and overpriced." The *Oregonian* said the food was improving but the service was over-eager. *Willamette Week* liked it, but the folks at *PortlandFood.org* leaned toward "I don't get it."

All I can say is that if a serious restaurant serving Mexican food for Sunday brunch sounds good, Trébol just might be your cup of tequila.

Wait: None.
Seating: About 80 inside and tables, a bar, and smallish booths. 20 in the small patio outside.
Large groups? Yes.
Portion size: Underwhelming.
Changes: Not so much.
Coffee: Self-serve Stumptown.
Other drinks: Several versions of Bloody Mary and Mimosa, plus 75 kinds of tequila.
Feel-goods: Ingredients are local, seasonal, and organic.
Health options: Good vegetarian options, and they sometimes serve fruit and yogurt (for $8).
WiFi? No.

Utopia Cafe

New/Hip/Veggie

Grown-up hippie, or hippie grown-up?
3308 SE Belmont (SE/Belmont)
503-235-7606
Breakfast served weekdays 7:00 a.m. to 2:00 p.m.; weekends
7:30 a.m. to 2:30 p.m.
$9–14 (Visa, MasterCard, no checks)

———————◆•◆———————

"Not as hippie as I expected."

That's the first line in my coffee-stained hand-written notes from a trip to Utopia. I don't recall whether it was good news or bad. I guess I was expecting something a bit more airy from a place called Utopia that's next to It's A Beautiful Pizza—run by Deadheads—in the heart of Belmont.

I was probably just being cranky. When I entered through the very cool old-timey screen door, though, I saw a long black bar, Formica tables, lovely wood floors, high ceilings, fused-glass art on the walls, and faux stained glass. It was all very clean and modern, and not a bit rustic. "This is nice," I thought—as if *hippie* and *nice* couldn't possibly coexist. Just being cranky, I'm sure.

Out came the menu, and it was pure Portland: eight scrambles ranging from Garden (with goat cheese) and no-egg Tofu (with tomato, onion, zucchini, mushroom, basil, and garlic) to the Baja (with chorizo) and the Camp (with bacon, mushrooms, and red and green peppers). There were also five house specials, French toast, three kinds of pancakes, and a couple of hot cereals.

I was eating with two women who called themselves the

Candida Sisters because they both had issues about eating sugar and wheat, and they had no problem finding stuff they could eat. And substitutions were easily made.

So here's the thing about Utopia. The first time I went I came home with no notes at all; chalk that up to eating with two women. The second time I was in the neighborhood and wanted to try the Brioche French Toast. It was amazing and bountiful. I still didn't have good notes on the place, so next time I invited some friends. Nobody showed up. I went, anyway, and got the Bacavo Scramble with bacon, tomato, avocado, and blue cheese crumbles. It, too, was amazing. Again, I took almost no notes.

I recognized there was a pattern developing. For some reason I could not get a handle on the Utopia Cafe. I couldn't put my finger on its essence, couldn't see how it fit in the Portland Breakfast Pantheon. So I decided to see what other writers had to say. Among all the Internet praise, I found this from the *Portland Mercury*: "There's no angle on the Utopia Cafe. It's not a good place to take Grandma, it's not great for a date, it's not healthy, it's not vegan, it doesn't have great ambiance and they don't allow dogs. It's just really good food."

So it wasn't just me! Then I found this in the *Willamette Week*: "Utopia offers a breakfast dish I have never seen before, and it strikes a very satisfying note: hot wild rice . . . a mix of long gray and black grains, thoughtfully served with raisins, hazelnuts and brown sugar."

Really? Utopia has that? Well, I dragged out the menu, and by golly it does. It's right under the From the Griddle section, which explains why I never made it that far. I also saw Fried Cornmeal, cooked on the grill and served with warm syrup. Somehow I had missed that, too. Clearly, I needed to go back.

And that's when I realized there were actually two patterns going on with me and the Utopia. It's true I had a hard time pegging it, probably because it fits so neatly into everything Portland breakfast is about: relaxed setting, neighborhood feel, good food, reasonable prices, and plenty of options.

But the other pattern was that I seem to keep going back—a pattern I have no intention of ending.

Wait: Pretty long on weekends, with some space inside but little cover outside. **Seating:** About 40 at tables plus 6 at two counters. **Large groups?** Yes, but no split checks for parties of five or more on weekends.
Portion size: Reasonable. **Changes:** Several options on the menu, and they're open to more.
Coffee: Portland Roasting, Utopia Blend.
Other drinks: Espresso, Kobos loose tea, juices, milk, soda.
Feel-goods: Lots of organic stuff.
Health options: Plenty of vegetarian options as well as egg substitute and egg whites available for a small charge. And they can make any scramble vegan.
WiFi? No.

Veritable Quandary

New/Classy/Weekend

Old-style class, new-style cuisine

1220 SW First Ave. (Downtown)

503-227-7342

Brunch served weekends from 9:30 a.m. to 3:00 p.m.

veritablequandary.com

$15–20 (all major cards)

Portlanders have been eating at the VQ for almost 40 years. It's also a visual anchor, perched near the end of the Hawthorne Bridge, and it's been a popular lunch, dinner, and happy hour hangout for a generation or two. That heritage is proudly trumpeted on the Web site, which claims "Old Portland charm . . . long before the Pearl District or South Waterfront hype."

I must confess that when I read about "Old Portland" stretching all the way back to the so-called foggy days of 1971, when the VQ was founded, I have to chuckle. I'm not opposed to marketing, and I don't even mind the Web site's claim that the VQ's garden patio is "the city's favorite outdoor dining venue." But somehow this all seems to fit with a place with a relatively long tradition that has also been a source of a long-running question: Just what kind of place is it?

Is the VQ a "serious restaurant" that wants to compete with the city's finest? Is it a casual lunch hangout? A happy hour where lawyers and downtown corporate types hit on one another? A tourist spot? A fancy bar? The answer to all seems to be yes.

My feeling is this: let's say there are three very general levels of restaurant. The low end places are the cafes and diners of the world. The high end places inspire foodie conversa-  tions about the presentation of the osso buco or the subtle mix of flavors in an *amuse bouche*. And then there's an area in the middle, whose inhabitants are trying to find a balance between casual and fine dining. Assuming an upward path through these places, you'd probably start at Stanfords, hit Mother's or the Bijou on the way up, and top out at the VQ, where your Benedict is $13 and your Frittata with Wild Mushrooms and Oregon Black Truffles, Brie, and Fresh Chervil is $15.

But I am probably over-thinking this thing. It just seems like to foodies the VQ is a small step below their usual haunts, and to the other 80 percent of people it's a fancy place that makes a fine start for a special cultural evening downtown.

The staff, which trends to young and cute, is everywhere and extremely helpful. The seating options include a dark, elegant bar; a light, airy dining room with tall windows; the famed flower-adorned patio; and a super-cool wine cellar with one table for about eight.

The menu is grounded in everyday breakfast tradition but with foodie twists—and prices. For example, there's a sausage-and-egg plate that's actually house-made Italian sausage, two local unpasteurized eggs, potato cakes, and "Peppers & Onions Agro Dolce tossed with fresh Mozzarella, Arugula and Basil." When I went with my friends Bob and Judy, none of us knew what Agro Dolce was, and for $14 we decided we could get something more interesting, anyway.

Bob got the Benedict, on house-made English muffins with house-smoked pork loin ($13), and he loved it. Judy had the Chilaquiles with Manchego, which the menu said was tortillas with chile sauce and scrambled eggs, guacamole, and crème fraîche. She also loved it. And I think it's the typical VQ brunch dish, because (a) it was really good, (b) it looked and sounded fancy, and (c) it could also, accurately, have been called Breakfast Nachos.

Now, am I saying the VQ is trying to be something it isn't? The thought has occurred to me. Am I saying it is a serious restaurant trying to "keep it real"? I'd say that applies, as well. What it seems to boil down to, though, is that whatever you're looking for in a slightly upscale brunch, it's probably a good idea to check out the VQ.

Wait: Tends to form later in the morning.
Seating: About 60 inside, 20 in the bar, and another 50 in the outside garden patio with a view of the Hawthorne Bridge.
Large groups? Yes, especially if you can get the wine cellar.
Portion size: Big.
Changes: Yes.
Coffee: Stumptown.
Other drinks: Full bar, espresso, and fresh-squeezed juices.
Feel-goods: Plenty of local ingredients and only local unpasteurized eggs.
Health options: A few things here for the nonmeat eaters.
WiFi? No.

Virgo and Pisces

New/Weekend

Not too serious a place, for good or for ill
500 NW 21st Avenue (NW)
503-517-8855
Brunch served weekends from 9:00 a.m. to 3:00 p.m.
virgoandpisces.com
$14–18 (all major cards)

------◆•◆------

When Jenny and I walked into Virgo and Pisces, she said what we were both thinking: "It's so young!"

We took a moment to take it all in: the color scheme was all bright and happy, with one wall covered by an under-the-sea mural and another by a big-screen TV that just happened to be playing the Cartoon Network.

The rest of the crowd tended pretty young as well, and the two folks working the floor couldn't have been 45 between them. When one greeted us with an almost Eddie Haskell-level of polite eagerness, Jenny and I giggled.

I should note that this was at about 10:30 on a pleasant Saturday morning and there was no line; almost every review I've read said the same thing. It's a certain good news/bad news feature of Virgo and Pisces; the good news is there's no line, even though it's in the middle of the busiest stretch of NW 21st Avenue. The bad news, according to at least two newspaper reviews, is that it's not a very good restaurant.

Initial reviews by the *Willamette Week* and the *Mercury* had a few things in common: they were both headlined "Star-Crossed," they both said the restaurant lacked focus, they both complained about the decor, and they both more or less panned the place.

Willamette Week saw "a menu whose aim is entirely unclear" and "an unlikely brunch/lunch menu where (Northwest and Pan-Asian) cuisines . . . battle for space." Of the decor, *WW* had this to say: "The dining room is best described as ornate Chinese food restaurant meets tacky tarot-card parlor." The *Mercury* (which said V&P's brunch looked better than its dinner) complained, "The menu is a mess, with a physical layout as confusing as the items it contains," and then added this nugget about the decor: "The booths appear to have been purchased at the same restaurant supply shop that outfits Chili's." Ouch.

For the record, both negative and positive reviews shared two insights: the staff is very nice, and it's a great happy hour place.

In our experience there's another way to look at all this good/bad stuff: Virgo and Pisces is a casual place with plenty of styles of food to choose from, and the prices are pretty reasonable. In other words, neither we nor the other folks eating there needed a restaurant to be "serious." And we thought the decor fit in perfectly with the youthful vibe of the place; in fact, the collection of kitchen-inspired Zodiac-sign paintings (a bull with a chef's hat, Libra with a scale and a head of lettuce) were done by an 18-year-old artist from Seattle. And everybody's impressed by the bathroom; ask the staff to make sure you see the right one.

We even though it was cute when our waiter, asked what the Manchego cheese in the Smoked King Salmon Benedict was like, struggled to remember and then told us, "It's Spanish . . . kind of like a mild Parmesan. It's a nice cheese." And it was nice—not the best Benedict either of us had tasted, but not the worst, either. Other Benedicts came with Oregon Dungeness crab, chèvre, and oven-roasted tomatoes; savory baked tofu with Shitake mushrooms; and bacon, roasted tomato, and Tillamook Cheddar.

The rest of the menu didn't have much of the seafood thing going on (apparently that's more prominent at dinner); it was just the usual lineup of scrambles, a frittata, and a couple of omelets, plus more than a dozen crepes, from savory (such as lox with capers, red onion, spinach, Dijon, and dill Provolone) to sweet (variations on Nutella, fruit, and nuts, plus a few with liqueurs).

So is that a scattered menu with too much variety and goofball décor, or plenty of options in a fun, youthful environment? I suggest you decide for yourself.

Wait: None that I've seen.

Seating: About 60 at tables and booths.

Large groups? Yes. **Portion size:** Big. **Changes:** Sure.

Coffee: RayJen Organic.

Other drinks: Espresso, hot chocolate, Pellegrino, juices, mimosas, Bloody Mary.

Feel-goods: Menu says "local and fine ingredients."

Health options: Decent vegetarian options; allergies can be accommodated.

WiFi? Yes; see server for password.

Vita Cafe

Hip/Veggie/Kiddie

A veggie palace, a local hangout, a Portland institution
3024 NE Alberta (NE/Alberta)
503-335-8233
Breakfast served weekdays 9:00 a.m. to 4:00 p.m.; weekends
8:00 a.m. to 4:00 p.m.
vita-cafe.com
$9–13 (all major cards)

———————————◆●◆———————————

Two of the most endearing moments of my breakfast research
project happened at the Vita Cafe. My old college roommate
was visiting from Dallas, and he brought his wife, their three
kids, his mom, and his wife's parents, who come from a town
in East Texas that has one streetlight. The group collectively
became known simply as the Texans.

My friends wanted to know how the Texans were liking
Oregon, where I was taking them, and so on. And I knew
before they came to town that I'd take them to the Vita Cafe,
a monument to what "my" Portland is all about: healthy food,
community, grassroots neighborhood development, hipsters,
hippies, leisurely breakfasts, outdoor dining, and local-sus-
tainable-organic-vegetarian and vegan food.

The first charming moment came when the eldest Texan,
after watching some of the human traffic stroll by on Alberta,
asked me sincerely, "Paul, where does a woman with tattoos
get a job?"

In the same way, I'm pretty sure nothing like the Vita
Cafe or Alberta Street has ever happened in Dallas. In the
mid-1990s most of Alberta's buildings were boarded up
and crime was common. Then came the artists, and soon

the restaurants followed.
The founding owner of
the Vita, who at the time
also owned the Paradox
Cafe on SE Belmont, set
up shop on Alberta for
two reasons: a lot of his
employees were moving
there, and New Seasons
Market was headed there,
as well.

What has since happened on Alberta is the stuff of
Portland legend; for its full expression just come by on a
Last Thursday in the summer. Or come into the Vita almost
any day of the year. As a *Willamette Week* article once put
it, "Regulars from the surrounding neighborhood wait for
tables elbow-to-elbow with suburbanites who haven't ven-
tured into this part of town for years."

What those folks will be ordering at the Vita is a vast
array of mostly vegetarian and vegan dishes—another reason I brought the Texans there. I wanted them to see that
organic, vegan food can be both good and filling. They pored
over the menu, expressing surprise at tasty-sounding dishes
like a Greek, Mediterranean, Mexican, or Italian scramble,
asking me "And it's *vegan?*" It is if you get it with tofu or
tempeh instead of with free-range eggs.

Then they asked what tempeh was, as well as tofu, jicama,
miso, and TVP. And how you get milk from rice or soy-
beans. Fortunately, all of this is explained in the "Food For
Thought" section of the menu, which brings me to another
of Vita's endearing qualities: it is by no means an elitist
place. It's practically an advertisement for a food movement

doubling as a kid-friendly restaurant and neighborhood hangout. There's a full bar and happy hour specials, and kids eat for a buck daily from 5 to 7 p.m. There's even a bocce ball court on the sprawling patio.

The best-known breakfast dishes are the corn cakes (including Mexican and Thai versions), the "Chicken" Fried Steak made with tempeh, and my favorite, the Tofurky Florentine, which is English muffins topped with slices of tofurky, spinach, vegan hollandaise (warning: it's brown), and either eggs or tofu. I'm not a vegetarian by any means, but I never feel like I'm being adventurous at the Vita; in fact, my favorite dessert in town is the super-sweet (and also vegan and wheat-free) carrot cake.

For me, the lasting image is sweet and wholesome. Late in the meal, with the kids romping on the patio with the not-too-hot sunshine streaming down, one Texan asked another with a slight grin, "How's your fake sausage?" Without even looking up from her rapidly emptying plate, she just mumbled and gave two thumbs up.

Wait: A little on weekends.
Seating: About 50 inside at tables and booths; picnic tables outside in spring, summer, and fall.
Large groups? Yes. **Portion size:** Big. **Changes:** Easy.
Coffee: Stumptown.
Other drinks: Smoothies, juices, cocktails, beer.
Feel-goods: Free-range, sustainable, local ingredients; 1 percent of sales is donated to local social and environmental groups. **Health options:** Everywhere!
WiFi? Yes.

Webber's Crossing

Mom and Pop/Old School

That place is still there?

7000 SW Beaverton Hillsdale Highway (SW/Outer)

503-292-3932

Monday through Saturday (7:30 on Saturday), 7:00 a.m. to
2:30 p.m.; Sunday, 7:30 a.m. to 2:30 p.m.

$6–10 (Visa, MasterCard, checks)

When I started telling my friends I was writing a book about
breakfast in Portland, my friend Allan told me, "Oh, I've got
a place *nobody* knows about—but you'd never want to put it
in a book." When I asked why, he said, "Well, it's just this
little place, been there forever, the kind of place you drive by
every day and never notice."

Just my kind of place, I said. So he tried to tell me where
Webber's Crossing is, and he said it's at Kamikaze Corner.
That meant nothing to me. Over by the Parr Lumber? Sorry.
Right where Beaverton-Hillsdale Highway crosses Scholls
Ferry? I had to tell Allan that I am a fairly recent transplant,
almost allergic to tools and manual labor, and my mind goes
squishy when somebody mentions Beaverton or any of the
Ferry roads.

Undaunted (and armed with Mapquest directions), I ven-
tured forth: west on US 26 and over the Sylvan Hill, left on
Skyline, then down Scholls Ferry Road and into a time warp.
"My" Portland is mainly a place of liberal politics, young couples, and urban planning. The old homes and tree-filled lots
down Scholls Ferry reminded me of visiting my grandparents, and when I got to the intersection in question, I felt like

 I was looking at what happens when there is *no* planning: a horrible five-way intersection that invited automotive chaos and where, somewhat fittingly, my Mapquest printout was utterly useless.

Within my view was a tanning salon, two pet shops, a mailbox place, dry cleaners, a donut place, and cars going in every direction at once. And right in the middle was a little place about 50 feet wide with a '70s-era sign outside that read, "Webber's Breakfast and Lunch." More signage painted onto the window panels read, "Breakfast—Lunch—Dinner—Hamburgers—Bento." Allan was right: even though I'd never been to this part of town, I'd driven by this kind of place a million times. And now I was going to eat in one!

I took my seat at a red vinyl half-booth, grabbed a paper from a wicker basket, and settled to wait for Allan and take it all in. The chairs were also of red vinyl, and one table had heart-shaped chair backs. The plants were plastic, and the art could have been lifted from a hotel. I noticed there were still some homes around the place, and one building across the street was the Animal Dermatology Clinic.

And here's the thing: I felt completely comforted. It was like dropping off the grid and traveling to the land of semi-country living. It didn't take much effort to imagine a field of corn on one of the side roads (even if I'm fairly sure there are tract homes instead). I couldn't find one online review of Webber's, which made some sites' claims for "the latest buzz on Webber's Crossing" that much more laughable. When

Allan arrived and told me the motto used to be By Golly, Our Soup Is Good!, I felt even better about the place.

By now, perhaps, you're wondering about the food—or maybe you already know or can imagine. The French toast is Texas toast soaked until it's yellow, the bacon is thin and crispy, the omelets are filling and cheap, there's Smuckers on the table, and you can plainly see both the microwave and the Bunn coffeemaker behind the counter.

What you really should know, though, is that the owners remembered Allan and a $10 bill he had dropped on the floor *a month* before, and that the food came out quick and hot thanks to an energetic and friendly waiter. And sometimes isn't that about all you want, along with some quiet time to visit with an old friend and a reminder that the old parts of town haven't been completely buried by the new?

Wait: Can't imagine.
Seating: About 70, mostly in fun half-booths.
Large groups? No.
Portion size: Decent for the price.
Changes: Within reason.
Coffee: Standard diner.
Other drinks: Milkshakes, juices and tea.
Feel-goods: It's still there!
Health options: Egg beaters, egg whites if you ask. There is a Garden Burger on the menu.
WiFi? Hardly.

Wild Abandon

Hip/Veggie

Mmmm, red velvet!

2411 SE Belmont (SE/Belmont)

503-232-4458

Weekdays 7 a.m. to 2 p.m., but closed on Tuesdays. Weekends
9:00 a.m. to 2:00 p.m.

wildabandonrestaurant.com

$12–15 (all major cards)

Six of us once tried to come up with the theme of Wild
Abandon. The mural on the wall says either Greek baccha-
nalia or Druid ritual. The dark red tones say New Orleans.
The sculpted hands holding candles on the walls say freaky.
The old-school country music playing says honky-tonk.
Somewhere we sensed a thread in there; we just couldn't put
our fingers on it.

Then Michael, the owner, told us he calls the place "garage
sale baroque." *That* was it! He explained that back in the '70s
his grandmother had a basement filled with frosted Mexican
lights — he assured us that grandma's was *"the* '70s basement"—and that was the feel he was going for. He got it. In
fact, one of grandma's original lights is on the right as you
walk out to the big, beautiful patio. Look for the hole around
back, where Michael accidentally hit it trying to toss a spoon
into a bus tray.

He also said the building was the original home of
Montage before that restaurant moved to its funky home
under the Morrison Bridge. So the theme kind of continued,
we thought. Before that it was a barber shop, and before that

Michael said it was (no lie) Ginger's Sexy Sauna. Some guy once told Michael he had lost his virginity on the premises.

Michael calls himself "an old restaurant hand" and has given his funky-feeling place a selection of old-fashioned breakfasts and a casual ambience. Basic omelets and scrambles run about $8, three Benedicts (spinach, ham, and salmon) average $10, and vegetarians and vegans will find several options. In fact, Wild Abandon offers a Vegan French Toast made with soy milk, soy butter, and real maple syrup.

The Old Fashioned French Toast, like the restaurant, had a little something we couldn't put our finger on; we thought it might be rum, fitting the theme, but Michael said it was orange juice. I guess we were just getting carried away. By that time our conversation had turned to a wacky combination of Humanism, Alaskan fishing, our server's tale of coffee sampling (known as "cupping") to get the blend just right, and my trivia contest to see if anyone else could tell Marty Robbins from Hank Williams and Hank Snow.

Like the mood, we thought the food was just right: the Benedicts had a little crunch to the muffins, a light sauce, and some bite in the spinach. I had to defend my French toast from inquiring hands. There's a little Mexican flair to the menu, as well: the S.O.B. (no explanation given) includes black beans, salsa, guacamole, and flour tortilla strips. Richard's Chilaquiles is an egg scramble with peppers, onions, Cheddar, and fried tortilla strips, all topped with black beans, salsa, sour cream, and cilantro. Both, as well as the breakfast burrito, come with or without chorizo.

Mexican food, Marty Robbins, grandma's basement, freaky hands holding candles, down-home food, cocktails, red velvet . . . I'm telling you, there's a theme in there somewhere. I guess we'll have to keep going back to nail it down completely.

Wait: Not bad.
Seating: 40 to 50 inside with booths and wall booths, 40 to 50 outside on a nice, clean patio.
Large groups? Maybe on the patio.
Portion size: Solid.
Changes: Sure.
Coffee: Bridgetown special blend.
Other drinks: Good Earth teas, beer, wine, cocktails.
Feel-goods: None in particular.
Health options: Garden sausage, soy products including tofu, and an entire vegan section on the menu.
WiFi? No.

scramble: hmm, don't care for asparagus in the morning. Avocado-bacon-tomato omelet? Don't care for avocados that much. Portobello-spinach-tomato-Asiago omelet? Getting warmer. Reuben scramble with pastrami, eggs, Gruyere, and Dijon-mayo on rye with potatoes and kraut? Good gosh, that's our early leader! A gingerbread waffle with Oregon strawberries and whipped cream? See, that's not fair! I'd have the best 15 minutes of my life eating that, then need a nap. Why can't somebody else be here to order it so I can have a bite, or seven?

No, it's a savory day. Back to the menu. Two Benedicts, one with baked salmon. A salami scramble, an imported Gouda and ham scramble, a smoked wild salmon scramble. I'm getting depressed. I pick one, I eliminate all the others! Huevos rancheros, Greek omelet, corned beef hash. Wait: Gorgonzola-mushroom-thyme omelet? Folks, we have a winner! And, of course, two seconds after I make my decision here's the waitress to pour water and take my order. Complete pros here, every time.

Now to just sit back and take it in. Moms are out with their kids. The two ladies by the window are clearly old friends. The couple by the register is definitely a first date. The group by the door is some kind of work team. The guy at the counter is just doing scones, coffee, and the paper. The clatter of dishes, the creaking wood floor, the subdued chatter of the crowd, the jazz playing—everything is in balance.

scramble: hmm, don't care for asparagus in the morning. Avocado-bacon-tomato omelet? Don't care for avocados that much. Portobello-spinach-tomato-Asiago omelet? Getting warmer. Reuben scramble with pastrami, eggs, Gruyere, and Dijon-mayo on rye with potatoes and kraut? Good gosh, that's our early leader! A gingerbread waffle with Oregon strawberries and whipped cream? See, that's not fair! I'd have the best 15 minutes of my life eating that, then need a nap. Why can't somebody else be here to order it so I can have a bite, or seven?

No, it's a savory day. Back to the menu. Two Benedicts, one with baked salmon. A salami scramble, an imported Gouda and ham scramble, a smoked wild salmon scramble. I'm getting depressed. I pick one, I eliminate all the others! Huevos rancheros, Greek omelet, corned beef hash. Wait: Gorgonzola-mushroom-thyme omelet? Folks, we have a winner! And, of course, two seconds after I make my decision here's the waitress to pour water and take my order. Complete pros here, every time.

Now to just sit back and take it in. Moms are out with their kids. The two ladies by the window are clearly old friends. The couple by the register is definitely a first date. The group by the door is some kind of work team. The guy at the counter is just doing scones, coffee, and the paper. The clatter of dishes, the creaking wood floor, the subdued chatter of the crowd, the jazz playing—everything is in balance.

And bang-o, here's my food! A wrap-style omelet, just browned on the outside, some Gorgonzola oozing out the side. I take a bite and mmmmm, perfect. Somehow, it's firm and soft at the same time. The potatoes are lightly seasoned, and some smaller pieces got just a little crispy. Again, everything in balance. Of course, now I'm thinking that if the omelet is this good, I really have to come back and hit that Rueben scramble or one of the Benedicts.

Now I've worked my way through the whole thing, going back and forth between the savory omelet, the crunchy potatoes, the sweet cider, the view, the sun, and the music. I managed to save one last little buttery bite of scone, too. I reach for the jam, at peace.

Mmmm, Zell's.

Wait: Long on weekends, with a padded bench inside and some cover outside.

Seating: About 50 at tables plus a counter at the bar.

Large groups? Possible, but would add to the wait.

Portion size: Reasonable.

Changes: On egg dishes, you can get fruit ($1.50), cottage cheese ($.75), or veggies ($1.50) instead of potatoes, or toast for 75 cents.

Coffee: Kobos.

Other drinks: Kobos loose-leaf teas, espresso, mineral water, Italian sodas, cocktails.

Feel-goods: The request that everyone refrain from using cell phones!

Health options: Tofu and egg whites available for 50 cents. Morning Star Patties and Soy Milk are available.

WiFi? No.

About the Author

I've always wanted to do interesting things, visit interesting places, meet interesting people, and then tell folks about them. As a teenager I found out that writers get *paid* for doing it, and my life's trajectory was set.

I started as a sports writer at the Southern Methodist University *Daily Campus* because I wanted to sit in the press box at football games. I also had a sports-desk job at the much-missed *Dallas Times Herald* for three wonderful years.

After college I screwed around and traveled for a few years, then retreated to my home town of Memphis and another fantastic sports-desk job at the *Memphis Commercial Appeal*. I also got hired at the weekly *Memphis Flyer* and wrote for every section of the paper: sports, news, book and film reviews, editorials, you name it. Good times!

And then in the mid-1990s I found the twin promised lands of freelance writing and travel writing. That was when I cut loose from the docks of life and set myself adrift; I've held exactly one "real" job since. Along the way I've slaved for money in between writing gigs at various places: an amusement park, a temp agency, landscaping (briefly), restaurant kitchens (more briefly), Alaskan fishing boats, social service nonprofits, FedEx, and an insurance company—yes, cubicle and all. Those are the jobs I can remember, anyway.

I moved to Oregon in 1996 because it's about four thousand times cooler than Memphis. I have written two hiking guidebooks, both published by Menasha Ridge Press of Birmingham, Alabama: *60 Hikes Within 60 Miles of Portland* (third edition, 2007) and *Day and Overnight Hikes on Oregon's Pacific Crest Trail* (first edition, 2007). I am in the process of revising Menasha's *Best in Tent Camping: Oregon*, which will be out in early 2009.

I published this book myself, and more titles are on the way from Bacon and Eggs Press.

I do appreciate your buying this book because I really don't want to have any more jobs.

The Author's Favorites

Fine.

I always get hit with "What's your favorite place?" so I forced myself to list my favorites. Note that I didn't say "the best in town." These places (listed alphabetically, by the way) all have some combination of good food, good memories, and a vibe that I dig.

Two disclaimers: I invested exactly three minutes in putting together this list, and if you ask me again, I'll have a slightly different list.

Beaterville Cafe because it's Portland-style weird and it's where this book was born.

Bijou, Cafe for its combination hippie-tourist-business vibe, and the oyster hash.

Fat City Cafe because the Fellas eat there all the time, and I get to say "Fat City Sizzle."

Genies Café because it has about 27 things I love.

Golden Touch Family Restaurant because of Corky.

Helser's for half-price early treats, good Benedicts, and my crush on the staff.

Milo's City Cafe because Bob and I go there to eat meat and talk politics and writing.

Original Pancake House because deciding which pancakes to get is pleasurable torture. And the pink skirts.

Simpatica Dining Hall because it's the best breakfast food in town and makes me feel good about Portland.

Stepping Stone Cafe because it was my original regular place, and 12 years later it still is. And because of the Thursday Night Boys.

Tosis because of Craig slumped in a booth and going on about theology, fishing, or French toast.

Zell's, just because it's Zell's.

Zell's

New/Classy

Relaxed elegance, Portland style

1300 SE Morrison St. (SE/Inner)

503-239-0196

Monday through Friday, 7 a.m. to 2 p.m.; Saturday, 8 a.m. to 2 p.m.; Sunday, 8 a.m. to 3 p.m. Breakfast available all day.

$10–14 (All major cards)

———————◆•◆———————

Ah, back at Zell's. It's a weekday lunch, nothing like the weekend breakfast madhouse. Haven't been here in a while, and I'm already wondering why. I'm halfway through one of my two soft, buttery and free scones, sipping apple cider, and soaking in the light that's streaming through tall windows and over luscious wood tables, chairs, and bar. It's an old pharmacy, drawers and soda fountain still intact, so folks have been sitting here in the sun for many a year.

I'm feeling rather savory today, and since I'm solo, there won't be any sweets. Well, other than this homemade raspberry jam and orange marmalade on the table. So I'll have to pace myself and leave some of that for the last few bites of my scone. As always, breakfast and lunch are both available, but I definitely want breakfast. I could go with the 2x2x2 and get the cake flour-cornmeal pancakes, but I want more substance. That rules out the French toast with honey oat bread and the ridiculous German pancakes, for which I shall now have a moment of silence. Man, Zell's just cries out for a group of friends!

So let's check the specials. Today the German pancakes come with hot rhubarb or strawberries. (A buttermilk waffle comes with the same.) An asparagus-prosciutto-Asiago